Making Social Worlds

Making Social Worlds

A Communication Perspective

W. Barnett Pearce

BLACKWELL PUBLISHING
350 Main Street, Malden, MA 02148-5020, USA
9600 Garsington Road, Oxford OX4 2DQ, UK
550 Swanston Street, Carlton, Victoria 3053, Australia

First published 2007 by Blackwell Publishing Ltd

1   2007

Library of Congress Cataloging-in-Publication Data

Pearce, W. Barnett.
   Making social worlds : a communication perspective / W. Barnett Pearce.
      p.   cm.
   Includes bibliographical references and index.
      ISBN 978-1-4051-6259-3 (hardcover : alk. paper) – ISBN 978-1-4051-6260-9
(pbk. : alk. paper)   1. Communication–Social aspects.   2. Interpersonal communication.   3. Social perception.   4. Meaning (Philosophy)   I. Title.

HM1206.P43 2007
302.2–dc22

                                                                2007005640

A catalogue record for this title is available from the British Library.

Set in 10.5/13pt Minion
by Graphicraft Limited, Hong Kong
Printed in Singapore
by COS Printers Pte Ltd

For further information on
Blackwell Publishing, visit our website:
www.blackwellpublishing.com

Contents

Preface

An Invitation . . .

Making Social Worlds: A Communication Perspective is an invitation to use some new concepts and tools to think about very familiar things and see them in a new way. If you accept this invitation, it will improve your ability to understand the situations in which you find yourself, increase your ability to act wisely in those situations, and provide scaffolding for your development as a person, in patterns of communication with others, and as part of organizations.

The concepts and tools come from the theory of the coordinated management of meaning (also known as "CMM"). Don't let the word "theory" make your eyes glaze over. As I explain in chapter 3, it is a very special kind of theory, both respectable in academic circles and useful for professionals. I've worked with CMM for over thirty years, and the line between my professional practice (as a facilitator, consultant, and trainer) and my academic work has become very faint. To see how scholarship and practice interpenetrate, take a look at the website for my business, www.pearceassociates.com, and for the nonprofit organization of which I'm a founding member, www.publicdialogue.org.

I invite you to use these concepts and tools to re-examine the most familiar things. These include yourself; your friends; your family; your school; the company in which you work or that produces the things that you buy; your church/synagogue/mosque/ashram/shrine; your favorite sports team; the people you think of as heroes, villains, and fools; your country; your birthdays, anniversaries, and favorite holidays; your highest hopes and deepest fears – in short all of the events and objects of your social world.

In chapter 2, I'll describe the "communication perspective" that sees these things as *made* (not found or discovered); as *made in processes of communication* of which you are a part; and, finally, made in ways *shaped and determined by how you act* in specific moments.

There's a sense in which any new perspective is refreshing, and I think you'll find this one intellectually exciting. But you'll also find it practically useful. In chapter 1, I introduce the idea that there are critical moments in which what you do (or what I do or someone else does) changes the world. I mean that literally: what happens "next" is contingent on what is done in that moment. Chaos theorists use the term "bifurcation moments" to name those points in a sequence when, if "this" happens, the rest of the sequence goes this way, but if "that" happens, it goes a different way. That's the idea of what I'm calling "critical moments." Sometimes these critical moments are seemingly random: you chose to ride the bus rather than take a taxi and because of that you met a person . . . and your life and the life of all those around you will forever be different. But sometimes these critical moments are ones in which you know full well that what you do will have an afterlife for you and all those around you. The tools and concepts of CMM will help you identify and act wisely in these critical moments.

In this book, you'll find some ideas and models that can help you seize the moment by first identifying those critical moments in which you have the choice of acting this way or that way, knowing that your choice will change your social world. These ideas and concepts will also help you choose wisely in those critical moments.

I believe that this ability to identify and act wisely in critical moments is important. The world is too crowded, diverse, and interconnected, and the tools and toys with which we play are too powerful for us to be complacent about missed opportunities and unwise choices either by us as individuals or by those who would lead us. Far too long, too many of us, and particularly too many people who control the reins of power, have fumbled clumsily with the process that makes the worlds in which we live. The tools and concepts in this book can function as a ladder for the "upward" evolution of society.

In Chapters 6, 7, and 8, I introduce the idea that the complex entities of our social worlds emerge from specific, situated, momentary instances of communication. I have a specific and important sense of "emergence" that is described more fully in chapter 3. I'm taking a both/and position to a question with which scholars often wrestle: the relationship between micro- and macro-social entities. To express this view requires a complex sentence with several parentheses and three clauses. Stay with me! In my view, macro-social entities (nations, cultures, economies, social classes, genders, etc.) are "real," but they do not and cannot exist apart from micro-social entities (specific moments in which real people coordinate their actions and make/manage meanings by doing and saying things), and these macro-social entities have properties not found in the micro-social entities of which they are comprised. That is, the wholes are greater than the sum of the parts. In chapters 6, 7, and 8, I'll name these "wholes" patterns of communication, forms of consciousness, and relational minds.

Taking the communication perspective, however, positions us in a certain way with respect to both what you and your friends do in the moment and to the cultural/social/organizational contexts in which you find yourself. CMM does not lead to propositions describing the properties of these events and objects of our social worlds. Rather, by describing the process by which these events and objects are made, it positions us to take actions that reproduce and/or change those events and objects. CMM invites you to ask, of the passing moment, "What are we making together?" and of the events and objects of your social worlds, "How is it made?" It invites you to ask, "How can we make better social worlds?" The tools and concepts of CMM provide a vocabulary for answering those questions, and function as enabling and disciplining heuristics for determining those answers. That is, as enabling heuristics, they function as tools saying "look here!" and, as disciplining heuristics, as reminders to continue looking past the first, easy set of answers.

I would not have spent the time writing this book if all it did was to invite you to learn another academic theory. In fact, I decided to write it because of an unusual coincidence. Within a week, three professionals – a city manager, an organizational consultant, and a teacher – told me that I needed to write something about CMM that made it easier for people to learn how to use it in their work. Their stories were eerily similar. Each said that he/she used CMM tools and concepts; two said that having learned CMM, they could not *not* use it; but all three said that learning it was too difficult – if not for some special circumstance (different in each case), they would not have invested the time and energy to learn it.

Even someone as insensitive as I am could take the hint: the materials that I had previously written were not sufficiently accessible. To use a concept from manufacturing, the "first-unit cost" was too high: people had to invest too much before they could use CMM for the first time.

I hope that this book will reduce the first-unit cost. I've included a flurry of examples throughout the book about how to use the ideas in it. I invite you to look over my shoulder as I examine specific critical moments (such as President Bush's speech about 9/11) and I describe how Ingrid and Tanya (you'll meet them in later chapters) use CMM in organizational consulting and in an important conversation in a relationship. And, just to make sure that I honor my colleagues' suggestion for a more accessible guide to using CMM, the Afterword in chapter 9 is something of a guide to using CMM.

Extended to . . .

I wrote this book for three groups of people: everyone, students, and professionals.

Everyone

Everyone is a communicator, of course, and the tools and concepts in this book are equally useful for parents and children, students and teachers, employers and employees, friends and spouses, leaders and followers, politicians and citizens, salespersons and customers, filmmakers and viewers, and rock stars and fans. If you are reading this book primarily for your own use, you'll probably find some portions more useful than others. You'll find that I've included a lot of examples, ranging from intimate conversations in a family and meetings of managers in a corporation to speeches by heads of state. Read through the book until you find an example that speaks to your specific purpose, and then delve more deeply into the ideas described there. You'll also find that the ideas in each chapter stand on the ones presented in the earlier chapters, so as you begin to explore the section that is most relevant to you, you'll probably want to re-read the rest of the book, this time through the lens of the section that you find most helpful.

Students

Many of you will read this book because it is required or recommended as part of a college course. As students, you'll be interested in the communication theory on which the interpretations and practices are based. If you've had other courses in communication, you'll see that I've played somewhat of a trick in the first chapter. That is, without calling attention to it, I've already taken sides in many of the controversies among social theorists. You'll see that I've given examples of communication at the interpersonal, organizational, and national political level, so you know that I don't have much patience for restricting theory to specific social contexts. You'll see that I've treated each of these instances of communication as a sequence of conversational "turns," so you know that my theory has affinities with the Language and Social Interaction approaches to communication. The title of the book, *Making Social Worlds*, should be a give-away that my thinking is deeply enmeshed with those who see communication as social construction. By inviting you to think about specific choices made by the persons in those situations – that is, taking a first-person perspective as one who acts into unfinished situations – I've aligned my treatment of these examples with the long history of communication studies stretching back to ancient Greece and away from those who seek general laws covering all situations.

Figure P.1 describes the conceptual structure of the book. Start reading the figure from the bottom. The first circle notes that there are many approaches to communication theory, many of which go in directions other than CMM. The second circle includes those theories that, like CMM, take what I call the "communication perspective." These theories all urge us to take communication itself seriously; to look *at* communication processes, not just *through* them to other things. In this view, communication is seen as generative: a way of doing things and making things, not just talking about them.

Continuing to read upward through figure P.1, the next circle specifies CMM as one theory that takes the communication perspective. It is distinguished from its intellectual cousins by its conceptualization of communication. If we've decided to look at communication, the next question is, "How shall we understand communication?" (Not all theories that take the communication perspective agree.) CMM suggests that we see communication *as* a two-sided process of coordinating actions and making/managing meanings.

"Speech acts" is one way of naming those moments when coordination and meaning making/management come together. An understanding of the way speech acts are made provides us with insights into the structure of our social worlds, and these insights are surprisingly useful. Chapter 5 ends

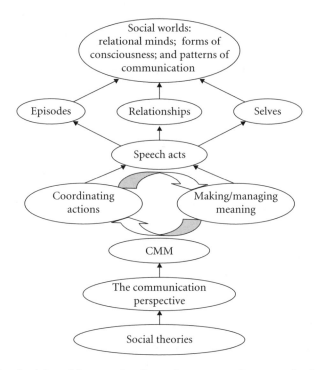

Figure P.1 Social worlds emerging from the process of communication
(Adapted from W. Barnett Pearce (2007), *Communication and the Making of Social Worlds*, Copenhagen: Danish Psychological Press)

with some specific suggestions about how to make better social worlds by acting in ways informed by a knowledge of the structure of speech acts.

Speech acts don't exist in isolation, however, and chapters 6, 7, and 8 focus on the contexts in which they occur: episodes, selves, and relationships. Each of these entities is complex, and as they evolve, emergent characteristics develop. We don't have a very good vocabulary for talking about these emergent characteristics, so I offer forms of communication (as organic clusters of episodes), forms of consciousness (as that which develops from selves), and minds (as that which develops from relationships). The topmost circle in the figure is labeled "social worlds." You might call it "cultures" as well, but I want to emphasize the notion that there are many social worlds, that they are made, and that we are agents in their making – which takes us back to the content of chapter 2.

In addition to this conceptual overview, please note the tone in which CMM is presented. You will misunderstand what is written here if you hear it said in ponderous, pontifical tones declaring that "this is the way it is!" You will grasp both the meaning and the spirit of CMM if you hear what is written in tones of wonder, curiosity, awe, and delight. CMM's tools and concepts are heuristics; they say "Look here! See this!" They summon you to explore, to inquire, to a kind of very serious playfulness; they do not try to elicit your submission or belief.

Professionals

Some of you are professionals. Perhaps you are a manager, supervisor, team leader, consultant, mediator, therapist, coach, or social worker. I hope that you'll find these concepts useful in your work.

Someone once said, "In theory, there is no difference between theory and practice. In practice, however, there is."[1] I am both a scholar and a practitioner, and I know that I read differently depending on which of those hats I'm wearing at the moment. If you are reading this book as a practitioner, I suggest that you read lightly until you get to an example that resonates with you. You may want to know that some of the examples are continued in several chapters. Read them carefully, reflect on what is being done in them, and then re-read the rest of the book. It will make more sense to you if you read it through the lens of your own experience and purposes.

With Appreciation for . . .

I had not planned to write this book now. I did so because three things converged. At about the same time that my colleagues urged me to write about CMM in a more accessible way, Danish Psychological Publishers invited me to revise an earlier book (Pearce 2007a) for translation and publication in Danish (Pearce 2007b). As I started the process of revision, I realized how much my thinking had developed. But I would not have been able to devote the quality time to the project without the sabbatical leave granted me by the School of Human and Organization Development of Fielding Graduate University. I'm grateful for the leadership of my Dean, Charles McClintock, and to my faculty and student colleagues who closed ranks while I focused on this project.

I owe special acknowledgment to several groups who have supported and challenged me as I've developed these ideas.

The theory of the coordinated management of meaning was originally developed in the company of a remarkably generous and creative set of colleagues. Vernon Cronen and I started working on CMM when both of us had dark hair and rather more of it. Our efforts were aided by working with an exceptional group of junior colleagues including Jack Lannamann, Sheila McNamee, Ken Johnson, Linda Harris, Arthur Jensen, Robert Branham, Kang Kyung-wha, Victoria Chen, Jonathan Shailor, Richard Buttny, Francis Buttle, and others.

My student and faculty colleagues at Fielding Graduate University constitute the most consistently stimulating environment in which I've ever had the pleasure of working. I owe particular debt to Frank Barrett, my coach in understanding Appreciative Inquiry and my colleague in offering graduate seminars in social constructionism.

The Public Dialogue Consortium has been the basis for most of my professional practice during the past decade, and I'm grateful for the example of applied scholarship and scholarly practice provided by the members of this organization. I've learned particularly from my colleagues Stephen Littlejohn, Shawn Spano, Kathy Domenici, Kevin Barge, Victoria Chen, Leslie Fagre, Liliana Castañeda Rossmann, Ralph Banks, Suzette Merchant, and Kim Pearce (whom I mention in other contexts below).

I've had the honor and pleasure of being a member of the faculty of the graduate certificate program in Dialogue, Deliberation and Public Engagement. Offered through Fielding Graduate University in collaboration with the Kettering Foundation and the University of Sydney, this certificate program has been an opportunity for intense work with colleagues from whom I've learned more than they might realize. For value added to this book, I thank Jan Elliott, Keith Melville, Hal Saunders, Phil Stewart, Lyn Carson, and John Dedrick.

I'm particularly grateful to friends and colleagues who read the next-to-last draft of the manuscript. Their thoughtful and useful suggestions have made this draft far different from the one they read, and much better. Big hugs go to Carey Adams, Victoria Chen, Cate Creede, Marie Farrell, Beth Fisher-Yoshida, Allan Holmgren, Jeremy Kearney, Keith Melville, Chris Oliver, Kimberly Pearce, Shawn Spano, Ilene Wassermann, and to four anonymous reviewers.

My gratitude to my wife and partner Kim exceeds my ability to express. I appreciate her patience while I worked on this project, her support throughout, the materials that we have developed together on which I drew, her willingness to talk with me when I needed a conversation partner, and her comments on the entire final draft. Besides all of that, she is my role model when I imagine good communication, highly evolved consciousness, and healthy relational mind.

W.B.P.

Note

1 I've seen this quotation attributed both to computer scientist Jan L. A. van de Snepscheut and to baseball player Yogi Berra. I haven't a clue who should be credited for it, but I'd bet on van de Snepscheut, although Yogi was no slouch with a quip.

References

Pearce, W. B. (2007a), *Interpersonal Communication: Making Social Worlds*, New Brunswick, NJ: University Publishing Solutions.

Pearce, W. B. (2007b), *Communication and the Making of Social Worlds*, Copenhagen, Denmark: Danish Psychological Publishers.

Chapter 1

Critical Moments that Shape Our Social Worlds

Preview

This chapter calls attention to "critical moments" in which what we do changes the social worlds in which we live. It urges us to develop our ability to identify and act wisely in these moments. This ability is important, both in our personal lives and for human society as a whole. Powerful forces are pulling us simultaneously backward, forward, and upward, and we need to enhance the forces that would move us upward.

Critical moments, and the ability to identify them and act wisely in them, are described in the context of two examples: a 911 emergency call and President Bush's speech on the evening of 9/11. Without commenting on them, many of the themes developed in later chapters are introduced in the analyses of these examples. Each example is described as turn-by-turn sequences in which the participants coordinate their actions with each other and make/manage their meanings about what is going on. Foreshadowing the final three chapters and as diagrammed in figure P.1 (in the Preface), the descriptions of these events are sensitive to differences in the forms of communication achieved, levels of consciousness embodied by the participants, and the quality of the relational minds that evolve.

A Critical Moment in a 911 Emergency Telephone Call

The normal high-speed congestion on Highway 85 in San Jose, California, was suddenly made worse when drivers started swerving to avoid a mattress in the road. Concerned that a serious accident was likely, one driver called "911" on her cell phone. After she explained the situation, she was told that the Emergency Response unit was not the appropriate government agency, and her call was transferred to the City of San Jose police dispatcher. After a wait of some time, her call was answered and this conversation occurred (the transcript was published in the San Francisco Chronicle, September 4, 1998):

(1) *San Jose police dispatcher:*   San Jose Police . . .
(2) *Driver:*   Um, yes. I wanted to report that there is a mattress in the middle of the freeway. Cars are dodging it left and right.
(3) *Dispatcher:*   In the middle of the freeway?
(4) *Driver:*   In the middle of the freeway on . . .
(5) *Dispatcher:*   OK. You'll have to call the highway patrol for that.
(6) *Driver:*   *(Sigh)* Why don't you call them for me? Or otherwise, I'll just leave the mattress in the middle of the freeway. I mean, it's 85! Highway 85!
(7) *Dispatcher:*   Is there a reason you're so upset?
(8) *Driver:*   Well, it took me forever to get through, and people are dodging this mattress and I just wanted to, maybe . . .
(9) *Dispatcher:*   OK. But what I'm telling you, ma'am, is that the San Jose Police do not respond to the freeway. It is the Highway Patrol's jurisdiction. I'd be more than happy to give you the number if you'd like.
(10) *Driver:*   Never mind. I'll just let someone get killed. *(Hangs up)*

A few minutes after the call ended, a car hit the mattress, flipped over, and a person in the car was killed.

In many ways, this conversation is remarkable for being so ordinary. It occurred between two busy people who acted reasonably from their own perspectives. Both ended the conversation frustrated with the other, and unsatisfied with what had been accomplished. At specific moments during the conversation, each person missed opportunities to change its trajectory. The conversation is unusual because we have a published transcript of an audio recording and because the apparent link between its quality and its (in this case, tragic) consequence is so clear.

Executive coach Hilda Carpenter (2006) suggested that we think of every conversation as having an "afterlife" in the memories of those involved and in the experience of those affected by it. I'm struck by how large an afterlife was generated by this short conversation between these two persons. There was an official investigation of the incident by the San Jose police department; the major regional newspaper published the details of what happened and the results of the internal police investigation; the dispatcher and the driver incorporated this experience into their stories of who they are and how they will act into[1] similar situations in the future; the person responsible for the mattress being in the road was never publicly identified but had to construct a story about the incident with which he or she can live; and the family and friends of the person who was killed must live not only with the fact of the accidental death but with the knowledge that, had the conversation above gone better and a police officer been sent to the scene promptly, it might have been prevented.

What might we gain if we thought about social reality itself as the afterlife of many such conversations? That is, if we looked at the relationships among friends and enemies, at families and corporations and nongovernment organizations, at the clash of cultures and the relations among nations as conversations that, although they differ in the number of participants and the length of time involved, have a structure similar to that of the one between the driver and the dispatcher? This is part of what I describe in chapter 2 as taking "the communication perspective".

The communication perspective gives us a distinctive and unusual way of thinking about the things that we love and hate, and about the things that inspire and frighten us. For example, the unequal distribution of wealth; the virtual eradication of dread diseases like polio and smallpox; the still-in-process full participation of women in political life; the sense of safety when you walk the streets of your neighborhood; or your relationships to your parents, colleagues, and family – all these can be seen as shaped in conversations very much like the one about the mattress in the road. Looking backward in time, we can see that what was said or done in specific moments prefigured the realities in which we live now.

In addition to its (perhaps refreshing) oddity, the primary reason for taking the communication perspective is that it serves practical purposes. By looking more closely at the turn-by-turn process of communication, we can enhance our ability to discern those critical moments in which, if we act wisely, we can change the trajectory of the conversation and thus create a different "afterlife." If we are very wise and at least somewhat lucky, we can make our social worlds better.

But the communication perspective is odd; it runs against the grain of some very resilient threads in contemporary Western culture. In many circles, there's a profound belief that we should focus our attention on the "hard stuff" (masculine issues like power, money, buildings, and equipment) and let the "soft stuff" (feminine issues like relationships and patterns of communication) take care of itself. To the contrary, as IBM global business development executive Yvette Burton (2001) noted in the oral presentation of her doctoral dissertation, "if you ignore it, the 'soft stuff' will be the hardest brick wall you ever hit."

Some people ignore the "soft stuff" because they don't have the tools for working with it. Those tools are now available and reward the effort spent on learning how to use them. Although farmer and carpenter Walter Pearce thought that idle moments were shameful if not downright sinful, he taught his son (who, in turn, taught his son – me) that "Time spent sharpening a tool is not time wasted."[2] Mindful of Grandpa's good advice, chapter 3 introduces some concepts that will sharpen the tools of our intellects, helping us find our way through the jungle of social theory and engage more incisively in the flow of communication.

The communication perspective is the knack of looking *at* communication rather than *through* it, but this isn't enough. In a real sense, we see what we know rather than the other way around (Steiner 1992), and our ability to discern critical moments and to make wise decisions about how to act into them requires some sharper conceptual tools for understanding communication. At this point, any number of communication theories could be built, but for over thirty years, I've been attracted to an evolving set of ideas encapsulated in the theory of the coordinated management of meaning, or "CMM." Chapter 4 invites you to consider communication from a CMM-ish perspective, seeing it as a two-faced process of making meaning and coordinating with others. But the point of this trip through these chapters is to increase our collective abilities to discern and act wisely into critical moments.

The afterlife of the conversation between the driver and dispatcher was shaped by their inability to coordinate their different ideas about what the conversation was about, or, in CMM terms, what was the highest context for the conversation. From the driver's perspective, it was about a mattress in the road; from the dispatcher's, it was about lines of interagency jurisdiction. Within this context, each enacted an appropriate role/identity: as a rough shorthand, call them "concerned citizen" and "professional switchboard operator." During the conversation, the driver's role/identity changed to something we might call "frustrated citizen" or even "feeling abused by faceless bureaucrats." Both participants felt frustrated and didn't understand why the other was so unreasonable.

We get a more useful understanding of the conversation if we ask, "How was it made?" rather than "What was it about?" Among other good things, this question directs our attention to critical moments in which what happened – or in which what might have happened – determined the trajectory of the conversation and the resulting afterlife.

In turn (6), the driver clearly expressed that she had reached the limit of her good-citizen concern and asked the dispatcher to take over the responsibility for dealing with the danger posed by the mattress in the road.

In one sense, every turn in a conversation is a bifurcation point. If either person were to do something other than they did, the conversation would go in a different direction. But some turns – in this case, turn (7) – signal themselves as particularly significant bifurcation points. Because the driver had asked the dispatcher to change her role/identity, no matter how the dispatcher responded to this request, it would determine the subsequent direction of the conversation.

As it turned out, the dispatcher's question in turn (7) ("Is there a reason you're so upset?") was ambiguous. The driver understood it as a response to her frustration in trying to get an official response to a dangerous situation, initiating a more personal conversation. Based on this interpretation, she said:

(8) *Driver:* Well, it took me forever to get through, and people are dodging this mattress and I just wanted to, maybe . . .

But she never got a chance to finish what she was saying, because the dispatcher cut her off. Turn (9) was a forceful restatement of the dispatcher's own concern about official jurisdiction:

(9) *Dispatcher:* OK. But what I'm telling you, ma'am, is that the San Jose Police do not respond to the freeway. It is the Highway Patrol's jurisdiction. I'd be more than happy to give you the number if you'd like.

I imagine that the driver felt irritated at being apparently invited into a personal conversation and then slapped down with a bureaucratic response. She ended the call with the disturbingly accurate prediction that someone would be killed.

If the driver and dispatcher had been more sensitive to the critical moments in their conversation, and if they had sufficient resources on which to draw that would have enabled them to act into them wisely, they might have created a different social world. This is one possibility: assume that the conversation went just as it did for the first eight turns. No matter what the dispatcher intended in turn (7), as she listened to the driver in turn (8), she clearly heard the driver expressing an unsettled emotional state. Perhaps it was her frustration with the call itself, or perhaps she was nervous about talking on the cell phone while driving on a dangerous road. The dispatcher might have said something like this:

> Alternate (9) *Dispatcher:* Hey, are you taking care of yourself? Are you calling while still driving or have you pulled over to make this call?
>
> Alternate (10) *Driver:* I'm still driving. The traffic is so heavy that I'm afraid to pull over.
>
> Alternate (11) *Dispatcher:* I'm going to take over from here; I'll alert the Highway Patrol and they'll get an officer out there right away. Now I want you to hang up and make sure that you are driving safely. And on behalf of the San Jose Police department, I want to thank you for making the effort to call us about this. I drive 85 myself and know how dangerous it is even without a mattress in the road! I'm sorry about the confusion; the 911 operator should have handled it or put you in contact with the Highway Patrol.
>
> Alternate (12) *Driver:* Thanks! Goodbye.

This would have made a different conversation with a different afterlife. What abilities would have made this possible?

Why Acting Wisely in Critical Moments is Important: We're in a Race that We Need to Win

Let's take a larger view. Our social worlds are in a state of disarray. Whether you celebrate or lament the changes that are happening, it would be hard to deny them. In one way of putting it, we are all being pulled in three directions at the same time; call them backward, forward, and upward.

As I write in late summer, 2006, the backward pull is described in the headlines of every major news source. Our social worlds are still mired in the same old patterns of territorial disputes, religious and cultural wars, and the all-too-familiar motives of lust, greed, hatred, fear, and pride. The stalemate called "the Cold War" (between the Soviet Union and the Western allies) has been replaced by a less stable antagonism – what some call a "clash of civilizations" between the West and (at least some) Muslims.[3] While billions of people diet for health and appearance, other billions are malnourished because they don't have enough to eat;[4] and while some ethnic groups reach out to facilitators who help them engage in dialogic communication with their traditional enemies (Saunders 1999), others are locked in the same old cycle of committing murder and other atrocities in revenge for murders and atrocities that have been committed against them.[5]

The pull forward is being driven by technology. In one sense, techno-logy helps us do "the same thing" more efficiently. But doing something "better" isn't always better for us. For example, John Arguilla (2006), a professor at the Naval Postgraduate Institute, recently described the devel-opment of military technology for fighting in space. As I read the essay, I was struck by the sense of doing the same thing (war) in a new place (space) with costlier, more deadly weapons. That seems a movement "forward" with-out any "upward" evolution.

Technology also drives us "forward" into situations for which we aren't prepared. I grew up with an environmental ethic that presupposed that there was little I could do that would seriously harm the planet. Now that I get the senior citizen discount at movie theaters, it's clear that the human species is very capable of affecting the planet. To survive, armed with such tools as we have, requires the development of a new ethic.

The pace of technological change is mind-boggling. As a useful way of gauging the rapidity with which things are happening, we might use a single human lifespan as a metric. As a child, my maternal grandmother rode an ox-cart when she and her family went into town; as a senior citizen, she watched the live televised broadcast of Neil Armstrong walking on the moon. My grandmother thought that that was fast, but my grandchildren won't, because the pace of change is getting even faster.

In many fields, the pace of change is exponential. The power of com-puters doubles every 18 months, the capacity of information storage and retrieval technology doubles every 12 months, and the bandwidth of the internet doubles every 9 months. If society isn't unraveled by the pull backward, some analysts suggest that in the next 30 years integrated devel-opments in genetics, robotics, information technology/artificial intelli-gence, and nanotechnology (a combination known by the acronym GRIN) will bring about unforeseeable changes as radical and unpredictable as those experienced when humans shifted from hunting and gathering to domes-ticated agriculture (Garreau 2005). They speak of virtual immortality (for some few people – how will they be chosen?), unlimited resources (unequally divided), and the ability to live in harmony with – or to destroy – the earth (Ratner and Ratner 2003). In their darker moments, they refer to the "Singularity," when artificial intelligence will outstrip human ability, ushering in an era that we are unable to imagine and which, when it occurs, we will be unable to comprehend (Singularity n.d.).

Genetics, robotics, information technology and nanotechnology (GRIN) have already changed the geometry of our social worlds. Five hundred years after Columbus's discovery that the world is round, *New York Times* columnist Tom Friedman (2005) visited the high-tech capitals of India and discovered that the world has been flattened. While most of us have had our attention diverted by the wasteful conflicts of the forces pulling us backward, a new "globalized" world has developed. New communication and information technologies have leveled the playing fields of education, business, and politics. Distance and national boundaries have been diminished or erased, and the issues determining success or failure in the globalized community involve connectivity, information processing capability, education, and, above all, intelligence. Before this level of globalization, Friedman argued, it was better to be a "C" student in Boston than an "A" student in Bangalore because the differential levels of opportunity were so great. Now, however, that isn't true – and this is changing individual opportunities and institutional structures in both Boston and Bangalore.

As the other three parts of GRIN (genetics, robotics, and nanotechnology) begin to affect society, we can predict with full assurance that we will have new challenges commensurate with the new opportunities they confer. The "development gap" and the necessity for making moral and practical decisions for which our resources are inadequate are two of those challenges.

One of the first effects of any new technology is to increase the gap between those who have access to it and adopt it and those who do not. We know that the distribution of any new technology is uneven, and in communities where it is available, some people adopt it sooner than others. To the extent that the new technology benefits those who use it, the gap between them and those who cannot or will not use it increases. So whatever else technological advances bring, it will include the challenge of dealing with the gap between rich and poor.

And the benefits of new technological capabilities carry with them new responsibilities. For example, if we are now *able* to use cosmetic surgery to change our appearance, we have to decide whether we *should*. If we now have the technological capability of making an inexpensive telephone call or send a virtually free email message to every person we know, regardless of his or her location, we have no excuse not to be in daily contact. Our failure to communicate has become a matter of *choice*, not one of *ability*, and that takes us into very different relational issues. When my mother was seriously ill, the hospital asked our family to instruct them about the extent to which they would try to prolong her life. The question paralyzed me. On one hand, I realized that modern hospitals have machines that can be used as surrogates for the organs of a human body, keeping blood flowing, lungs pumping, and liver filtering long after those organs have lost their power to function independently. But on the other hand, I knew that there are limits to what we should call "life," and there comes a point where mechanically aided functioning is something less than life. But, on what resources could I draw to make the decision about how much was "enough" and what was "too much" when my mother's life was at stake? Although I am a thoughtful person and have studied philosophical and theological ethics, I found myself without a clue about how to make this kind of judgment.

I don't think I am alone in my discovery that the pull forward – "progress" but on the same plane – confronts us with irresolvable issues. In addition to "more," we need something "different." Many of us resonate with the observation attributed to Albert Einstein: "The significant problems we have cannot be solved at the same level at which we created them."[6] In addition to extricating ourselves from the pull *backward*, we need to transform the pull *forward* with something that will take us *upward*.

The pull upward consists of new ideas, institutions and practices that elevate and enhance human beings and society. Although we might not know it from reading news headlines, we have accomplished a great deal in this upward direction. At no previous moment in human history have so many people been so well fed, well clothed, politically free, relatively safe from criminal acts, educated and healthy. Both government and nongovernmental organizations (even if often at cross-purposes with each other!) are exploring possible ways of living together that are sustainable, inclusive, peaceful, and supportive.

But is the evolution of our ability to act wisely keeping pace with tech-nological developments in GRIN or sufficient to overcome the downward pull of the old, familiar ways of being? Again, assessing the rate of change depends on the metric that we use. If we divided the past 4,000 years of human history into 200-year increments and plotted innovations in this "upward" direction, we'd rightly say that our era is experiencing a dizzyingly rapid rate of social development – very likely faster than advances in technology.

The idea that we could be citizens of a state rather than subjects of a monarch is only a few hundred years old, as is the idea that a state could be religiously diverse. Not so long ago, the execution of criminals was done in public for the entertainment of spectators; when did it become something done privately or, in more advanced societies, not at all? Slavery was legally abolished less than 200 years ago, and women were empowered to vote only about 100 years ago. As recently as 1862, Jean-Henri Dunant saw the injured soldiers at the Battle of Solferino as victims in need of medical attention regardless of which army they served in and started what became the International Red Cross and the Geneva Convention of 1864 in which signatory nations pledged to care for the wounded in war, whether friend or enemy.

Whole new professions exist that did not even 100 years ago, including psychotherapists, mediators, coaches, mentors, arbitrators, and organizational development consultants. Despite their differences, all of these share a certain sensibility that communicating is a form of action and that certain forms of communicating produce desirable effects. They all celebrate the power of, as Stephen Littlejohn put it during a workshop, "listening in such a way that others want to talk and talking in such a way that others want to listen." In these forms of communication, individuals are called to listen, inquire, understand, explain, and find ways of moving forward together (Stein 2004). In many families (Orem 2003), some organizations, and a few governments, disagreements and differences are seen as sites for mutual learning, not intellectual pugilism. In some professions, the art of posing questions is valued at least as highly as that of expressing one's own opinions, and you can find a whole shelf of books and even commercially available training to learn how to do it (I'm thinking of workshops offered by the Public Conversations Project, among others). Even in some corporate settings, dialogic communication is prized (Boogaard 2000) and, when it occurs, generates an afterlife that participants describe as having "better relationships, different ways of being in the world, change of perspectives, personal transformation, self-acceptance, continuous learning, more curiosity, more awareness of self and others, and finding more meaning for their lives" (Gonzáles 2004).

We've come a long way, very fast. And we have miles to go. The good news is that the pace of the development of social sophistication is something that we can increase. Psychologist Edward Sampson (1993) said: "All that is central to human nature and human life – and here I mean mind, self, and society itself – is to be found in processes that occur *between* people in the public world of our everyday lives." If so, then we can increase the rate of our social evolution by giving explicit attention to these processes.

The bad news, or at least the cautionary tale, is that this is a race that we must win. Civilizations have collapsed before (Diamond 2004), and not every wild-eyed prophet warning of barbarians at the gates is mistaken. New technologies present equally strong opportunities for new abuse as well as for enlightenment, and some of the technophobic warnings about the evils of the next generation of widgets and practices will likely turn out to be correct. We need all the help we can get – and I think the "communication perspective" is a hitherto neglected, potentially very useful resource.

I wrote this book with a sense of urgency. We are locked into a race against two powerful opponents. One opponent would mire us in old, unproductive ways of being in relation to each other; the other would link the morality of "if we can, we must!" to engines of technological development and hurl us unprepared into an unforeseeable future. But I think that we are making much more "upward" progress than conventional wisdom acknowledges. When I started working as a practitioner of dialogic communication, I met far more like-minded people than I expected, and each of them led me to several others. I'm encouraged by the fact that the United States Institute of Peace already exists, even if not given a seat in the President's cabinet like the Department of Defense. The National Coalition for Dialogue and Deliberation brings together hundreds of individuals and organizations with scholarly and practical knowledge about how to call better forms of communication into being. Is it possible that we will soon hit what Gladwell (2000) called a "tipping point" and "suddenly" discover that, while most people's attention was diverted by the factors pulling us backward and forward, we've laid the infrastructure for a great leap upward?

Maybe. If we lose this race, it won't be because not enough people cared enough. It will be because too many of those who *want* to support the "upward" evolution of society don't know *how*. And my energies are summoned because I see us repeatedly missing opportunities to act wisely into the critical moments of our personal, social, institutional, and cultural histories.

Critical moments occur wherever people make meaning and coordinate actions with each other. That is to say, they occur everywhere: at dinner tables, in conference halls and boardrooms, during employment interviews, when responding to emergencies, in classrooms and consultations, during political campaigns and public hearings, in churches and in hospitals, etc. In my opinion, the single best leverage point for stimulating the "upward" evolution of ourselves as individuals and as a society comes from increasing our ability to discern those critical moments and to act wisely into them.

9/11: A Missed Opportunity to Act Wisely in a Critical Moment

I've made some large claims for the importance of learning to discern and act wisely into critical moments, and you would be quite right to be skeptical. Let me show you what I have in mind.

The tragic events of September 11, 2001, comprise the most momentous critical moment in recent memory. Unfortunately, the way the American government acted into it missed an opportunity to escalate the upward evolution of our society. Instead, the response created an afterlife that magnified the effects of the terrorist attack and deteriorated the quality of life around the world. Using the terms of the previous section, the American response moved us simultaneously backward and forward by doing more of the same old things (polarization, centralization of power, war) with more powerful, high-tech tools.

What happened?

Four commercial airliners were hijacked. At 8:45 A.M., one crashed into the North Tower of the World Trade Center in New York City. At 9:03, another crashed into the South Tower. The Federal Aviation Agency ordered all civilian flights grounded at 9:40; at 9:41, the third airliner crashed into the Pentagon, outside Washington, DC. At 10:10, the passengers of a fourth hijacked airliner, having learned that other airplanes had been used to attack buildings, attempted to seize control of the plane. In the struggle, it crashed in western Pennsylvania.

More Americans were killed or injured by these terrorist attacks than in any single day in any war since our Civil War in the middle of the nineteenth century.

One of the roles of a leader is to help people understand tragic events like this. At 7:00 P.M., President Bush addressed the nation. In this short speech (17 paragraphs in the transcript made by the program *NewsHour with Jim Lehrer*), he described the attacks, named our response as "disbelief, terrible sadness, and a quiet, unyielding anger," and promised that we would "stand together" to "defend freedom and all that is good and just in our world." We were attacked, he explained, "because we're the brightest beacon for freedom and opportunity." Those who attacked us are "evil" and "intend to frighten [us] into chaos and retreat." He promised that the attacks would be unsuccessful (we have "stood down enemies before and will do so this time") and named constructive steps already taken by emergency response teams, government agencies, and financial institutions. In retaliation, he announced a new doctrine in which the US will make "no distinction between the terrorists who committed these acts and those who harbor them."

The following morning, after a meeting with the National Security Council, the President addressed the nation again. This speech was even shorter; only nine paragraphs in the transcript posted by AOL News. In this speech, he described the attacks as "acts of war" in which "freedom and democracy are under attack." We are engaged, he said, in "a monumental struggle of good versus evil, but good will prevail." He demonized the perpetrators, calling them "a different kind of enemy" who "hides in shadows and has no regard for human life" and "preys on innocent and unsuspecting people and then runs for cover." The speech featured tough talk. The terrorists, he promised, "won't be able to run for cover forever . . . to hide forever . . . be safe forever"; the "US will use our resources . . . rally the world . . . be patient . . . be focused and steadfast"; and we are more alert, have heightened security, and are taking precautions.

How was the story told?

In a period of crisis, any leader needs to help others understand what is happening, reassure them that they are being competently led, and suggest the trajectory of their response. These were clearly among President Bush's intentions for these speeches.

Where does the story begin?

In both speeches, the President's official narrative started when the first plane hit the building – at 8:45 A.M. on September 11. This manner of storytelling left out everything that led up to this dramatic event and made the actions of the hijackers appear senseless, adding to the confusion and anxiety about what was happening.

His story could have started with other times and other places.[7] Here are some possibilities. Although it might seem a bit of a stretch, he could have begun by recalling Pope Urban II's speech in November 1095, calling for Christians to mount a Crusade to aid the Byzantine emperor in his war against the Seljuk Turks.[8] In a speech at the Council of Clermont, the Pope used words eerily similar to those of the people who encourage contemporary suicide bombers. Urban told the Franks: "God himself would lead them, for they would be doing His work. There will be absolution and remission of sins for all who die in the service of Christ. Here they are poor and miserable sinners; there they will be rich and happy. Let none hesitate; they must march next summer. God wills it!" The phrase "God wills it" became the battle cry of the First Crusade (Knox n.d.).

Another possible starting point would be the period immediately following the end of World War I. The victorious European allies created new nations (Iraq, Pakistan, Iran, Jordan, and Lebanon) without regard to geography or ethnic and tribal structures, and achieved the unlikely effect of, as Fromkin (1989) put it, *A Peace to End All Peace*. Some Muslims believe that they are still struggling with political problems created or exacerbated by European interventions and resent Europeans who cite those struggles as evidence that the Muslim nations are not capable of good government.

Yet another starting point might be the American decision to fight a surrogate war against the Soviet Union in Afghanistan. As a way of discomforting its enemy in the Cold War, the United States covertly made Pakistan a staging area and provided training and weapons to radically conservative Muslims who would fight a guerrilla war against the USSR because they hated the presence of infidels on the land they considered their own (Mamdani 2004). One such person was an independently wealthy Arab named Osama bin Laden. After the Soviet Union first withdrew from Afghanistan and then collapsed as a nation, bin Laden turned his attention to the United States, becoming the leader of a loose confederation of people willing to use the tactics learned in Afghanistan to achieve their political purposes, including getting the US to remove its military bases from Saudi Arabia.

The first terrorist attack on the World Trade Center did not occur on September 11, 2001. It happened on February 26, 1993, and that might be a good starting point for the story of what happened. Six people were killed and more than 1,000 injured.

This attack was framed as a "crime" rather than a war, and five years later, a New York City jury found Ramze Ahmed Yousef guilty. Before being sentenced to spend 240 years in prison, Yousef proudly identified himself as a terrorist and explained his actions as responding to the terrorist acts invented by and practiced by the United States. In an impassioned pre-sentencing statement, he accused the United States of "inventing this kind of terrorism" that "kills innocent people or civilians in order to force the government to change its policies." As supporting evidence, he cited the atomic bombs and fire bombings of cities in Japan, the use of Agent Orange in Vietnam, and economic embargoes on Cuba and other countries that "[kill] nobody other than children and elderly people." He concluded:

> The government in its summations and opening said that I was a terrorist. Yes, I am a terrorist and I am proud of it. And I support terrorism so long as it was against the United States Government and against Israel, because you are more than terrorists; you are the one who invented terrorism and are using it every day. You are butchers, liars and hypocrites. (Wanniski 2001)

If President Bush had told the story this way, he would have been criticized for not sounding a clear and comforting note to a frightened and confused people. However, he would also have established the groundwork for a more nuanced and subtle American policy and a foreign policy that might invoke less negative reaction from Muslims around the world.

How should we frame what happened?

About 17 hours intervened between the two speeches, during which the frame that the President offered for understanding the tragic events shifted from "a response to a terrorist act" to "a war on terrorism." In comments made on September 12, President Bush announced that this was the first war of the twenty-first century and, by the end of the week, Congress had granted the President extraordinary powers, similar to a state of war.

Consistent with the "war" metaphor, the world in Bush's speeches is divided into "us" and "them," and the conflict between the two is legitimated. In a characteristically American way, the war becomes one in which "we" are good, the embodiment of civilization and freedom, and "they" are evil, cowards, and inexplicably opposed to our virtues. Other nations were asked to cooperate in this "war"; they were told that this was a time when our "friends" were clearly distinguished from our "enemies." There was no third category. Both speeches were filled with promises of victory, although the shape of that victory was left fairly vague.

The clear subtext of all of this was that our response to the terrorists' attacks would not be in a legal context of trying individuals for their actions but in the context of an international war, using all of the resources of the United States' government and its allies, including military force. Later in the week, Bush's rhetoric toughened still more, with promises to "smoke out" the terrorists, with allusions to what we in the United States call "the old west" posters saying "Wanted: Dead or Alive."

How did President Bush respond?

Terrorism isn't a new technique. It is no mystery that the purpose of terrorism is to provoke a response that is more damaging to the target than the terrorist act itself. President Bush interpreted the events of 9/11 as an opening act in a new kind of war and responded by promising tough action leading to victory. I don't know why he made that choice; perhaps he sincerely believed what he said or perhaps he was already planning to use the attack as a justification for reducing civil liberties in the United States, diverting vast sums of money to political and personal friends, and attacking Iraq. But regardless of his motive, his actions seemed calculated to accomplish Osama bin Laden's purpose of dividing the Western alliance and rallying large groups of Muslims to oppose the West.

If you will permit me a play on words: English is a language spoken by lots of people, many of whom don't speak the same language. Beyond matters of pronunciation and vocabulary, there are cultural ways of communicating and these manners of speaking (and to a lesser extent, writing) are crucial in determining whether we recognize others as "one of us."

With this in mind, we can say that President Bush's response to 9/11 was, in Donal Carbaugh's (1988, 1996) phrase, "talking American." He used a style of speech that relied on certain cultural conventions about what to say and how to say it, made certain assumptions about shared values and knowledge, and worked within a complex set of rules – that neither he nor his audience could articulate – about what is good, true, beautiful, and appropriate. This distinguished his remarks from those made on the same day by, for example, Tony Blair (the Prime Minister of the United Kingdom) and Yasser Arafat (leader of the Palestinian government), even though they, too, spoke in English.

So what? Well, three things. First, the fact that he spoke "American" permitted most Americans to identify with him. This was a necessary goal if he were to function, as the occasion required, as the national spokesperson. Second, his speech was shaped, limited, and facilitated by the discursive properties of American culture. For example, this cultural discourse made it easy to use the dichotomy between "good" and "evil" and to quote a Psalm in a way that clearly claimed that God is on our side. Third, by speaking "American," he reproduced this culture, extending its hegemony just a bit further. That is, its strengths and weaknesses were reinforced rather than challenged.

As a speaker, the President was both enabled and limited by the necessity to speak "American." My guess is that he did not find the limitations vexing, because his message was fairly conventional. Had he attempted to do something more ambitious, he would have needed to find ways of transcending these limitations or of changing the rules in a way that would bring his audience along with him (Branham and Pearce 1985; Pearce and Littlejohn 1997).

Could President Bush have responded in another way?

Could President Bush have done something other than "talking American?" I think so. By looking at 9/11 as one move in a sequence of turns, he might have seen these tragic events as a critical moment, a major opportunity to restructure a conversation that has gone on, usually not particularly well, for almost a thousand years (since 1095). And if he had drawn on some available knowledge about the kinds of things that transform troubled relationships into dialogic communication, he might have had some touchstones for acting more wisely. For example, in our studies of moral conflicts, communication theorist and consultant Stephen Littlejohn and I (Pearce and Littlejohn 1997) found that moving forward together productively usually requires breaking out of the "normal" patterns of interaction. That is, someone, sometime, must respond in something other than the expected way that simply reproduces the pattern.

Where "talking American" is a perfect recipe for continuing the bloody conflict, these are some ways in which this, and any other similar pattern of interaction, can be transcended. We don't have to invent alternatives, and changing from unproductive aspects of "talking American" to something more useful is not an impossible task. Those involved in the "alternative dispute resolution movement" or the rediscovery of the virtues of dialogic communication in organizations, politics and personal relationships have found that "ordinary people" – that is, those without extensive formal training – can communicate more productively if they are in a well-designed meeting or have the services of a skillful mediator or facilitator. Or simply learn/experience other, better, and more productive forms of communication. Here's one way of describing what the alternative form of communication looks like:

1   Constructing a richer story about what happened, including:
    • an understanding of the other;
    • an understanding of ourselves; and
    • an understanding of the historical context.

2   Constructing a more systemic description of what happened:
    • beyond "us" and "them" to the patterns that "we" are involved in; and
    • beyond "win" and "lose" to win–win outcomes.

3   Facilitating an increased awareness of the roles the participants play in making the world in which they live:
    • noting their responsibility for making the patterns in which they find themselves, not just blaming the other; and
    • noting their opportunities for acting in novel ways, not just responding in the most obvious ways.

4   Changing the context:
    • providing a new interpretation of what's important or relevant (including "common ground");
    • moving to a different space or place; and
    • changing the set of participants.

5   Minding and caring about the kind of energy that is involved. Following the maxim that what we pay attention to grows, it makes a difference whether the participants in a moral conflict attend to that which is wrong/missing/bad or to that which is right/present/good. These differences in attention summon very different kinds of energy and thus resources to act into difficult situations. In general, "appreciative" energy is far more productive than "deficit" energy.

Examples of acting wisely in critical moments

Not only do we know what makes better social worlds, there are well-known examples of people who have acted this way. In what follows, note how the five principles above were – or were not – applied.

President Abraham Lincoln's "Gettysburg Address"

On November 19, 1863, President Lincoln spoke at the dedication cere-
monies of a Union cemetery at the location of what was already recognized
as the decisive battle of the long, bloody American Civil War. Speaking to
a partisan audience at the site of a great Union victory (in which far more
Americans died than on 9/11), Lincoln never referred to "us" or "them,"
to "Confederates" or "Union," or to "winners" and "losers." In his brief
speech (shorter than either of Bush's speeches on September 11 or 12),
he framed the situation as a test of whether this nation or any other,
dedicated "to the proposition that all men are created equal," could "long
endure." Naming the specific task as that of establishing the cemetery, he
claimed that the oratory of the day was less important than what "those
brave men" have done here. The significance, he concluded, was to ensure
that "government of the people, by the people, and for the people, shall
not perish from the earth."

Four aspects of this speech are noteworthy. First, Lincoln changed the
context. Instead of a partisan rally celebrating a Union victory, he located
the day's events as part of a historic exploration of the possibilities of
democratic government.

Second, he constructed a more systemic description of what happened.
By conspicuously refusing to "speak American" – in this instance by
differentiating "us" good, successful Union supporters from "them," bad,
losing Confederates – he called into being that which he was striving
to achieve – a Union consisting of one nation, undivided. His speech
flouted the rhetorical conventions of his day and appealed, as he put it
himself in another major speech, to "the higher angels of our nature."

Third, he focused on positive or "appreciative" energy. Committed to
honoring those who fought at Gettysburg, he called on his audience to
join him in insuring that "government of the people, by the people, and
for the people, shall not perish from the earth."

Fourth, the entire speech was self-reflexive; a meditation on its own
circumstance and means of meeting the requirements of the situation.
As such, it invited the audience to be more mindful of their own role in
making the world in which they would subsequently live. Without naming the alternative, Lincoln spoke as if that future – a day in which the
warring sides were reconstituted into a Union – were already present.

The immediate reactions to the speech were critical, even contemp-
tuous. Only with some distance has it been identified as one of the great

orations in history, in part because it transcended the divisiveness of the moment and appealed to noble sentiments in a situation that was at the time dominated by smaller emotions. This speech is perhaps best understood as the first announcement of Lincoln's plan for postwar reconciliation. Lincoln recognized that winning the war on the battlefield was not the same as achieving peace. Before the fighting ended, he spent considerable time in secret consultations with his generals about how the fighting should end in order to set the stage for peace (Winik 2001).

The Treaty of Versailles

The treatment of Germany by the victorious Allies at the end of World War I provides an example of not recognizing a crucial moment and/or of acting unwisely into it. Those with the power to impose their decisions on others acted out of their desire for vengeance and short-term benefits; the afterlife included the Holocaust and World War II.

After the fighting stopped on the battlefield and before the formal meetings at which the Treaty was signed, Germany created a new government (the Weimar Constitution, February 6, 1919) that differed significantly from the government that had been in place before and during the war. Most Germans saw the new government as a move toward a democratic republic, breaking with their past. They imagined the program of self-determination and equality of rights originally set out in President Woodrow Wilson's Fourteen Points to be binding on both sides. However, the Treaty signed on May 7, 1919, was punitive, imposing extremely harsh terms on Germany. Among other things, the terms of the Treaty weakened the Weimar government and led to the legend that the German Army had never been defeated but was stabbed in the back by the Republicans, the Socialists, and the Jews.

Notice that this Treaty ignored changes in the German state from the end of hostilities to the time it was signed. Among other things, this disempowered the Germans as agents of their own political and social change and, by rendering them incapable of participating in the construction of their own future, legitimated their refusal to accept responsibility for the conditions in which they found themselves. The ground was prepared for Hitler to rise to power on the basis of a story that the Germans were victims of a plot and had the right to strike back at those who had tricked them. The "official story" among the Allies – at least for public consumption – was that the Treaty was fair and honorable. As a result, many people among the Allied nations were subsequently surprised by the aggressiveness of the Germans, who themselves knew quite well what had happened to them.

The European Recovery Program (Marshall Plan)

In sharp contrast to the Treaty of Versailles, the authors of the European Recovery Program following World War II were aware of the role they were playing in the creation of the future, and elevated this concern above the harsh emotions that had dominated the fighting. In order to create stable conditions in which the institutions of free nations could survive, the United States initiated a massive plan of rebuilding 16 European nations. The success of the plan led President Truman to extend it to many other nations as his Point Four Program, starting in 1949.

Like Lincoln's Gettysburg Address, the Marshall Plan transcended the previous divisions between "us" and "them" and between "winners" and "losers" in the war. Through its attention to the kind of future that it was creating, it called into being previously unthinkable patterns of cooperation and productive interdependency. By focusing on the conditions that would make a better world, it unleashed productive energies that did much more than solve the problems envisioned by its founders.

Could President Bush have acted more wisely in the critical moment of 9/11?

I think so. Had President Bush (with his advisors) taken the communication perspective, learned from historical examples such as those cited above, and/or used some of the concepts and tools presented in this book, he would have at least had the opportunity to choose among various responses.

As a way of expressing my own sense of horror and sadness at what I perceived as yet another missed opportunity to make a better world, I wrote the speech that I wished President Bush would have given on the evening of September 11. As you read the speech, take note of how it puts into practice the five principles, listed above, for making better social worlds. Also, assume that this isn't "just" a speech, but is the announcement of a set of policies pursued with the same consistency and vigor that the Bush Administration has implemented what the President said in his speeches on September 11 and 12. Since those speeches, the Bush Administration has invaded Afghanistan and Iraq, bullied and threatened other nations to obtain their support for the invasion of Iraq, established the Department of Homeland Security, led Congress to pass the Patriot Act that gives unprecedented powers to the Executive branch of government at the expense of civil liberties, circumvented legal process in order to monitor private conversations on telephones and internet, and violated international rules of war in using torture and secret detention of prisoners (then Presidential legal advisor, Alberto Gonzales, now Attorney-General of the United States, described the Geneva Conventions for the treatment of combatants as "quaint" and "outmoded"). Finally, ask yourself what social worlds would have been made if this were the speech to which the whole world listened on that fateful evening.

The first three paragraphs and the final paragraph are the same as those delivered by the President. My revisions begin in the fourth paragraph.

Today, my fellow citizens, our way of life, our very freedom came under attack in a series of deliberate and deadly terrorist acts. The victims were in airplanes or in their offices. Secretaries, business men and women, military and federal workers. Moms and dads. Friends and neighbors.

Thousands of lives were suddenly ended by evil, despicable acts of terror.

The pictures of airplanes flying into buildings, fires burning, huge structures collapsing, have filled us with disbelief, terrible sadness, and a quiet, unyielding anger.

Making all of this worse, at this moment, we don't know who is responsible or why such savagery was directed at us. But we will find out, and we will respond.

Our first response is to prevent additional attacks. Your government, law enforcement, and military forces continue to operate, and we are taking every step possible to protect our citizens and our country from further destruction.

In addition, we are meeting the needs of those injured in these attacks. I immediately implemented our government's emergency response plans. Our emergency teams are working as I speak in New York and in Washington, DC, to help local agencies in their rescue efforts.

We join in grief those families who have lost loved ones. Nothing we can do is enough to console those whose parents, friends, children, brothers, or sisters are missing or have died, but we can and will join them in their sorrow. We are all bereaved; we are all shocked; we are all saddened. Let us comfort and support each other in this time of tragedy.

While we protect ourselves, care for the injured, and grieve for our dead, we are also searching for those who did this horrible thing. We will find them and bring them to justice.

And, we will do more.

We Americans like to think of ourselves as a good and generous people, and so we are. Nowhere has this been shown more clearly than in the courageousness of those who have rushed into burning buildings to save others; the concern of those who have given blood and donated skills and supplies; and the compassion of those who treated wounds and embraced those who are hurt and hurting.

But we live in a complex and dangerous world. And in this world there are people who are not like us; who do not like us, and who seek to harm us. Some of these people think that whatever they can do to hurt us is morally right; some even claim God's blessing for what they do.

The fires and chaos in New York and in Washington are unprecedented – and yet they remind us of images that we have seen from other places: among the Palestinians and Israelis, from Beirut and London, and, I say with deep regret, from many other places around the world.

For many years, our intelligence and law enforcement officials have successfully protected us from attacks such as we have seen today. For many of us, terrorism has been something that afflicts other people or affects us only when we travel to other countries. And we have been generous in our support for the victims of terrorism as we have of natural disasters. We have given food, clothing, equipment; many of us have gone to the sites of terrorist attacks and offered medical help. But until today, most of us had not experienced it ourselves.

But now we, too, are the victims. This is not the first terrorist attack on US soil, but it is the most heinous. And it ends our ability to rest comfortably behind our own protective walls in such a dangerous world. Its sets before us a daunting task – a task different from those that confronted other generations, and one to which we must rise.

This terrorist attack, like all the other ones that have occurred during the past decades, does not come out of nothing. Our stories about the world, and about our place in the world, will have to become more complex. If we are to understand why people hate us so much, we will have to understand how the world looks from their perspective. And if we are to respond effectively to protect ourselves, we must understand those whose sense of history and purpose are not like our own.

It is tempting to see this vicious attack as the result of madmen trying to destroy civilization, and our response as a war of "good" against "evil." But if we are to understand what happened here today, and if we are to act effectively in the days to come, we must develop more sophisticated stories than these about the world, about our place in it, and about the consequences of our actions.

This is a terrorist attack. If we are in a state of war, it is a different kind of war than we have ever fought before. Terrorists are not capable of occupying our country or meeting our armies on the field of battle. They hope to destroy our confidence; to disrupt our way of life. They hope that we will destroy ourselves by the way we respond to the atrocities that they commit. Our first reaction, that of wanting revenge, to lash out at those who have injured us so, is almost surely the wrong response because it makes us accomplices of what they are trying to achieve.

Instead of doing the obvious thing that they are trying to provoke, the more difficult task before us is to work on two levels simultaneously. First, we will identify, seek out, and punish those who did this horrible thing. As President Kennedy said in a different situation: let the message go out from this place that we will pay any price and bear any burden to prevent and punish those who make war on our citizens and our country. Let there be no uncertainty, no room for ambiguity, no doubt about that. We have enormous resources on which we may draw, and we will use them.

But no matter what we do in retaliation and prevention, it will not bring our dead back to life; it will not heal our wounds; it will not wipe the tears from our eyes. And if only our grief and our pain motivate us, we run the risk of becoming that which we hate.

Let us today renew our commitment to our highest values – what President Abraham Lincoln called "the higher angels of our nature" – and resolve that we will not defeat ourselves by becoming indiscernible from terrorists as we battle against terrorism.

So the second level of our task is to identify and seek to change the conditions in the world that call forth such hatred and permit it to flourish. Even as we struggle with our grief at the wounds inflicted on us as a nation, I call us to a renewed effort to achieve peace and justice throughout the world. The world is now too small, too interrelated, and too complex for us to hope that we can insulate ourselves from those who hate us, or to ignore the consequences of our actions that cause grief and pain to others.

In the next few days, I will set into motion two initiatives.

First, I will support the initiative already in Congress to create a cabinet-level Department of Peace. We now know a lot about peace, and we know that it is not simply the absence of war. My charge to this Department and to the Secretary that I will name to my cabinet is a formidable one: to help create a world in which hatred and terror have no place. And I pledge my full support to this good work.

Second, to help create a world in which hatred and terror have no support or places to hide, I will ask for all nations of the world to join us in a campaign to identify and prosecute terrorists, to deny them support and materials, and to coordinate efforts to maintain the freedom of citizens throughout the world to live and move about in safety.

Almost forty years ago, a great American stood not far from where I now sit, and said that he had a dream of "the day when all of God's children will be able to sing with a new meaning, 'My country, 'tis of thee, sweet land of liberty, of thee I sing. Land where my fathers died, land of the pilgrim's pride, from every mountainside, let freedom ring.' "

Today, as our nation rebounds from this vicious attack, I have a dream of the day when all of God's children will be able to sing, with full meaning, that their country is a "sweet land of liberty" and that from every mountainside in every country, freedom will ring. And as Martin Luther King, Jr., told us: "When we let freedom ring, when we let it ring from every village and every hamlet, from every state and every city, we will be able to speed up that day when all of God's children, black men and white men, Jews and Gentiles, Protestants and Catholics," – and, yes, Muslims and Buddhists and Hindus and agnostics and all the rest – "will be able to join hands and sing in the words of the old Negro spiritual, 'Free at last! Free at last! Thank God Almighty, we are free at last!' "

My fellow Americans, let us accept the task that has been so tragically thrust upon us, to bind up our nation's wounds and to work together to create a world in which such wounds are not inflicted on anyone.

Thank you, and good night.

Notes

1   You may find the term "act into contexts" unfamiliar – the grammar-check on my word processing software certainly does! Let's start with the distinction between "texts" or "acts" – what we say and do – on the one hand, and "contexts" on the other.

The term "contexts" is a linguistic place-holder indicating specific places, such as church, pub, or school; specific relationships, such as friends, spouses, or business acquaintances; specific events, such as a job interview, a performance review, a flirtation, or watching a football game on television; etc.

We all know by now that the meaning of what we say or do is shaped by the context in which we say or do it. So far, so good. But where do contexts come from? How do we, sitting in a bar with our employer, know which event – watching a game, a performance review, a flirtation – is the context that provides the meaning for what is being said and done? How are contexts changed?

The answer: not only do contexts shape the meaning of what we say and do, but what we say and do also shapes the contexts in which we act. The relationship is a reflexive one, and that challenges our standard linguistic repertoire for explaining "why" we do the things we do as well as the grammar for describing it. In an attempt to stimulate the evolution of our language, Branham and Pearce (1985) borrowed from Gregory Bateson the notion of a "zig-zag dance" between text and context, and expanding on Ludwig Wittgenstein, John Shotter (1997) suggested that we think of what we say and do in each moment both as "acting out of contexts" (those that existed "before" our action) and "acting into contexts" (those that are brought into being as a consequence of our action).

I find Shotter's paired expression – acting into and out of contexts – a useful way of describing this reflexive relationship between the acts that we perform and the contexts in which they occur. By the time you've read more deeply into this book, I hope that you will be comfortable with these ways of talking – and find yourself explaining to your puzzled friends what you mean by these phrases.

2   The influence of this bit of family wisdom might have been why, although neither of my parents or any of my grandparents had done so, I was encouraged to go to college. However, my clumsiness with the tools more commonly found on farm and construction site might also have had something to do with it.

3   Although it is in popular use in some circles, I hesitated even to mention this term because it presumes a totalizing way of thinking about both "the West" and "Islamic nations" that can prevent us from discerning many critical moments. This is evident in the analysis (in chapter 2) of the response to cartoons depicting the Prophet Muhammad.

4   As I write in late February, 2006, millions of people are in danger of starving in the Sudan. The American government has officially designated this as the result of a policy of genocide, not because there is too little food in the world.

5   As I write these lines, Sunni and Shi'ite Muslims in Iraq are on the point of civil war; Israel and the Palestinians are still fighting; an ethnic minority is fighting against the central government in Pakistan, etc.

6   Many people repeat this quotation and attribute it to Einstein. I've been unable to find the original statement.

7   These comments assume that the President had more knowledge of the likely suspects than he revealed in these speeches. Given subsequent revelations of the amount of information possessed by the Administration and by intelligence agencies, this seems a reasonable assumption.

8   For one brief, unshining moment, President Bush actually used the word "crusade" to describe our side of what he later called the "war on terrorism."

References

Arguilla, J. (2006), Rods from God, *San Francisco Chronicle*, March 12, 2006, section E: 1, 8.

Boogaard, D. (2000), Leading dialogically: being authentic, aware and compassionate in the corporate world. PhD dissertation, Fielding Graduate University. Santa Barbara, CA.

Branham, R. J. and Pearce, W. B. (1985), Between text and context: toward a rhetoric of contextual reconstruction, *Quarterly Journal of Speech*, 71: 19–36.

Burton, Y. (2001), Understanding the significance of socially constructed conditions and business information exchanges in group task–goal dynamics. PhD dissertation, Fielding Graduate University, Santa Barbara, CA.

Carbaugh, D. (1988), *Talking American: Cultural Discourses on Donahue*, Norwood, NJ: Ablex.

Carbaugh, D. (1996), *Situating Selves: The Communication of Social Identities in American Scenes*, Albany: State University of New York Press.

Carpenter, H. (2006), Reconceptualizing communication competence: high performing coordinated communication competence (HPC3): a three-dimensional view. PhD dissertation, Fielding Graduate University, Santa Barbara, CA.

Diamond, J. (2004), *Collapse: How Societies Choose to Fail or Succeed*, New York: Viking.

Friedman, T. L. (2005), *The World is Flat: A Brief History of the Twenty-first Century*, New York: Farrar, Straus, and Giroux.

Fromkin, D. (1989), *A Peace to End All Peace: The Fall of the Ottoman Empire and the Creation of the Modern Middle East*, New York: Henry Holt.

Garreau, J. (2005), *Radical Evolution: The Promise and Peril of Enhancing Our Minds, Our Bodies – and What it Means to be Human*, New York: Doubleday.

Gladwell, M. (2000), *The Tipping Point: How Little Things Can Make a Big Difference*, New York: Brown, Little.

Gonzáles, A. L. (2004), Transformative conversations: executive coaches and business leaders in dialogical collaboration for growth. In I. F. Stein and

L. A. Belsten (eds.), *Proceedings of the First ICF Coaching Research Symposium*, Mooresville, NC: Paw Print Press, pp. 94–103, 97.

Knox, E. L. (n.d.), Online materials for a course on the history of the crusades at Boise State University. Retrieved on February 26, 2006, from http://crusades.boisestate.edu/1st/02.shtml

Mamdani, M. (2004), *Good Muslim, Bad Muslim: America, the Cold War, and the Roots of Terror*, New York: Pantheon Books.

Orem, S. (2003), Relationships that grow: disagreeing as a site for learning. PhD dissertation, Fielding Graduate University, Santa Barbara, CA.

Pearce, W. B. and Littlejohn, S. W. (1997), *Moral Conflict: When Social Worlds Collide*, Thousand Oaks, CA: Sage.

Ratner, M. and Ratner, D. (2003), *Nanotechnology: A Gentle Introduction to the Next Big Idea*, Upper Saddle River, NJ: Prentice Hall.

Rogers, E. M. (1995), *The Diffusion of Innovations* (4th edn.), New York: Free Press.

Sampson, E. E. (1993), *Celebrating the Other: A Dialogic Account of Human Nature*, Boulder, CO: Westview Press.

Saunders, H. H. (1999), *A Public Peace Process: Sustained Dialogue to Transform Racial and Ethnic Conflicts*, New York: St. Martin's Press.

Shotter, J. (1997), Dialogical realities: the ordinary, the everyday, and other strange new worlds, *Journal for the Theory of Social Behaviour*, 27, 2 and 3: 345–57.

Singularity (n.d.), retrieved on June 26, 2005, from http://www.aleph.se/Trans/Words/s.html#SINGULARITY

Stein, I. F. (2004), The "coach-approach" as dialogic discourse. In I. F. Stein and L. A. Belsten (eds.), *Proceedings of the First ICF Coaching Research Symposium*, Mooresville, NC: Paw Print Press, pp. 130–9.

Steiner, R. J. (1992), Believing is seeing, *Art Times Journal*, retrieved on December 22, 2005, from http://www.arttimesjournal.com/peeks/believingisseeing.htm

Toulmin, S. (1992), *Cosmopolis: The Hidden Agenda of Modernity*, Chicago: University of Chicago Press.

Wanniski, J. (2001), The mind of a terrorist, *Future Edition*, 4, 19.

Winik, J. (2001), *April 1865: The Month that Saved America*, New York: HarperCollins.

Chapter 2

Taking a Communication Perspective on Social Worlds

Preview

Chapter 1 introduced the topic of "critical moments" and argued that what we do in them has an afterlife that shapes social worlds. This claim is more radical than it might seem. It presumes particular concepts of communication, of social worlds, and of the relationship between them.

In this way of thinking, communication is a process of doing things and making things, not just talking "about" them. This concept of communication runs against the grain of commonsense notions of how communication works and of what work communication does.

Because we are immersed in them, we have to somehow "discover" social worlds. This chapter describes how my experience with the cultures of my parents' and grandparents' families taught me that social worlds exist, they are world-like, and that there are many of them. This chapter also develops the ideas (that I did not learn until much later) that social worlds are made and that we are agents in their making.

The communication perspective is more a way of looking at things than a set of assertions about the things looked at. As a result, those who take this perspective ask certain sorts of questions. This chapter ends by identifying some of these distinctive questions and applying them to the relationships between wives and husbands.

Everybody Has a Theory of Communication, Although Most People Don't Know It

If you look carefully, you can see an implicit theory of communication in everything that people say or do with each other. That theory matters. It prefigures the content and quality of the conversations people have with each other and these conversations have afterlives. As the afterlives from many such conversations extend and intertwine, they comprise the social worlds in which the people involved in those conversations – and you and I – live.

I know that some people go whole days at a time without reflecting on their implicit communication theories! But you should know that I believe that all of us would be better off if we all paid a bit more attention to what we think about communication. I didn't start out believing this way; in fact, it is very far from where I started my intellectual journey. Even if the idea that a "communication perspective" is the first step toward better social worlds seems implausible, I invite you to explore it with me.

If Communication is so Important, How Should We Understand It?

I've found two concepts of communication in the talk and action of the people I've studied. When I say "two concepts," I'm not doing a scholarly review like Craig's (1999). There are far more than two concepts, but my purpose is to call your attention to the one that is most deeply embedded in common sense and contrast it with the concept that I propose as an alternative. For convenience, let's call one the "transmission model" and the other the "social construction" model.

As an oversimplification, the transmission model defines the purpose of communication as the transfer of information from one mind or one place to another. It works best when messages clearly and accurately represent the meaning in the mind of the person who says, writes, draws, or performs them; those messages are transmitted without distortion, and are interpreted in the manner in which they were intended. In the social construction model, communication is more a way of making the social world rather than talking about it, and this is always done with other people. Rather than "What did you mean by that?" the relevant questions are "What are we making together?" "How are we making it?" and "How can we make better social worlds?"

These concepts of communication direct our attention in different ways. Let's see how they work out in real life.

On September 30, 2005, Flemming Rose, culture editor of *Jyllands-Posten*, asked the members of the Association of Danish Cartoonists "to draw Muhammad as you see him." Twelve of the 25 active members of the association responded, with a wide variety of cartoons, some of which were published in the paper.

Rose's actions have certainly had an afterlife! The newspaper has been threatened; the cartoonists have gone into hiding; the prime minister has been involved; embassies and Danish flags have been burned; whole countries have stopped importing Danish goods, people have been killed, and – in some places, at least – the tensions between Muslims and the West have been exacerbated.

As Flemming Rose tells the story, his decision to solicit and publish these cartoons was a response to his observation that people were censoring themselves for fear of angering Muslims. He noted that the "cartoons do not in any way demonize or stereotype Muslims. In fact, they differ from one another both in the way they depict the prophet and in whom they target" and asked, "Has *Jyllands-Posten* insulted and disrespected Islam? It certainly didn't intend to."

There's more to the story than just this, of course. At the moment, however, I want to focus on his statement that his actions in soliciting and publishing the cartoons should not be understood as insulting and disrespecting Islam *because that's not what he intended.*

This is a coherent, persuasive argument *if* we understand communication in terms of the transmission model, in which the meaning of a message is determined by its correspondence to the meaning of the person who made it, and "good" communication occurs when the meanings in "your" mind are exactly the same as the intentions in "mine." If this clarity and agreement are not achieved, we have a regrettable and potentially correctable communication problem. Perhaps the message wasn't clear (and the speaker/writer/performer should explain further); perhaps the message was distorted in the transmission (and we should look for a medium with higher fidelity); or perhaps the problem is with the people who interpret the message (what's wrong with those people anyway?).

It is not surprising that Flemming Rose would assume the transmission model as his implicit theory of communication. It has been the dominant concept in northern European and Anglo-American culture since the Enlightenment. Our culture was persuaded by the idea that good communication consists of a perfect correspondence between messages and clear thoughts, even though that means that we must fight a continuing struggle against "the imperfection of language." This phrase comes from the title of a chapter in John Locke's (1690/1998) *Essay Concerning Human Understanding*. In this chapter, Locke said, "The chief end of language in communication being to be understood, words serve not well for that end, neither in civil nor philosophical discourse, when any word does not excite in the hearer the same idea which it stands for in the mind of the speaker." Two hundred and fifty years later, philosopher and social activist Bertrand Russell (1922) was even more specific: "The whole function of language is to have meaning, and . . . the essential business of language is to assert or deny facts. Given the syntax of a language, the meaning of a sentence is determinant as soon as the meaning of the component words is known." I've looked at most of the major dictionaries and many of the encyclopedias published in English, and this is always the first and sometimes only concept of communication they offer.

However, many of us believe that this concept of communication does not serve us well. Among other things, this theory of communication makes sense in an intellectual context that envisions individuals as separate from each other, each with a theater of the mind in which meanings exist. Most of us now believe that individual minds are murkier and less private than the Enlightenment philosophers thought – well, that's what *they* might say about *us*, at least. Another and more important critique is that this way of thinking leads to serious impasses if those involved in communication disagree about whether the meaning of particular messages is clear. Or, what happens if I understand clearly what you've said, but we continue to disagree about its implications? If we rely on this concept of communication, we will strive to explain ourselves more and more clearly, but this may make our conflict worse rather than better, and then we are stuck.

I think that this is what happened in the cartoon imbroglio. In his thoughtful essay "Why I published those cartoons," Rose spent considerable time explaining his intentions. I assume that this was based on his hope that, if he could express his intentions clearly then, as Locke and Russell implied, our "communication problem" would dissipate. Let's see how it worked out.

In clarifying his intentions, Rose (2006) described the commitment to freedom of speech and press in democratic states like his native Denmark.

> We have a tradition of satire when dealing with the royal family and other public figures, and that was reflected in the cartoons. The cartoonists treated Islam the same way they treat Christianity, Buddhism, Hinduism, and other religions. And by treating Muslims in Denmark as equals they made a point. We are integrating you into the Danish tradition of satire because you are part of our society, not strangers. The cartoons are including, rather than excluding, Muslims.

He explained that he was particularly sensitive to these freedoms, because he had worked in a country – the Soviet Union – in which these freedoms did not exist.

He celebrated the "constructive debate in Denmark and Europe about freedom of expression, freedom of religion and respect for immigrants and people's beliefs" that was initiated by the publication of the cartoons, particularly the participation of Danish Muslims.

> Never before have so many Danish Muslims participated in a public dialogue – in town hall meetings, letters to editors, opinion columns and debates on radio and TV. We have had no anti-Muslim riots, no Muslims fleeing the country and no Muslims committing violence. The radical imams who misinformed their counterparts in the Middle East about the situation for Muslims in Denmark have been marginalized. They no longer speak for the Muslim community in Denmark because moderate Muslims have had the courage to speak out against them. (Rose 2006)

I think that Rose's implicit concept of communication – the transmission model – leads him to conclude that anyone who continues to disagree with him after he has stated his intentions this clearly are (in the terms of the paragraph quoted just above) "radical," engaged in "misinforming their counterparts" and are (and should be) "marginalized."

Nowhere in this well-reasoned essay does Rose acknowledge that Muslims are offended by *any* depiction of the prophet Muhammad, whether satirical or not, or that there might be principled reasons why Danish Muslims would object when "we" choose to "integrat[e] you into the Danish tradition of satire." It is at least possible that some Danish Muslims might wish to be invited to integrate rather than having it forced upon them by a journalist, and that some processes of cultural integration might be more mutual than the one he initiated.

At any rate, when confronted with the impasse of those who understand clearly what he meant but continue to object to what he did, this concept of communication points to no further actions than to apologize for having given offense if not for the actions which offended (which the newspaper did) or to blame the other, as Rose did in the final lines of his essay. Rose differentiates the narrative in Europe (which he thinks has benefited from publication of the cartoons) from that in the Middle East, which he describes as "more complex, but that has very little to do with the cartoons." That is, it's their fault that they misunderstood me.[1]

I am not interested in participating in a discussion about whether the transmission model is right or wrong. Rather, I'm content to point out that it works best in conversations among people who already share deep cultural beliefs about what is true, morally right, and politically prudent. It doesn't provide a way of moving forward together when there are deep moral conflicts as there are in contemporary society (Pearce and Littlejohn 1997). For this, I want to turn to another, less familiar concept of communication, one whose unusual properties enable us to deal more effectively with certain aspects of the world in which we live.

Let's continue to focus on the need to deal constructively with the "Other" – people who are not only not like us, but who do not want to become like us. As sociologist Peter Berger (2001: xi) put it, virtually every society on earth has been affected by "the process of modernization," and one of the most important consequences of modernization is "pluralism." This means simply that "people with very different beliefs, values, and lifestyles come to live together in close proximity, are forced to interact with each other, and therefore are faced with the alternative of either clashing in conflict or somehow accommodating each other's differences."

The usual results of pluralism, Berger said, are "relativism," in which everything is just an opinion or taste and it is embarrassing to have real convictions, or "fanaticism" in which, to avoid relativism, the "comforting certainties of the past" are reasserted confrontationally against those who appeal to alternative certainties and, with even greater energy, against those who apparently have none. Surprisingly, there is a strong commonality between relativists and fanatics. Since neither believes that there can be "reasonable communication between different worldviews," there is "no middle ground between challenging nothing that those others are saying and hitting them over the head until they surrender or disappear" (Berger 2001: xi–xii).

While "theologians and other accredited theorists" might well find themselves stranded in this polarized discourse, Berger (2001: xiii) notes, "meaningful conversation" has been hammered out by ordinary people "over lunch break conversations between fellow-workers, over backyard fences by neighboring housewives, or by parents coming in contact because of shared concerns for their children's schools or recreational activities."

The stakes are too high to allow us to be hamstrung by limiting concepts like relativism and fanaticism. Like Berger, I take comfort in knowing that ordinary people, confronted with specific challenges, are often able to achieve communication that looks impossible – at least if we look from the perspective of the transmission model. But I want to go further and articulate an alternative concept of communication, and later in this book a set of practices, concepts and models, that make it easier. Let's start with a specific instance.

On January 16, 2006, Dr. Michelle Bachelet was elected President of Chile. This was a remarkable event for several reasons: she is the first woman elected president in her country, she and her mother are survivors of state-sponsored terrorism under the rule of former President Augusto Pinochet (her father died of injuries suffered during torture), and she made an unusual proclamation in her victory speech. She said, "Because I was the victim of hate, I've consecrated my life to turning hate into understanding, tolerance, and why not say it – love." In an interview just a few days after the election, she was asked: "As President, what policies will you follow to promote this kind of understanding and tolerance between those who were tortured and killed in the past and those tortured – like you." She replied:

It's the idea of how we're able to build places in our society where tolerance, understanding of diversity, integration – and not discrimination – will be main policies. When I'm speaking of love, when I'm speaking of reversing hate, I'm speaking not only of reconciliation – I don't use that word – I use "reencuentro" – it's not exactly reconciliation . . . because "reconciliation" is related to forgiveness, and that's very individual. Some people forgive and some people do not. But let's use the word reconciliation here. . . . We'll have to continue advancing in reconciliation between people who were victims and their families and people who were responsible for that.

But not only that. I am also thinking of re-coming together of people left behind, people who need to have equal opportunities. In one sense, reconciliation in the political arena, but also people who are poor and haven't had opportunities. (Bachelet 2006)

The interviewer, Elisabeth Farnsworth, wanted to pursue President-elect Bachelet's personal story. During the victory celebration, Farnsworth said, many people said to me – even people who suffered a lot under the dictatorship – "We really appreciate the fact that Dr Bachelet is willing to forgive." You suffered a lot, you don't like to talk about it. Your mother spent six days in a cage the size of a square. Your father died because of the tortures inflicted on him. He wrote letters – the saddest letters one could imagine, about what happened to him.

How do you forgive – I'm not going to say whether you forgive, I don't know – but how do you come to this position of being so positive about the possibility for reencuentro – the coming together of the nation?

President-elect Bachelet replied:

I wouldn't be honest if I told you that in some moments of my life I [didn't have] a lot of rage, probably hate – I'm not sure of hate – but rage. But, you know what happens is that you then realize you can't do to others what you think nobody has to do to anybody. Life is important for me. And not just any life. Quality of life. It's probably strange or difficult to understand but everything that happened to me made me not only rationally but emotionally get to a deep conviction, and that is I have to create all the conditions in our country, political conditions, social conditions, cultural conditions – in order that we can guarantee to further generations that they will never have to live what we have had to live. And that is a feeling that is so profound in me, so deep in me, that it's something natural. (Bachelet 2006)

If we were looking at Dr. Bachelet's comments from the perspective of the transmission model, the appropriate questions might have to do with her sincerity (does what she says correspond to what she really intends?) and the clarity of her statements. For example, in the hours following 9/11, President Bush announced his policy of preemptive strikes against those presumed to constitute a threat and his intention of treating nations that don't cooperate with him as if they were allied to the terrorists, and he has been commendably consistent in implementing these policies. In fact, when challenged by the consequences, his public pronouncements turn to the importance of being unwavering and clear in the pursuit of stated objectives. These are all virtues from the perspective of the transmission model.

But Bachelet began her presidency with a different sensibility. I think she is clearly hoping to do what Albert Einstein suggested: to avoid simply perpetuating problems by addressing them with a more complex and, in this case, more compassionate level of thinking. Two aspects of President-elect Bachelet's position seem noteworthy. First, she identifies her goals in terms of what she and others are able to make together. That is, she wants to create new patterns of social relationships that bring together groups who have reason to hate and fear each other, and to bring into society those who have been marginalized. These are goals that she cannot accomplish by actions that she will take alone; they require coordinating with other groups.

Second, she sees herself as an agent of the social world she wants to create. That is, her actions cannot be based (only) on her own personal feelings ("a lot of rage, probably hate – I'm not sure of hate – but rage") but in terms of what she wants to call into being. Now that she has the power of the presidency, she could take revenge on those who tortured her and her family, but because she asks something like "what kind of social world would I be making if I did?" she is able to focus on the higher calling of creating a society in which no one is tortured.

There will be countless times during President Bachelet's administration when her implicit theory of communication will be tested. Her policy decisions will be challenged, and it will be tempting for her to fall back into a way of thinking that defines the meaning of what she says and does by its correspondence with her intrapsychic mental state or an abstract principle rather than with its place within the emerging patterns of interaction between herself and others.

Based on our life experiences, reflections, and – perhaps – formal training, all of us develop an implicit theory of communication that guides and governs the way we act in the situations in which we live. Even if we are not an editor of a major newspaper or the president of a country, we live, play, and work in patterns of social relationships that call for us to be at our best. We will face situations similar in structure if not in content to those addressed by Flemming Rose and Michelle Bachelet: we see a pattern of interaction occurring (whether self-censorship or state-sponsored terrorism) that we want to change for the better, and we either decide or are required to act. But what should we do? We know that many well-intentioned attempts to make things better either have no discernible effect or actually make things worse. How can we act wisely in these situations?

One way of addressing that question is to make our implicit theories of communication explicit, and to develop useful models for understanding specific situations so that we can discern the critical moments and make good decisions about how to act wisely. This book is based on my best efforts to articulate a theory of communication that is productively different from those that created the problems that confront us, and to offer a set of concepts and heuristic models that you can use to explore specific situations.

My Discovery of Social Worlds

Both Flemming Rose and Michelle Bachelet referred to important learning experiences (he as a journalist in the Soviet Union; she as living in a dictatorship) when explaining their present commitments. In a similar way, my own commitments are grounded in my life, not just what I've found and read in libraries.

My belief that an enriched understanding of communication is useful in developing our collective capacity to act wisely was something to which I came eventually and a bit reluctantly. I began at quite a different place – as a child confused and frustrated by being in (although I did not then know how to name them) different social worlds.

When I was between about 3 and 10 years old, my family visited my grandparents on Thanksgiving and Christmas, spending half a day with each set of grandparents. My father's parents were deeply religious; everything was seen through the perspective of conservative Protestant beliefs and practices. Their religious practice was strict and forbidding. I don't remember laughing much in their home but I do remember many instances of being told that I had done something wrong (and often being punished for it). It was a strictly patriarchal family structure: my grandfather's whims were law. They recited a verse from the Bible before each meal. Before breakfast, with long faces and in a slow, plodding, monotone, we would say together the wonderful invocation "This is the day that the lord has made! Let us rejoice and be glad in it." The ironic mismatch between content and manner was unintentional and it would have been scandalous to comment on it – but I did notice it, and wondered.

The International Order of Odd Fellows played a much larger role than religion in my mother's parents' life. My grandfather served as president and had visited Havana, Cuba, for their annual convention. In the rural world in which we lived, this was exotic stuff! Unlike my other grandparents, he was physically large and enormously vital. His characteristic expression was to throw both arms into the air in a "victory" signal and shout "wow!" He practiced medicine without bothering about such things as having a medical degree or state license, dispensing a listening ear, placebos (I think), advice and probably some post-hypnotic suggestions to a clientele consisting exclusively of African Americans – a fact significant because he was white and lived in a racially segregated society. My grandmother and he sustained a perpetual conflict, not least because of his long relation to the African-American woman who lived in his office (a homemade building several hundred meters from their home) and served as his nurse. To comment on this relationship in front of my grandmother was strictly forbidden. They had a traditional division of labor and responsibilities: my grandmother was queen of the house (Grandpa seldom came inside) and my grandfather ruled the rather extensive property outside the house – except for the chicken yard, that somehow was my grandmother's possession. I had to be aware of where I was, because they often gave conflicting commands, and I had to obey the one in whose "place" I was. I remember laughing a lot with them, but always separately, as they competed with each other to be the favorite grandparent.

At the end of each of these days, I sat alone in the back seat of our family car and asked myself "what the heck happened?" Although I had no language in which to express these perceptions, I was well aware that my grandparents lived in different social worlds. In one, I was praised for doing the same thing for which I was punished in the other. I was aware that there were unspoken motives and relational currents at work in each family, and that what was said and done meant more than it seemed. But I had no vocabulary for describing these differences, or conversation partners with whom I might explore them. I remember trying to discuss what happened with my parents, but what I intended as "questions" were heard as "criticisms" and, since in our family children were not supposed to criticize adults, I was told to "stop that!" and instructed to "act respectfully." I did stop talking about it, but I continued to wonder, but without an adequate vocabulary in which even to pose my questions, much less to answer them.

The work described in this book represents an effort to develop a vocabulary in which to pose and answer those questions. In the process, I've joined a larger community of people who have posed similar questions and wrestled with answers. We haven't developed a set of answers that describe all social worlds. In fact, we've come to the principled decision that such a quest is in itself wrongheaded. Instead, we've developed a set of tools that enable us to explore in some detail any given situation and our role in it.

Social worlds

The ability to use the concepts and models of this approach is grounded in a very specific way of looking at the world. One way of presenting that worldview is to imagine a conversation between me, now a grandfather in his sixties, and me at age five, confused by his experience with his grandparents. To make this scene vivid, imagine us walking on a beach with our dog, throwing stones so that they skip on the water, and talking.

I would want to tell this little boy four things. First, he *should* have been confused when he moved through these different social worlds, because they really were social *worlds*. All of us create worlds that are "complete" or "whole" within their own horizons and that are structured by a geometry of "oughtness" that tells us what things mean and what we should, could, must, or must not do about or because of them. I imagine the boy heaving a sigh of relief; his confusion does not mean that there's something wrong with him.

Second, there are *many* social worlds. His grandparents' worlds are far more alike than not, and occupy the smallest fraction of the great array of ways of being human. I'd test his comprehension by asking if he can imagine an infinite set of possible social worlds, each one different from the others. If so, can he see the social worlds of his grandparents as just two of the infinite number of social worlds that exist or might exist. I imagine him struggling a bit with this concept, so I move on, with a wink and a chuckle, to tell him that by the time he's a grandfather, he will have deliberately sought out social worlds very different from any he'd known, and enjoyed being in them. I imagine him not quite believing this, perhaps wondering if I'm teasing him.

Third, I tell him that each of these social worlds is *made*. They are shaped by the things that we do to and with each other. They start and they end, and they change over time. Even things that seem so real and powerful, like Grandpa Pearce's strictly enforced standards for children's behavior, wasn't and won't always be this way, and there are people who act differently in other social worlds. He will learn things about all of his grandparents that will show them to be much more complex and interesting people than they let him know when he's five years old. He may not respect them as much, but he will like them more. When I see the look of absolute incredulity on his face, I hurry on to the next point.

Finally, I tell him that he, like everyone else involved, is an agent in the making of these social worlds. Although no one can "control" what happens, everyone in those social worlds affects what happens by their actions. I suspect that this is where our conversation ends – "yeah, right!" he says, sarcastically – and we turn to the serious business of seeing who can make a rock skip the most times, because it is hard for a five-year-old to conceptualize an unfolding pattern with bifurcation points into which he might act wisely. But I know that he will some day – I wish it happened sooner and easier! – develop the ability to accept the opportunities and responsibilities conferred by this way of thinking.

Let me make these same four points without having to fit them into what a five-year-old boy can understand.

The worldliness of social worlds

I studied philosophy in college. As usual, we started with a brief look at the "pre-Socratics" and then plunged into Plato, then Aristotle, and then the rest of the Western philosophical heritage. I noted that virtually all philosophers accepted Plato's notion that "knowledge" is good, mere "opinion" is bad, and that the difference between the two had to do with what they are about: eternal and unchanging things in the case of knowledge and things that change and come to an end in the case of opinion.

We studied chronologically, so it wasn't until my senior year that I encountered the twentieth-century philosophers. I can still remember my excitement when I read William James's (1909) concept of the "pluralistic universe," in which the world that each of us creates is perceived as a meaningful whole, although each is, in fact, just one of many such wholes within the totality.

I took two things from my reading of James. First, it liberated me from the philosopher's curse of trying to find a set of propositions into which to force everything. That's a game that one can play for as long as one chooses, but why would I want to? Second, it helped me realize that, within each of these subuniverses, people live lives of meaning and honor even though those lives may not resemble anything coherent or honored in other subuniverses. For those living in each social world, it seems complete. Here is where philosophy and anthropology merge. One of the great contributions of twentieth-century anthropology was the ethnographies (literally: writing cultures) that described many cultures in ways that made them accessible by those living in other cultures.

Alfred Schutz's (1962) concept of "multiple realities" provides some useful concepts for understanding the wholeness of social worlds. Each "finite province of meaning," as he put it, has a specific way of thinking and a form of consciousness that are different from those in other finite provinces. It has a peculiar sense of reality that can't be fully translated into the language of any other province of meaning. We can only understand another "reality" by something like a Kierkegaardian "leap" – a discontinuous joining of the other rather than a logical progression of steps. Each finite province has its own specific form of spontaneity, self-experience, sociality, and time.

But can a "finite province of meaning" such as my grandparents' family or the corporate culture of IBM function as a "world"? Looked at from outside, each of these worlds seems small, arbitrary, and restrictive. If the limits of our social worlds are perceived as "boundaries," then we are aware of imposed restrictions. Boundaries function as bars on a cage that mark off distinctions within the array of what we know and what we don't, and between where we can go and where we cannot. But the fact is that most of us are comfortable – sometimes *too* comfortable – within the limits of our social worlds. Philosopher Hans-Georg Gadamer (1979: 143) provides a key concept: our "horizon of understanding," he said, is "the range of vision that includes everything that can be seen from a particular vantage point." From our perspective inside them, our social worlds appear to have what we might call "horizons" rather than boundaries. Horizons are the natural limits of sight; they mark the end of what can be seen, but with no sense of confinement or impediment. Within "horizons," our social worlds appear rich and complete with no visible limits.

Living within one's horizons constitutes a kind of wisdom. But the material and social conditions of our era make this increasingly difficult. More and more often, we are required to encounter those who see our horizons as boundaries to be broken, and whose own horizons are invisible to them. And this brings us to the notion of multiple social worlds.

There are many social worlds

The issue here isn't the number of social worlds. There are an infinite number, because new ones are being made in each moment.

Don't pass too quickly by the thought of an infinite number of social worlds, each evolving in every moment. This concept runs powerfully against the grain of the "finite provinces of meaning" that have dominated Western thought for most of our history. Whether clerical or scientific, theorists have usually launched themselves into a quest for "all-embracing schemas, universal unifying frameworks . . . vast structures in which there should be no gaps left open for spontaneous, unattended developments, where everything that occurs should be, at least in principle, wholly explicable in terms of immutable general laws" (Prigogine 1984: 2). Such a question makes sense if there is one "real" social world out there that is unchanging.

However, if social worlds are made, and remade in each moment, then we live in a more complex, dynamic, and interesting place than could be contained in such "all-embracing schemas." I'm a little uncomfortable with the ease with which I can see governments, economic systems, power relations, and multinational corporations as temporary configurations of an ongoing process. Maybe this is an occupational hazard of someone who reads as much as I do. Science fiction writer Gordon Dickson remarked: "Trouble rather the tiger in his lair than the sage among his books, for to you kingdoms and their armies are things mighty and enduring, but to him they are but toys of the moment, to be overturned with the flick of a finger."[2] But maybe it isn't just that I'm such a bookish person, but that the tools built on the communication perspective are sufficiently powerful to display the ebbs and flows of social worlds. I hope so.

But I'm confident that we live in a pluralistic universe in which there are many finite provinces of meaning. If so, then the task before us has more to do with making better social worlds, and finding ways of coordinating with people who live in other social worlds, than with finding an all-embracing schema that would explain everything.

Protagoras said, "Man is the measure of all things." Most people would agree if we understood him to mean that things appear differently depending on the perspective from which they are perceived. (But, they hasten to add, the things-in-themselves haven't changed.) But what if the things that we take as important are not so much the *objects* that we perceive but the *meanings* we make of them, and the *actions* we take on the basis of these perspectives? If we *act* on the basis of how we perceive things, those actions are things in the universe and they have an afterlife. This is, of course, a new expression of an old idea. Thomas and Thomas (1928: 572) put it this way: "If men define situations as real, they are real in their consequences." The common thread is that reality itself is made, and continues to evolve as we act and make/manage meanings.

Once we perceive that there are many social worlds, the fact that they are different isn't particularly surprising. The interesting aspect of the plurality of social worlds is the nature of their difference and how we will handle those differences.

The simplest way of dealing with these differences, of course, is to judge that my world is right, good, and beautiful, and to the extent that any other social world differs from it, that social world is wrong, evil, and ugly. This seems to be the substance of most of the news headlines that I read, and it is all too obvious what kind of social world that creates.

Things get more interesting when we are open to the possibility that our social worlds differ not just because we think differently about the same things, but also because we think similarly about different things. That is, people in different social worlds may be honorable, but each may deem honorable that which the other finds dishonorable or simply incoherent. It may be impossible to translate one social reality into another; or, better said, to understand someone else, it may be necessary for us to adjust our horizons. In a sense, engaging and understanding another social world means becoming, to some extent, another person. One of the reasons for doing ethnographies (or reading them) and seeking out the "other" is to stimulate the evolution of our own consciousness. As Clifford Geertz (1986: 113–14) put it:

> The reach of our minds, the range of signs we can manage somehow to inter-
> pret, is what defines the intellectual, emotional and moral space within which
> we live. The greater that is, the greater we can make it become by trying
> to understand [what others] are all about . . . the clearer we become to
> ourselves. . . .
>
> It is the asymmetries . . . between what we believe or feel and what
> others do, that make it possible to locate where we now are in the world,
> how it feels to be there, and where we might or might not want to go. To
> obscure those gaps and those asymmetries by relegating them to a realm of
> repressible or ignorable difference, mere unlikeness . . . is to cut us off from
> such knowledge and such possibility: the possibility of quite literally, and
> quite thoroughly, changing our minds.

My first introduction to this way of thinking was in an essay by William James (1899/2001: 133–4) called "On a certain blindness in human beings." While traveling in the rural mountains of North Carolina, in the middle of an unspoiled forest covering mountains as far as the eye could see, James found a devastated landscape in which all the trees had been cut down, holes dug, and here and there some corn was growing. When he commented on it, the settler who had, with great effort, cleared the forest to make room for a farm, said, "Yes, isn't it wonderful to have a patch of civilization!" With some effort, James was able to transform his perception of what he had previously called "devastation" to, through the eyes of the settler, the results of "duty, struggle, and success." The "blindness" to which he referred in the title of the essay is our inability to see the social world of the other: "I had been as blind to the peculiar ideality of their conditions as they certainly would also have been to the ideality of mine, had they had a peep at my strange indoor academic ways of life at Cambridge."

James's experience of his encounter with the culture of the Appalachian mountain settlers was the closest thing I had found to my experience as a five-year-old. For the first time, I had some vocabulary for naming and comprehending the situation in which I found myself in our biannual holiday trips to my grandparents' houses. I was also struck by James's call for tolerance and compassion for the other – something far beyond my ability as a five-year-old. In his advice to students and teachers, James (1899/2001: 264) said that the existence of multiple social worlds

> commands us to tolerate, respect, and indulge those whom we see harm-lessly interested and happy in their own ways, however unintelligible these may be to us. Hands off: neither the whole of truth nor the whole of good is revealed to any single observer, although each observer gains a partial superiority of insight from the peculiar position in which he stands. Even prisons and sick-rooms have their special revelations.

I've deliberately woven a thread through my presentation of these first two characteristics of social worlds: the possibility and desirability of what might be called intercultural communication. I've chosen to emphasize this for several reasons, including the fact that the same skills that make one a good member of a culture often disable one for achieving what Gadamer called "the fusion of horizons" or for displaying that respectful tolerance that James described. I want to take a communication perspective on a particular conversation because it displays so well the subtle dance of horizons of the participants.

The conversation was a research interview as part of a major study of the language of morals used by Americans; when published, it was widely heralded as shedding important light on the inability of contemporary Americans to engage in moral reasoning. The authors concluded that Americans' first moral language is "individualism" and that this moral language is incapable of sustaining the public order. They urged a renewal of "biblical" and "civic republican" moral languages as a way of keeping individualism in check, trusting that individualism would limit the tendencies of these moral languages to sanction discrimination and oppression (Bellah et al. 1985: 20, 161, 163). One of the data points for this study was an interview with Barry Palmer, conducted by Ann Swidler.

The interview focused on moral choices that people make, such as: Why do you work? Why did you change jobs? Why did you marry and start a family? According to the researchers, they "did not seek to impose our ideas on those with whom we talked" but they "did attempt to uncover assumptions, to make explicit what the person we were talking to might rather have left implicit. The interview as we employed it was active, Socratic" (Bellah et al. 1985: 304). The researchers believed that this interview procedure revealed the horizons of the respondents' cultures, and that the respondents' cultures did not include resources that enabled them to articulate good reasons why they made the moral choices that shaped their lives. Specifically, when Brian Palmer said

(1) *Palmer:* Lying is one of the things I want to regulate.
(2) *Swidler:* *[Trying "to get [him] to clarify the basis of his moral judgments."]* Why?
(3) *Palmer:* Well, it's a kind of thing that is a habit you get into. Kind of self-perpetuating. It's like digging a hole. You just keep digging and digging.
(4) *Swidler:* So why is it wrong?
(5) *Palmer:* Why is integrity important and lying bad? I don't know. It just is. It's just so basic. I don't want to be bothered with challenging that. It's part of me. I don't know where it came from, but it's very important.
(6) *Swidler:* When you think about what's right and what's wrong, are things bad because they are bad for people, or are they right or wrong in themselves, and if so how do you know?
(7) *Palmer:* Well, some things are bad because . . . I guess I feel like everybody on this planet is entitled to have a little bit of space, and things that detract from other people's space are kind of bad. (Bellah et al. 1985: 304–5)

The researchers interpreted this conversation as showing that Brian Palmer lacked a sufficiently powerful moral language; that when confronted by a "Socratic" interviewer, he was quickly reduced to incoherent babbling ("I don't know. It just is," and "I guess I feel that everyone on this planet . . ."). They characterized Palmer as using the moral language of individualism that they believed was rampant in the popular culture of the United States at the time of the study but which is philosophically defective.

Is there some other way of understanding this interview? If we look closely at what Swidler and Palmer are doing – perhaps letting the content of what they are saying move into fuzzy focus – another interpretation is possible. Let's start with the whole notion of "Socratic questioning." At its best, Socratic questioning invites a person to pursue a line of thought further than he might otherwise have done, and this was clearly what Swidler intended when she interviewed Palmer. But are there moments when inquiry should come to an end? At their worst, the persistent queries "Why?" or "How do you know?" that constitute Socratic questioning can be a tool for intellectual bullying. As ethicist Jeffrey Stout (1988: 34–5) put it, the interview protocol of this study relentlessly continues until the person interviewed "either becomes confused or starts sounding suspiciously like a philosopher." He warned that

> [t]here are many propositions that we are justified in believing but wouldn't know how to justify. Anything we could say on behalf of such a proposition seems less certain than the proposition itself. By now, it is hard to debate with flat-earthers. What real doubt do they have that can be addressed with justifying reasons? . . . we ought to be suspicious of people who want reasons even when they can't supply reasonable doubts.

To understand this conversation, we need to know a bit more about Brian Palmer. He is a middle-aged man who has been successful in business, whose first marriage failed (in part because he neglected his family for his business and had a dishonest relationship with his wife), who has remarried and is deliberately restructuring his life to make sure that his second marriage succeeds.

Palmer's statement in the fifth turn seems to be a critical moment in this conversation. Without apparently realizing it, Swidler and her colleagues were working within the horizons of a particular notion of what moral reasoning looks like: articulating universal principles and linking specific decisions to those principles through clearly articulated reasons. Further, they don't recognize this as part of one social world, but treat their horizons as if they were the ends of the social universe. Swidler doesn't even hear Palmer's statement in the fifth turn as an answer to her question. In the next turn, she explains the question she asked in the fourth turn, and asks it again.

There are other finite provinces of meaning in which Palmer's answer might be heard as very meaningful. For example, some people argue that moral judgments are, and should be, grounded in the experience of a person in the context of their community. If heard from this perspective, we might note that in the third and fifth turns, Palmer used a moral vocabulary of reciprocity, involvement, shared goals, and mutual respect. He grounded his moral judgment by describing his position within a matrix of rights and responsibilities. When Palmer says that the wrongness of lying is "just so basic," what he means is – in Stout's (1988: 195) interpretation – that "he can't think of anything more certain than the wrongness of lying that might be introduced to support the idea that lying is wrong. He'd rather not be bothered with the sort of challenge that the question implies . . . but his interviewer won't stop" and his problem is that he "doesn't know how to answer questions that aren't connected to real doubts."

When Swidler pushes him (in the sixth turn) for a different kind of answer, Palmer tries to oblige . . . and starts babbling like a third-rate philosopher. After the interview, Swidler changed from interlocutor to author and represented him this way:

> His description of his reasons for changing his life and of his current happiness seems to come down mainly to a shift in his notions of what would make him happy. His new goal – devotion to marriage and children – seems as arbitrary and unexamined as his earlier pursuit of material success. Both are justified as idiosyncratic preference rather than as representing a larger sense of the purpose of life. (Bellah et al. 1985: 6)

As I read this summary, I felt that Palmer has been trivialized. The summary shows how something that can seem rich in one social world can appear shallow and thin in another, and how a technique such as Socratic questioning can conceal the horizons of one's culture as well as revealing them.

Social worlds are made

If we take the communication perspective, a funny thing happens. Many of the things in our social world that seem permanent and powerful are

Figure 2.1 Raphael, *The School of Athens*, from the Stanza della Segnatura, 1510–11 (fresco). Vatican Museums and Galleries/Bridgeman Art Library.

transformed in front of our very eyes into temporary configurations of a continuous process.

Figure 2.1 is a reproduction of a painting titled *The School of Athens*. In it, the artist Raphael set out to portray all of the great philosophers of antiquity.[3] Striding confidently side by side and in deep conversation, Plato and Aristotle are at the center of the painting. Their gestures represent their epistemologies. Plato points upward, to the realm of ideas in which truth is obtained through philosophic insight and reality is eternal, unchanging, and immutable. Aristotle points outward, at the world of politics, public speaking, and household management, where knowledge comes from observation, categorization, and experience.

What would it look like if one of us who took a communication perspective were to be added to the painting? Let's call her Mara. Imagine her standing next to Plato and Aristotle and included in their conversation. What gesture would she be making that would represent her epistemology?

Rather than upward or outward, she'd be making a self-referential gesture; one that says "look at *us*; look at the work that *we* are doing!"

If I were touching up the painting, I'd depict her as making two gestures. The first would be a kind of circling gesture that includes Plato, Aristotle, and herself, indicating the conversation in which they are engaged. The second would be even more inclusive, embracing all of the persons in the whole room.

If we could add sound as well as movement to the painting, we might hear her tell Plato and Aristotle that by pointing upward and outward, they are ignoring the most immediate and relevant thing: the conversation in which they are engaged. This conversation isn't just "about" things up there or out there; it is itself a material substance. Is it a debate? A deliberation? A dialogue? An argument? Are their minds opening or closing as the series of turns continues? We see them speaking and gesturing, but who is listening? And *how* are they listening? To find the flaw in the other's argument or to achieve a fusion of horizons? Just as much as the realities to which they are pointing, they are *making* things in the conversation. Among other things, they are making *themselves* as people, their *relationship* (it might be improved or threatened, depending on how the conversation goes), and the *event* itself (I assume that students of each are watching what is happening and making sense of it in ways that will shape their own interactions with persons from other schools). We might even say that conversations of this sort constitute the "school."

And what they "know" is shaped by the manner in which they speak of it. Who are they describing as agents who act intentionally and who as helpless victims who are acted upon? What theories about nature are embedded in their discourse? Is the earth alive or dead? How are they naming the things that they are talking about? What distinctions are they making or not making among those things?

As Mara moves to her second, more inclusive gesture, she asks about the nature of this place. What is the consequence of calling it a "school" rather than any of the hundreds of other things that it might be called? Who is excluded? Who decided, and by what process and with what consequences, that Gorgias of Leontini (more about him in a minute) should be excluded? Would it still be a "school" if Gorgias were present? And where are all the women? What is being made by putting this "gentlemen's philosophy club" as a fresco on the wall of the Vatican? Does this reproduce a pattern of gender-based discrimination? What other categories of persons are excluded?

I'm confident that Aristotle and Plato would find these questions tiresome. But those of us who take the communication perspective believe that important things happen in the give-and-take between real people; that the language we use has consequences; that epistemologies are expressed in gestures and decisions about whom to invite to the party; and that important things – like schools and other social institutions – are made in decisions about who is included, who is featured as the central speakers, and even whether speaking itself is featured rather than listening.

In the painting, Diogenes – unkempt and poorly dressed – is sprawled on the steps just in front of Plato and Aristotle. Should he be in the painting? How do we decide whether he is a great philosopher who deserves such prominent positioning, or just another homeless person muttering or raving nonsense, to be avoided when encountered on the street? That's not just a rhetorical question; if we take the communication perspective, we are interested in just *how* Diogenes and other disorderly persons are *made* into great philosophers to be invited to schools or into mad persons to be confined to different kinds of institutions. What is this process? Are we sufficiently comfortable that we know what we are doing that we are willing to live with the results?

Remember Gorgias of Leontini? I noted that he is not included in the painting. Should he be? Gorgias is best known as a character in Plato's dialogue *Gorgias* (where Socrates soundly beats him in argument – proving that it is good to be friends with the author!) and for a book titled *On the Nonexistent*. Ironically, this book is, well, nonexistent. We know of it only in references to it in other documents. But these references tell us that in his own era Gorgias was famous for teaching that:

Nothing exists.
If anything did exist, we would be unable to know it.
If we could know anything, we would not be able to communicate it.
(Gorgias n.d.)

It's probably not a stretch to imagine Gorgias's statements as somehow related to his arguments with Plato. But how might they connect? If you take these statements as attempts to describe the same eternal, unchanging reality to which Plato pointed, they are absurd. But if you take them as a parody of Plato's concept that reality is timeless and unchanging, then they are an elegant statement that Plato's arguments themselves are absurd.

Note the sequence of what Gorgias said: first, he made a statement about ontology (what exists); second, about epistemology (how we know); and then, third, something about communication. One way of understanding

Gorgias's comment is as a way of showing the absurdity of this sequence itself. How are we to know anything about "reality" before we have worked our way through epistemology? And how can we know anything about epistemology except by communicating with each other and with the events and objects around us? Clearly, Gorgias might be understood to be saying, "communication" is first. The "reality" that presents itself to us is – as Mara indicated with her gestures – the experience of being in communication with other people and with the world around us. Any notions we might have about epistemology or reality occur within the framework of that experience. Our first and most important topic of study, it logically follows, is communication.

Each of us is an agent in the process of making social worlds

I wish that I had realized, when I was five years old, that I was a part of the process by which the social worlds in which I lived were made. Granted, I was not allowed to participate in some of the crucial conversations, and my opinions were neither sought nor respected about major decisions, but had I been sufficiently clever, I could have found some ways of acting into those social worlds that would have made life better for me . . . and I think for the others in my family as well.

As schools disciplined me, like almost everyone else, I was taught and tested on "spectator" knowledge – knowledge of things "out there" that I was to represent in the theater of my mind. Like most of us, I never thought about the kind of knowledge that was being taught me as part of my initiation into adult society. The "best" knowledge, so it seemed, took the form of geometric proofs, valid logical reasoning, or the empirical test of predictions made by a general law. It took me a long time to realize that this form of knowledge is at best not very useful when the question is "what should I *do* in this situation?"

The kind of knowledge that we need to participate in a process is very different from that which we need to be observers (Rorty 1979). Specifically, spectator knowledge is summarized in propositions; participatory knowledge is expressed in wise actions. The propositions of spectator knowledge have an affinity for the verb "to be"; participatory knowledge has an affinity for words describing oughtness (Rorty 1979). The grammar of the verb "to be" fits the conceptualization of reality as eternal and unchanging. It also fits the medium of writing, in which propositions can exist independently of the speaker/writer or listener/reader, thus creating the sense of a reality outside of human interaction (Ong 1982). If we try to use spectator knowledge to describe our experience within social worlds, we wind up describing ourselves as alienated or as victims; in the language of participatory knowledge, we can at least sometimes act wisely and effectively (Shotter 2000).

Recently, my colleague Vernon Cronen (2001: 26) has worked out the implications of taking a participant's perspective in social theory. He calls it a "practical theory" and summarizes it like this:

> A practical theory informs a grammar of practice that facilitates joining with the grammars of others to explore their unique forms of situated action. The proximal reason for joining is the cocreation of new affordances and constraints for participation in the instrumental and consummatory dimensions of experience. Practical theory itself is importantly informed by data created in the process of engagement with others.

Questions Asked by Those who Take a Communication Perspective on Social Worlds

If someone taking the communication perspective could enter Raphael's painting and join the conversation, what would she say? I think she'd say something like this: The key is to see the events and objects of the social world, like this school but also all of the things that Plato and Aristotle are talking about, as communication. That is, we look *at* what they are doing and saying, not through it to what it is supposedly *about*. We start with a set of questions and a well-developed curiosity.

If I'm a participant in a communication situation, and I have the opportunity or requirement of acting into it, these are the kinds of questions I'd pose:

- What are we making together?
- How are we making it?
- What are we becoming as we make this?
- How can we make better social worlds?

If I'm an observer of a communication event involving other people, and I want to understand and/or evaluate it, these are some of the questions I might ask:

- How was it made? How is it re-made in the ongoing process of social construction?
- Who participated in making it? Who didn't?
- What was the quality of the process by which it was made?
- Having been made, what does it, in turn, make? That is, how does it affect the ongoing process of social construction?

If I have a role in which I am both a participant and an observer – for example, I'm the manager and I want my company to run better, or I'm designing and facilitating a meeting, I can increase my probability of making better social worlds by asking questions like these:

- How can I/we act in ways that prevent the occurrence of undesirable events and objects?
- How can I/we act in ways that intervene in and improve already existing undesirable events and objects?
- How can I/we act in ways that call into being preferred events and objects?

For a few days in summer, 2006, "What Shamu taught me about a happy marriage" was one of the most frequently emailed articles that appeared in the *New York Times*. The author, Amy Sutherland (2006), describes how she used techniques learned from animal trainers to get her husband to put his dirty clothes in the hamper, to avoid crowding her when she was cooking, and to find his keys himself rather than ask her to find them. While taking a class in animal training, she says, she "began to analyze my husband the way a trainer considers an exotic animal" and would frequently write in the margins of her notes "Try this on Scott!" The results were good, she reported:

> After two years of exotic animal training, my marriage is far smoother, my husband much easier to love. I used to take his faults personally; his dirty clothes on the floor were an affront, a symbol of how he didn't care enough about me. But thinking of my husband as an exotic species gave me the distance I needed to consider our differences more objectively.

It's no wonder that this article was popular. And yet . . . what if we asked "what are Amy and Scott making when they use the animal-training technique of LRS (least reinforcing syndrome) on each other?" Granted, they are modifying each other's behavior, but what relationship are they making? What persons are they becoming? And is LRS the preferred pattern of communication for life-long partners?

Notes

1   A full examination of the cartoon controversy would take much more space than I am willing to allocate in this book. If you recall the two examples in chapter 1, you would want that analysis to include the sequence of turns, and analyze each one. I hope that someone will write that book, and I just want to acknowledge here my understanding that events subsequent to the publication of the cartoons had a major influence on how the conversation developed and its afterlife. For example, the prime minister's refusal to meet with concerned Muslim ambassadors, for whatever reason, seems to have been a critical moment (*Copenhagen Post* 2006).

2   I've long lost the reference to this quotation, but it is posted – also without citation – on several websites.

3   For an interactive identification of these philosophers, see http://un2sg4.unige.ch/athena/raphael/raf_ath4.html. Retrieved on February 2, 2006. The painting was done in 1509–1510.

References

Bachelet, M. (2006), Interview on the *NewsHour with Jim Lehrer*, January 25, 2006. Transcript retrieved from http://www.pbs.org/newshour/bb/latin_america/jan-june06/chile-ext_1-25.html on February 26, 2006.

Bellah, R. N., Madsen, R., Sullivan, W. M., Swidler, A., and Tipton, S. M. (1985), *Habits of the Heart: Individualism and Commitment in American Life*, Berkeley: University of California Press.

Berger, P. L. (2001), Foreword. In R. C. Neville (ed.), *The Human Condition*, Albany: State University of New York Press, pp. xi–xiv.

Copenhagen Post (2006), Twisted text gives government headache in cartoon crisis, February 20.

Craig, R. T. (1999), Communication theory as a field, *Communication Theory*, 9: 119–61.

Cronen, V. E. (2001), Practical theory, practical art, and the pragmatic-systemic account of inquiry, *Communication Theory*, 11: 14–35.

Gadamer, H.-G. (1979), *Truth and Method*, London: Sheed and Ward.

Geertz, C. (1986), The uses of diversity, *Michigan Quarterly Review*, 25: 106–23.

Gorgias (n.d.), Retrieved from http://www.missouri.edu/~engjnc/rhetoric/gorgias_bib.html on February 2, 2006.

James, W. (1899/2001), *Talks to Teachers on Psychology and to Students on Some of Life's Ideals*, Mineola, NY: Dover Publishing.

James, W. (1909), A pluralistic universe: Hibbert Lectures at Manchester College on the present situation in philosophy. Available as a Project Gutenberg Ebook at http://library.beau.org/gutenberg/1/1/9/8/11984/11984-8.txt. Retrieved February 28, 2006.

Locke, J. (1690/1998), *Essay Concerning Human Understanding*, New York: Penguin.

Ong, W. (1982), *Orality and Literacy: The Technologizing of the Word*, London: Routledge.

Pearce, W. B. and Littlejohn, S. W. (1997), *Moral Conflict: When Social Worlds Collide*, Thousand Oaks, CA: Sage.

Prigogine, I. (1984), *Order out of Chaos: Man's New Dialogue with Nature*, New York: Bantam.

Rorty, R. (1979), *Philosophy and the Mirror of Nature*, Princeton, NJ: Princeton University Press.

Rose, F. (2006), Why I published those cartoons, *Jyllands-Posten*, February 19. Retrieved from http://www.jp.dk/english_news/artikel:aid=3566642/ on February 26, 2006.

Russell, B. (1922), Introduction. In L. Wittgenstein, *Tractatus Logico-Philosophicus*, Retrieved from http://www.kfs.org/~jonathan/witt/aintro.html on February 26, 2006.

Schutz, A. (1962), On multiple realities. In *Collected Papers*, vol. 1, The Hague: Nijhoff, pp. 207–31.

Shotter, J. (2000), Inside dialogic realities: from an abstract-systematic to a participatory-wholistic understanding of communication, *Southern Communication Journal*, 65: 119–32.

Stout, J. (1988), *Ethics after Babel: The Languages of Morals and Their Discontents*, Boston, MA: Beacon Press.

Sutherland, A. (2006), What Shamu taught me about a happy marriage, *New York Times* online, July 22, 2006. Retrieved from www.nytimes.com/2006/06/25/fashion/25love.html on July 22, 2006.

Thomas, W. I. and Thomas, D. S. (1928), *The Child in America: Behavior Problems and Programs*, New York: Alfred A. Knopf.

Chapter 3

Paradigms and the "Physics" of Social Worlds

Preview

We develop very basic notions of how things work; we comprehend easily those things that "fit" those notions but have great difficulty getting our minds around things that are differently organized. Most of us have developed a practical sense of physics; we may not know the equations but we know that dropped pots fall and where to move our foot to keep ourselves from falling if we stumble. The term "paradigm" is used in this chapter to name these often-unstated senses of how things work.

The concept of paradigms makes it easier to point out that the physics of social worlds is not the same as that of the physical world, and we get confused if we attempt to understand one with tools appropriate for the other. In the physics of social worlds, questions are powerful, everything has multiple meanings, being playful is serious business, and what we do makes things real.

These characteristics make social worlds quite interesting places, and have consequences. In order to know things (epistemology), it helps to be systemic, to pay primary attention to processes rather than to the products of those processes, and to be sensitive to the emergence of sophisticated entities from less sophisticated ones. Ironically, the practice of this epistemology has challenged the traditional paradigm for understanding the physical world; apparently the physical world is more like our social worlds than we once thought.

This epistemology makes virtues of certain habits of the heart and mind that are not necessarily prized in other paradigms. Among these virtues are a principled and insatiable curiosity, the ability to identify one's own perspective, and a commitment to learn and to take into account multiple other perspectives.

What was That?

Chapter 2 ended with a set of questions that a person taking the communication perspective might ask.

Questions? Not statements? What's that all about?

When we think of someone who knows something, we usually think of their ability to state something rather than ask questions about it. Imagine an entry in an encyclopedia that was content to pose questions rather than answers!

Clearly, the ability to take the communication perspective on social worlds is something other than the ability required to win a spelling bee, quiz show, or even the Scholastic Aptitude Test (the scores that determine where you get to go to college). These abilities don't involve what you know *about* a topic nearly as much as they involve what you can *do*, in any specific moment.

In this chapter, I take the affinity for questions as an opening to focus on the "paradigm" shared by those who take a communication perspective on our social worlds.

Paradigms

About one hundred years ago, William James (1907/1975: 9–10, 13), commented on the unproductive and uncivil forms of communication between those with different ways of thinking about the world. This sounds familiar, doesn't it! James approached the situation obliquely. Rather than join in the conflict by supporting one position against the others, he made a meta-level analysis. He introduced the idea that what separates people is not so much the *content* of specific beliefs but their *temperaments*, which he defined as "our more or less dumb sense of what life honestly and deeply means. It is only partly got from books; it is our individual way of just seeing and feeling the total push and pressure of the cosmos." James introduced the terms "tenderminded" and "toughminded" and these have entered into an old paradigm as "types" of people – one "is" either tender- or toughminded. This is not the paradigm that I find useful. Rather, I see James as beginning to develop a vocabulary to describe the manner in which people engage in meaning-making and coordination. This changes it from describing what they "are" to "how they act" in specific circumstances.

In order to build on what I find valuable in James's thinking, let's use the term "paradigms" rather than "temperaments" to describe these more or less dumb senses of what life really means. Paradigms refer to social groups who understand the world roughly the same way and have similar expectations about how they – and each other – should act into it. When members of a social group listen to or watch others and say "yes, she's one of us" or "what a strange person he is," they are acting on the basis of a paradigm. This concept of paradigm was introduced by Thomas Kuhn (1996). Responding to criticisms that he used the term equivocally, he suggested that there are two aspects of a scientific paradigm: a cluster of assumptions and examples of practice. Although he was speaking of science, if we use a gentle touch, these two features might be used to articulate paradigms in other forms of life.

In this sense, all social groups are held together by a common commitment to a paradigm. About 2,500 years ago, Protagoras made his living by teaching people how to construct and evaluate good arguments. Protagoras was perhaps the first and certainly the highest-priced consultant of his era (c. 490–c. 420 BCE). Some say that Plato's theory of ideal forms was an attempt to find a way to achieve "certainty" in rebuttal to Protagoras's claim that "man is the measure of all things." Because Protagoras offered to teach people how to make the weaker argument appear to be the stronger, he earned Plato's scorn and the title "the Father of Debate." According to legend, a potential client challenged him, saying, "Prove to me that I should study argumentation." He replied, "Without studying argumentation, how would you know that I had given you a good proof?" This sounds arrogant, and probably was, but it might also be an accurate statement that what counts as a "good argument" or "good reason" for doing something differs in various paradigms.

Every family, corporation, government, and culture makes a similar set of judgments based on its paradigm. For example, each accepts certain patterns of explanation as sufficient and satisfactory but not others. When stopped from fighting on a playground, each child may tell the adult "he hit me first!" and expect that to be accepted as a convincing explanation about why he should not be blamed for misbehaving. Sometimes the adult frustrates the children by refusing to accept "he hit me first" as a good reason and instructing them about a different paradigm in which there is no acceptable excuse for fighting at school. In the best case, the children eventually adopt this paradigm as their own.

Paradigms function as the architecture of how we think; the scaffolds along which our thoughts run; or the underground channels that, when thought emerges again above ground, we call insight and intuition. In a culture, the paradigm might consist of the myths or stories that everyone knows, such as the Bible when Europe was known as "Christendom" (Frye 1983) or the Mahabharata and the Ramayana epics for Hindus. In an organization, the paradigm might be a story about the Founders or a deliberately constructed "mission statement." The organization for which I work encourages us to develop entrepreneurial initiatives, and we are explicitly told that one criterion for approval of these initiatives is that they conform to the mission statement – that is, that they fit the paradigm.

Consultants work with different paradigms. Some work as "experts," following a paradigm that goes something like this: the clients have a problem requiring expertise that they don't possess, they hire a consultant who knows more than they do (or who knows how to do the research required to find out what they need to know), the consultant presents findings or opinions, and the clients make the decisions they need to make and move on.

Other consultants see themselves as dealing with "process." Their paradigm might be described like this: the clients are functioning in a way that they identify as a problem, they hire a consultant to help them find out how to move forward, the consultant assumes that the clients are the experts about what they are doing and create new processes of interaction among them so that they can discover and bring this expertise to bear on the situation, the clients participate in these processes, and the clients themselves make the decisions they need to make and move on.

Still other consultants work within a "reflexive" paradigm in which they interact with the client in such a way as to provoke growth/desired change on the part of the client with little or no direct connection to a problem.

Certain confusions arise when a client hires a "process" consultant to do "expert" or "reflexive" work, or vice versa.

I believe that all of us should reflect, from time to time, on the paradigm we use in our work. Our choice is not whether to have a paradigm, but which paradigm to have and whether to explicate it clearly or allow it to work behind our backs.

So: what paradigm is appropriate for acting wisely in social worlds that (drawing on chapter 2) we understand to be world-like, multiple, made and continually being remade in social interaction, and in which we are agents?

Questions and Questioning

I'm using the phrase "questions and questioning" as a reminder that what we are talking about is the activity of an inquirer, not a grammatical form of language. That is, anyone can read and recite the questions with which I ended chapter 2, but not everyone can, in the sense that I'm meaning here, *ask* them as part of a genuine inquiry.

Much of my time is spent helping doctoral students design their dissertations. Framing their research question is one of the most challenging parts of this process for many students. We wrestle with the words. A good research question is thoughtful about the interrogative. It makes important differences whether one asks "how," "why," or "what." We are very careful with verbs. The choice between asking whether one thing "causes" another, "follows" another, or "is" another brings in clouds of assumptions and requires different research methods. Nouns have to be chosen so that they have just the right aperture – they point to a way of collecting and analyzing data that is as precise as possible, given the rationale for the study, but not so precise as to blind the research to serendipitous findings.

But this entire struggle with grammar is in service to the development of the doctoral student as a finely tuned inquirer. Usually, there comes a point when the student "gets it" and the struggle with grammar is over, having served its purpose. In the final analysis, the researcher himself or herself is the research method, and the wording of the research question and the method of collecting and analyzing data are a means for them to engage in conversation with what they are studying.

My first career (although an unpaid one) was as a competitive intercollegiate debater. My teammates and I spent weeks preparing to attack and defend all possible positions about important topics of public policy, and then went to tournaments in which we debated equally determined teams from other colleges. Asking questions was an important part of debating, as was skill in *not* answering them in the way that they were intended. But these questions had nothing to do with inquiring. They were an attempt to force the other person into a position where he or she would have to make an admission that was damaging to their position.

It has taken me a long time to unlearn the art of using questions as clubs with which to bludgeon other people. My first step was to learn that there are many different ways of questioning. For instance, Socratic questioning (as used by Swidler and her colleagues in the example I described in chapter 2) explores the grammar of the verb "to be" and relentlessly seeks the reason behind every judgment. For example, Plato's dialogue *Protagoras* may be read as a contest between Protagoras's notion that virtue (what they were apparently talking about) is best understood in stories and Socrates's notion that it is best understood in formal definitions (Levine 1998). This seems to me a direct parallel to the conversation between Swidler and Palmer that I analyzed in chapter 2, where Swidler kept pressing Palmer for an abstract definition and he responded (at first) with a story about his experiences and personal commitments.

My encounter with the Milan School of Systemic Family Therapy in the early 1980s was perhaps the single most important learning experience in my professional life. I had read some of the same books as had Gianfranco Cecchin and Luigi Boscolo, but could not have translated them into elegant practice as they did. When I saw them using circular questioning, this introduced me to a whole new form of inquiry. To play with metaphors: in debating, questions are used as clubs to defeat an opponent; in Socratic questioning, as shovels to uncover that on which your current belief stands; but in circular questioning, questions function as signposts, alternatively directing the listeners' attention to things that they would not otherwise see, or containing embedded suggestions, reframings, or simply "look here." (I talk more about this form of questioning in the Afterword.)

Many of the people with whom I now work can be described as artists of inquiry. They are appropriately considered experts, but their expertise is in how to inquire, not in the results of previous inquiries. Like any artist, they have studied the tools of their trade, trained their own performance ability, engaged in coached practice, taken on new dimensions of practice as a result of experience and exposure to striking models of artists in other schools.

Using narrative techniques developed by Australian therapist Michael White, professionals are developing ways of interviewing that focus on the problems rather than the person. By externalizing the story that is interfering with the client's preferred direction, the consultant can help the client to develop a new story that is less problematic (Zimmerman and Dickerson 1996).

In organization development, Frank Barrett and Ronald Fry (2005: 36, 39) stress the importance of questioning in appreciative inquiry (AI).

> To inquire means to search and discover. Inquiry is the act of exploration, a questioning with an agenda to see new possibilities. *AI always begins with a question – an honest desire to learn about something – at its premise* ... AI involves, at its root, the art and practice of crafting questions that support a system's capacity to apprehend, anticipate, and heighten positive potential.... The questions asked about a human system will lay the groundwork for the direction of the system's growth. As noted above, what we dwell upon expands. The pragmatic core of AI proposes that *it is the questions that count most.*
>
> If we really valued the power of inquiry – the powerful and fateful potency of the questions we ask – we might not need the word "appreciate" at all. In our work with AI we have come to see time and time again that *we live into the world our questions create.*

The Public Conversations Project was formed to help polarized groups engage in dialogue with each other. Much of their work is based in asking genuine questions in which members of both groups participate. Although they customize their work to each specific group, these are some of their standard questions: How did you come to hold the position that you hold today? What is the heart of the matter for you? What are your gray areas, those things you are not sure about? These questions are deceptively simple, but it is not just the grammatical form of the question that makes them work; it is the facilitator's modeling of deep and respectful listening.

Teacher and facilitator Kim Pearce (2002; see also W. B. Pearce 2002) has explored ways of training other people to facilitate dialogic communication about difficult topics. Using combinations of modeling, instructing, and coaching, she teaches them about forms of questioning that open up conversations and those that close them down. Two features distinguish her work from the others referred to here. First, she spends considerable time guiding the persons being trained to reflect on their own experience in conflict. They are led to discover their own assumptions about communication and their own comfort-zones with various things that can happen in conflicted situations. Second, she focuses not only on asking questions but on responding to the answers that people give to those questions. The importance of a sense of presence, active listening, and reframing responses is part of the training. But none of these techniques will work if they are not genuine. Dialogue consists of a way of being in the presence of the other, she insists.

Those who take the communication perspective are fully in agreement with these artists of inquiry. The most important aspect of the questions at the end of chapter 2 is that they are vehicles for genuine inquiry. But it isn't just the question that is important; it is also important to be able to hear and respond to the answers.

On November 21, 1995, US Secretary of State Warren Christopher, President Milošević of Serbia, President Tudjman of Croatia, and President Izetbegovic of Bosnia-Herzegovina signed the Balkan Proximity Peace Talks Agreement which ended the fighting in Bosnia. (This treaty is better known as the "Dayton Accords"; it was signed in Dayton, Ohio.) The meeting had been carefully designed to promote a "win–win" solution. Everyone knew that the Agreement would not be observed if any of the presidents felt that they "lost" while others "won."

After the documents were signed, a representative of the United States State Department met with reporters and gave a carefully worded announcement that an agreement had been reached that was a victory for all parties involved. I watched the live telecast of the interview. As I recall, the first question from a reporter was: "Yeah, but who won and who lost?"

The spokesperson shook his head and replied: "Everyone won. There were no losers. We worked carefully to achieve a decision that is in everyone's best interest."

Undeterred, the reporter persisted, "Yeah, OK. But who won?"

I think that the reporter was asking his question from a paradigm about conflict that saw it only as a zero-sum game, in which whatever one wins, another loses. From that paradigm, he simply couldn't hear "everybody won" as an answer to his question, and would not be able to unless he changed his paradigm.

The interaction with this reporter is very similar to the interview Ann Swidler had with Barry Palmer. Swidler's question came from a paradigm for understanding moral languages, and she simply couldn't hear what Palmer was saying as an answer to her question.

The paradigm that supports the communication perspective encourages us to remain profoundly curious about the other. I was asked by a person in one of my trainings: "How can I make the person to whom I'm listening perceive me as interested in what they say?" My response: "By being interested in what they say." He replied: "But it is so boring! I keep hearing the same thing over and over again, and I wasn't interested in it the first time." I felt good about my response: "I see the problem. You are listening to what is being said. Of course you've heard that before. But you should be listening to the person who is saying it. You've never heard this person say this before, and it means something else coming from just this person. Your curiosity should be about what this person means when he or she says the same old thing, and what he or she is 'making' while telling that story." I felt good about this reply because it was a paraphrase of an answer that Martin Buber gave when someone asked him how he could have possibly had a lengthy conversation with a person with whom he disagreed.

One reason to remain curious is that it helps us take the communication perspective. If we can resist the temptation to force "their" answers into "our" preconceived templates, we are better able to hear them. Another reason to remain curious is that it makes us more interesting people, both to others and to ourselves. The more open we are to the universe, the earth, and our social worlds, the more interesting it all becomes. As we sharpen our abilities to question, as literature teacher Giles Gunn (1992: 16) put it, we manage to "be interested and perhaps even interesting, or at least not boorish."

Playfulness

In chapter 1, I argued that we are engaged in a fateful race to see which of the forces driving our cultural evolution will win. There's no contradiction between taking that very seriously and being playful in manner. In fact, I believe that a certain kind of playfulness is a constitutive part of the paradigm supporting the communication perspective.

Perhaps because he was all too familiar with the heavy hand of an oppressive government (his work was suppressed in his native Soviet Union), Mikhael Bakhtin (1968: 6) spoke of the unique perspective afforded by laughter.

> Laughter has a deep philosophical meaning, it is one of the essential forms of the truth concerning the world as a whole, concerning history and man, it is a peculiar point of view relative to the world; the world is seen anew, no less (and perhaps more) profoundly than when seen from the serious standpoint. . . . Certain essential aspects of the world are accessible only by laughter.

I take Bakhtin's last statement very seriously. If social worlds are shape-changing depending on the perspective from which we view them; if the way we form a question shifts our perspective; and if perfectly valid answers to our questions can fly right over our heads because we don't recognize them as answers – in such a world, laughter is an appropriate response.

I hesitated to be so explicit about the seriousness of play because I've lived and worked among highly esteemed professional colleagues who perceived me as being intellectually shallow. Perhaps they are right about the lack of depth of my thinking, but there's at least one alternative hypothesis. As I've talked with them, I find that they don't respect my willingness to find humor in the human condition, or at least to be playful with my perceptions of it. To exaggerate, from my perspective, some of these colleagues mistake depression for profundity and somberness for seriousness.

But what "essential aspects of the world" are "accessible only by laughter"? Sociologist Peter Berger (1997: x) says that "the comic is experienced as *incongruence* . . . the comic conjures up a separate world, different from the world of ordinary reality, operating by different rules." Berger uses the very simple metaphor of a jack-in-the-box, which provokes laughter from children because one first sees an ordinary box, something familiar and unthreatening. Suddenly, something quite unusual pops out of the box and it becomes obvious that this something else was present in the box all along. Things are not what they seem (Berger 1997: 34).

In this sense, the child's understanding of a jack-in-the-box is not so different from seeing our social worlds as "worlds," recognizing that there are many of them and that they are made, and – the biggest joke of all! – that we are agents in their making.

In the more complex world of adult life, Berger shifts metaphors from jack-in-the-box to

> an untranslatable German word . . . *Doppelboedigkeit*. It is derived from the theater, where it denotes a stage that contains more than one level. While the actors go through their motions on one level, very different and putatively sinister actions take place on the other level, which lies below the surface. The dividing structure is fragile. All sorts of unexpected things may pop up from "downstairs," just as holes may suddenly open up and make things and people disappear from "upstairs" in the alien world below. The comic discloses that everything that is taken for granted in ordinary life

possesses this character of *Doppelboedigkeit*. For this reason, the comic is always dangerous. (Berger 1977: 35)

To carry this metaphor into the communication perspective, we would have to make this a participant's theater, with each of us simultaneously a member of the audience, a member of the cast, and – inevitably – a theater critic evaluating the performance. What a hoot!

Systemic

If you are trying to understand a forest, you can't just look at one tree. In fact, you won't understand much about a forest if you look at all the trees in the forest, one at a time. You will do better in understanding a forest by looking at the spaces between trees, and the relationships between forests and other ecologies such as grasslands, deserts, farms, and cities. Forests and other complex things – like me and you, families, corporations, and nations – are best understood systemically.

The distinction between thinking systemically about wholes instead of analytically about parts marks one of the great divisions among paradigms. The word "science" comes from the word "to cut," and science has traditionally featured a process of separating the parts and paying intense attention to them. On the other hand, to think systemically is to look for patterns of connections and relationships among the parts.

But note that I'm saying "systemic" rather than looking "at systems." I want to keep the emphasis on what *we are doing*, not on *the thing we are talking about*. This is in the spirit of Mara, the woman whom I painted (in our imaginations!) into Raphael's "The School of Athens" in chapter 2. Her gestures were self-reflexive, pointing to the "us" who are in a conversation before indicating what we were talking about.

This is an important reminder, because there are many schools of thought and traditions of practice that say that they are about systems, and some of these are very different from others (W. B. Pearce 2002). For present purposes, it suffices to say that the communication perspective always looks for connections and relationships, that it expects reflexive relationships rather than straight forward lines of causes and responses, and that it assumes that everything is both contextualized by something else and is a context for something else.

Process

When you first read the title of this book (*Making Social Worlds*), my guess is that your eye was drawn to the term "social worlds." And while our social worlds are important, the innovation that I'm proposing in this book is to focus more on the process by which these social worlds are made, believing that this gives a unique perspective on those social worlds. So let your eye turn toward the word "making." Say the title out loud, first emphasizing "social worlds" (that would be a more common book). Now say it again, this time emphasizing the word "making." Yes, that's this book!

There are many technologies for measuring objects, fewer for naming and measuring processes. But there are some. The remainder of this book is an attempt to provide a vocabulary for naming the process of communication and for describing how it is making social worlds, so in this particular instance, let me simply cite some other areas in which the focus is more on process than products.

Even serious physicists say that no two snowflakes are exactly alike. If that's the case, then it would not be very productive to try to collect, count, and categorize them. If sufficiently precise, a taxonomy of snowflakes would have as many categories as there are snowflakes . . . and what a useless way to spend our time! But we can know something very useful about snowflakes if we focus on the common process by which an infinite variety of snowflakes are made. For more than you ever thought there was to know about snowflakes, see the online Snowflake Primer (n.d.).

The communication perspective resembles the approach that the physicists at Cal Tech took toward snowflakes. While no two persons, relationships, or situations are alike, the same process – communication – forms them all. If we are willing to be surprised by each new snowflake and revel in its uniqueness, we can understand it as a "singleton," a one-of-a-kind product of a common process. In the same way, we can understand each moment in our social worlds as unique but also as the product of a common process.

Rivers provide another example of thinking primarily about process. Think of a white-water river cascading down a steep slope with furious rapids and foaming shoals. If you have ever been in a canoe in such a river, you know that there are many things in it that can ruin your whole day. Whether you hit a rock or an eddy, you can find yourself out of the boat and in the water.

For our purposes, it is possible to differentiate two kinds of things in this river, both of which can overturn your canoe. Rocks have the same shape and properties whether in the river or taken out of it; eddies, whirlpools, and standing waves do not.[1] The latter are dependent on the movement of the water. If you dam the river, eddies, whirlpools, and standing waves disappear; if you take them out of the river, they just turn into placid puddles of water. They are constituted by their energy and organization, not the "matter" which is energized and organized.

To understand eddies, whirlpools, and standing waves, we must attend to process. We are less interested in the composition of these things than we are in speed, volume, angles, and the like. We need a whole different vocabulary than we do for a chemical analysis of water or a mineralogical analysis of rocks.

To what extent are our social worlds like a white-water river? Which of the things in our social worlds are like rocks and water, and which are more like eddies, whirlpools, and currents? How can we tell the difference between them? What are the consequences of treating objects as if they were configurations? What might be gained and lost by treating at least some object-like things as if they were configurations?

A final example of an illuminating moment based on attention to process is provided by Thor Heyerdahl's story about how he came to know how the giant carved stone faces appeared on Easter Island. I find it so elegant that I sometimes refer to the "Heyerdahl Solution" for understanding puzzling things.[2]

These stone carvings have perplexed many people. Some have suggested that their construction required an inhumanly advanced technology, so – obviously! – they prove that Earth has been visited by aliens from outer space. Others note that they are similar in scale to the stonework of the ancient Egyptians and wonder how these builders got from the Nile River to the South Pacific. Similarly amazed but apparently much less sophisticated in the arts of speculation, Heyerdahl asked the mayor, Petro Atan, if he knew how the carvings had been raised into place.

Atan: Yes, Señor, I do know. There's nothing to it.

Heyerdahl: Nothing to it? It's one of the greatest mysteries of Easter Island!

Atan: But I know it. I can raise a *moai*.

Heyerdahl: Who taught you?

(The mayor grew solemn and drew himself up in front of me.)

Atan: Señor, when I was a very little boy I had to sit on the floor, bolt upright, and my grandfather and his old brother-in-law Porotu sat on the floor in front of me. They taught me many things, just as in school nowadays. I know a lot. I had to repeat and repeat it until it was quite right, every single word. I learned the songs, too. (Heyerdahl 1960)

Heyerdahl bet the mayor that he couldn't do it and brought his camera to record what happened. Atan gathered his helpers, performed the appropriate rituals, and, 18 days later, a new stone face stood facing the sea. Heyerdahl gladly paid the bet and developed the photographs showing how it was made.

What is gained by attention to the process by which these stones were made? Well, it eliminates the conceptual need to invoke aliens or ancient Egyptians. It gives a sense of what we would need to do if we wanted to make one more stone head. It answers a lot of questions about how they were made. And perhaps it enhances our sense of wonder. We might look at Easter Island and see impressively large, carved rock heads suitable for taking a photograph to help remember our trip to the Islands. But just maybe, if we adjust the structure of what we observe and how we explain and reflect, we might see them as momentary configurations of a process of coordination and meaning-making involving clashing cultures, improbable religions, bold actions by desperate people, limited natural resources, blazing visions in the minds of earthly men, and a lonely bit of land standing in a very large ocean – because, as Atan reminded us, he learned the songs, too.[3]

Emergent Characteristics

Just as we can gain some perspective from looking at those areas that focus on process, so we can draw insight and support from the development of chaos theory and theories of complex adaptive systems. There was a time when the social world was thought of as messy and disordered in contrast to a clock-like physical world, and artists painted mind-expanding and consciousness-enriching visions of the world. However, now it is the physicists who create the most fantastic models of the universe – complete with computer simulations.

In his history of the emergence of chaos theory, Gleick stressed the discontinuous nature of what we've learned about self-organizing systems, far from equilibrium and with emergent characteristics.

Where chaos begins, classical science stops. For as long as the world has had physicists inquiring into the laws of nature, it has suffered a special ignorance about disorder in the atmosphere, in the turbulent sea, in the fluctuations of wildlife populations, in the oscillations of the heart and the brain. The irregular side of nature, the discontinuous and erratic side – these have been puzzles to science, or worse, monstrosities.

But in the 1970s a few scientists in the United States and Europe began to find a way through disorder. They were mathematicians, physicists, biologists, chemists, all seeking connections between different kinds of irregularity. Physiologists found a surprising order in the chaos that develops in the human heart, the prime cause of sudden, unexplained death. Ecologists explored the rise and fall of gypsy moth populations. Economists dug out old stock price data and tried a new kind of analysis. The insights that emerged led directly into the natural world – the shapes of clouds, the paths of lightning, the microscopic intertwining of blood vessels, the galactic clustering of stars.

Now that science is looking, chaos seems to be everywhere. A rising column of cigarette smoke breaks into wild swirls. A flag snaps back and forth in the wind. A dripping faucet goes from a steady pattern to a random one. Chaos appears in the behavior of the weather, the behavior of an airplane in flight, the behavior of cars clustering on an expressway, the behavior of oil flowing in underground pipes. No matter what the medium, the behavior obeys the same newly discovered laws. That realization has begun to change the way business executives make decisions about insurance, the way astronomers look at the solar system, the way political theorists talk about the stresses leading to armed conflict. (Gleick 1987: 3–4)

Chaos theory and complex adaptive systems theory have had radical impacts on practice in a wide variety of fields. There has been a sometimes-giddy sense of vertigo as fundamental senses of order and disorder have been toppled, enabling practitioners to develop new tools for understanding and working. As Dora Fried Schnitman (2002: 5) put it, order and disorder were

traditionally seen as opposites. Order was that which could be classified, analyzed and incorporated within rational discourse; disorder was associated with chaos and, by definition, could not be expressed, except through statistical generalizations. The past 20 years have witnessed a radical reevaluation of this perspective because contemporary science, culture, and therapy have conceptualized chaos, disorder, and crisis as complex information rather than the absence of order. . . . Chaos can lead to order, as it does in self-organizing systems. . . . The world, such as it is seen by chaos theory, is rich in unpredictable developments, full of complex forms and turbulent fluxes, characterized by nonlinear relationships between cause and effect, and broken up among multiple scales of varying magnitudes that make globalization precarious. Clouds and waterfalls are turbulent metaphors, unpredictable, irregular, and infinitely variable small fluctuations expand into large-scale changes.

Ours is a pretty heady moment in the development of science. Nobel-prize winning physicist Ilya Prigogine (2002: 23) said: "our concepts of laws of nature have to be revised to include probability and irreversibility. In this sense, we come to the end of conventional science, but we are also at the privileged moment of the emergence of a new vision of nature. We are only at the beginning. Much remains to be done."

By now, the idea that sufficiently complex systems develop emergent properties should be no surprise. But even though the concept is now well known, emergence remains hard to fit into ordinary language.[4] Ironically, although he titled his book *Emergence*, John Holland (1998: 3) said: "It is unlikely that a topic as complicated as emergence will submit meekly to a concise definition, and I have no such definition to offer." Less daunted by the challenge, Ralph Stacey (1996: 285) offered this high-level description:

> Emergence is the production of global patterns of behavior by agents in a complex system interacting according to their own local rules of behavior, without intending the global patterns of behavior that come about. In emergence, global patterns cannot be predicted from the local rules of behavior that produce them. To put it another way, global patterns cannot be reduced to individual behavior.

I like Stacey's emphasis on the nonsummative nature of emergence, but I want to go beyond his phrase "patterns of behavior." Sometimes it makes sense to think of what emerges as a new entity or function; that is, as a thing in itself. For example, the human *brain* consists of neurochemical activities, but human *consciousness* is filled with blazing visions, doubts, hopes, and ambitions that are qualitatively different from the electrical flows that make them possible. The mind cannot exist without the brain, but having emerged, the consciousness's own actions can account for its continued development through study, reflection, and thinking. For this reason, I like Kevin Mihata's (1997: 31) use of the term "structures" in his definition. Emergence, he said, is "the process by which patterns or global-level structures arise from interactive local-level processes. This 'structure' or 'pattern' cannot be understood or predicted from the behavior or properties of the component units alone."

The discovery that complex functions emerge from simple processes has been truly revolutionary, upsetting centuries-old concepts of science and of the universe. Not coincidentally, it also runs against the grain of common sense. The recognition of how the authority of science has shaped common sense led Sir James Lighthill and his colleagues (1986: 35), speaking for the International Union of Theoretical and Applied Mechanics, to apologize for having misled us all.

> We are all deeply conscious today that the enthusiasm of our forebears for the marvelous achievements of Newtonian mechanics led them to make generalizations in this area of predictability, which indeed we may generally have tended to believe before 1960, but which we now recognize were false. We collectively wish to apologize for having misled the generally educated public by spreading ideas about the determinism of systems satisfying Newton's laws of motion, that after 1960 were to be proved incorrect.

Those working with organizations and people have sounded similar claims that a new epistemology is needed.

> Our normal way of thinking cheats us. It leads us to think of wholes as made up of many parts, the way a car is made up of wheels, a chassis, and a drive train. In this way of thinking, the whole is assembled from the parts and depends upon them to work effectively. If a part is broken, it must be repaired or replaced. This is a very logical way of thinking about machines. But living systems are different.
>
> Unlike machines, living systems, such as your body or a tree, create themselves. They are not mere assemblages of their parts but are continually growing and changing along with their elements. (Senge et al. 2004a: 2–3)

Drawing on de Gues (1997), Senge et al. (2004b) suggest that "large institutions, notably, global corporations" are best understood as living systems. Indeed, they constitute a "new species" that is "proliferating" and "affecting life for almost all other species on the planet."

> As long as our thinking is governed by habit – notably by industrial, "machine age" concepts such as control, predictability, standardization,

and "faster is better" – we will continue to re-create institutions as they have been, despite their increasing disharmony with the larger world.

In short, the basic problem with the new species of global institutions is that they have not yet become aware of themselves as living. Once they do, they can then become a place for presencing the whole as it might be, not just as it has been. (Senge et al. 2004a: 5)

I suspect that all of this talk about discontinuous developments in science functions better to help us identify and set aside unproductive aspects of our paradigms than to build a new one. My own learning of a paradigm appropriate for social worlds progressed most rapidly when I had specific examples to model. So let's turn to a computer simulation for a more tangible example of how complex entities, in this case a "flock," emerge from less complex entities, in this case "boids."

Watch a flock of birds. They do some amazing things. They wheel and turn in intricate patterns, they maneuver through and around obstacles, and they can land, practically simultaneously, on separate branches of a tree. And they do all of this without crashing into each other or forcing each other into the objects they pass.

How do they do that? Here are three explanations, each representing a different epistemology:

- Strong leadership: one bird knows what the whole group should do and somehow gives orders that they follow.
- Pattern matching: all the birds "know" the patterns that they are to fly and each carries out its specific tasks.
- Flocking: these abilities of the flock are emergent properties in a system in which each individual follows a few simple rules.

There's no evidence for the command and report pattern of communication envisioned in the first explanation, and the cognitive demands of the second exceed anything that anyone believes about birds. However, in 1986, Craig Reynolds (see Reynolds 2001) developed a simulation in which computer symbols he called "boids" duplicated the abilities of flocks of birds. Each boid followed three simple rules for "steering";

- separation: steer to avoid crowding local flockmates;
- alignment: steer towards the average heading of local flockmates; and,
- cohesion: steer to move toward the average position of local flockmates.

If you've seen the *Batman* movies or *The Lion King*, the computer-generated images of the flocking of bats and the stampede of wildebeests were based on these rules.

Flocking is an emergent characteristic. The abilities of the flock are different from and exceed those possessed by any individual member of the flock. Once we start thinking this way, we can change the parameters of the simulation and create flocks, herds, or schools with different and greater abilities. Or, we can reason "backward," observing flocks, herds, or schools with greater abilities and tinker with our simulations until we find the rules that, if followed through many iterations, will produce the complex behavior that we observe.

Now, find a comfortable seat and watch a group of human beings communicate. Note first how their turn-taking ebbs and flows; how it takes different configurations from time to time; how certain things cause it to change speed, pattern, length, etc. Watch the patterns of physical movements as the participants sit, stand, shift position, gesture, make facial expressions. Can you see this as a complex patterned behavior something like the flocking of birds? CMM suggests the term *coordination* as a place-marker for understanding how this works; in the next chapter, I argue that this is one essential part of communication.

Now begin to listen to what is being said by these people that you are watching. Story-lines enter into the conversation, are interrupted, resumed, trigger counter-narratives. People respond to each other before the other is finished. Each person expects the others to have heard more than they said, and sometimes things other than what they said, and get irritated when this doesn't happen. Can you see the flow of meaning-making as a complex flocking behavior? I'm suggesting the term *making/managing meaning* as a place-marker for understanding how this works, and in the next chapter, I argue that this is the second essential part of communication.

Is it possible to understand the events and objects of our social worlds as even more complex entities emerging from the process in which we coordinate actions and make/manage our meanings? Chapters 6, 7, and 8 explore this possibility. Let's see how far these ideas can take us.

Notes

1   I'm making the contrast sharper than I might in order to make a point. If we were to shift the scale, rocks and water appear more like configurations than immutable objects. For example, in geological time scales, rocks come and go.

At the subatomic level, rocks and water are configurations of smaller particles in intricate dances whose properties are perhaps closer to eddies, whirlpools, and currents than to the commonsense notion of thing-ness.

2   My appreciation for this story does not mean that I necessarily believe it! Victoria Chen told me of a television documentary in which various scientists and anthropologists commissioned the natives to build a stone head. While they succeeded, it seemed a much more laborious process than Heyerdahl's account would indicate.

3   This last comment – that Atan learned the songs, too – is included to open the door to a discussion of what Heyerdahl apparently did *not* learn from his study. We don't know what was going on at the time that made the Easter Island residents think to make these great heads. We don't know what making these stone carvings (or the carved stones, once they were finished) meant to those who made them. We don't know how the residents organized themselves and accomplished the task. Etc. I'm grateful to Victoria Chen for sharing these thoughts with me, based on the way she uses the story in her classes.

4   It is hard to fit any new idea into ordinary language. The language we use today is the product of previous generations of human struggles to fit their experience into words. That's why languages change over time and successive editions of dictionaries include thousands of new words and drop thousands of words that have fallen out of use.

References

Bakhtin, M. (1968), *Rabelais and His World*, tr. Helen Iswolsky, Cambridge, MA: MIT Press.

Barrett, F. J. and Fry, R. E. (2005), *Appreciative Inquiry: A Positive Approach to Building Cooperative Capacity*, Chagrin Falls, OH: Taos Institute Publications.

Berger, P. L. (1997), *Redeeming Laughter: The Comic Dimension of Human Experience*, Berlin: Walter de Gruyter.

de Gues, A. (1997), *The Living Company*, Cambridge, MA: Harvard Business School Press.

Frye, N. (1983), *The Great Code: The Bible and Literature*, Orlando, FL: Harcourt.

Gleick, J. (1987), *Chaos: Making of a New Science*, New York: Penguin.

Gunn, G. B. (1992), *Thinking Across the American Grain: Ideology, Intellect and the New Pragmatism*, Chicago: University of Chicago Press.

Heyerdahl, T. (1960), *Aku Aku: The Secret of Easter Island*, New York: Pocket Books.

Holland, J. (1998), *Emergence: From Chaos to Order*, Reading, MA: Helix.

James, W. (1907/1975), *Pragmatism: A New Name for Some Old Ways of Thinking*. Reprinted in *Pragmatism and the Meaning of Truth*, ed. A. J. Ayers, Cambridge, MA: Harvard University Press.

Kuhn, T. (1996), *The Structure of Scientific Revolutions*, 3rd edn., Chicago: University of Chicago Press.

Levine, P. (1998), *Living without Philosophy: On Narrative, Rhetoric, and Morality*, Albany: State University of New York Press.

Lighthill, J., Thompson, J. M. T., Sen, A. K., Last, A. G. M., Tritton, D. T., and Mathias, P. (1986), The recently recognized failure of predictability in Newtonian dynamics, *Proceedings of the Royal Society of London, Series A: Mathematical and Physical Sciences*, 407 (1832): 35–50.

Mihata, K. (1997), The persistence of "emergence." In R. A. Eve, S. Horsfall, and M. E. Lee (eds.), *Chaos, Complexity and Sociology: Myths, Models and Theories*, Thousand Oaks, CA: Sage, pp. 30–8.

Pearce, K. A. (2002), *Making Better Social Worlds: Engaging in and Facilitating Dialogic Communication*, Redwood City, CA: Pearce Associates.

Pearce, W. B. (2002), Systems: schools of thought and traditions of practice. Retrieved from http://www.pearceassociates.com/essays/story_about_systems.pdf on August 25, 2006.

Prigogine, I. (2002), The end of science? In D. F. Schnitman and J. Schnitman (eds.), *New Paradigms, Culture and Subjectivity*, Cresskill, NJ: Hampton Press.

Reynolds, C. (2001), *Boids: Background and Update*. Retrieved from http://www.red3d.com/cwr/boids/ on January 26, 2006.

Schnitman, D. F. (2002), Introduction: science, culture and subjectivity. In D. Schnitman and J. Schnitman (eds.), *New Paradigms: Culture and Subjectivity*, Cresskill, NJ: Hampton Press.

Senge, P. M., Scharmer, C. O., Jaworski, J., and Flowers, B. S. (2004a), Awakening faith in an alternative future, *Reflections: The SoL Journal on Knowledge, Learning and Change*, 5: 1–16.

Senge, P. M., Scharmer, C. O., Jaworski, J., and Flowers, B. S. (2004b), *Presence: Human Purpose and the Field of the Future*, Cambridge, MA: SoL, Society for Organizational Learning.

Snowflake Primer (n.d.), Retrieved from http://www.its.caltech.edu/~atomic/snowcrystals/primer/primer.htm on August 26, 2006.

Stacey, R. (1996), *Complexity and Creativity in Organizations*, San Francisco, CA: Barrett-Koehler.

Zimmerman, J. L. and Dickerson, V. C. (1996), *If Problems Talked: Narrative Therapy in Action*, New York: Guilford.

Chapter 4

Communication: Coordinating Actions and Making/Managing Meanings

Preview

The conceptual structure of this book is shown in figure P.1 (in the Preface). It begins with the very broad concerns in chapter 1 about the personal and social importance of identifying, and acting wisely in, critical moments. The second and third chapters become a bit more specific, describing the perspective and paradigm taken in this book. The current chapter sets out the broad outlines of the specific theory that I'm inviting you to explore. If figure P.1 resembles an hour-glass, then this chapter is the smallest point in the middle of the figure.

The theory of the coordinated management of meaning (CMM) does not try to offer a set of propositions about the events and objects of the social world. Rather, it is a set of concepts and tools focusing on the process by which those events and objects are made. It functions to discipline and enable inquiry into specific moments of that process for the purpose of understanding, acting wisely, and intervening to improve the process.

CMM describes communication as having two inseparable but different aspects: (1) coordinating actions, and (2) making/managing meaning. This chapter concludes by inviting you to see the dynamic dance between the two aspects of communication as the site where social worlds are made.

Theory as a Way of Seeing Things

Art critic Raymond Steiner (1992) was contemplating a gallery filled with people intently looking at the carefully displayed paintings. He wondered what they were seeing, and observed that they were seeing, in a certain sense, what they already knew how to see.

> Seeing is believing, or so they say, but I'm more than a little convinced that the reverse is equally true, that believing is seeing. How else to account for those people who can be brought to look at an exhibition of blots, squiggles and smears and come away thinking that they've seen "art"? Surely someone made them *believe* before they *saw*.

Taken together, chapters 1, 2, and 3 make a sustained argument that good things may come if we take a communication perspective. But even if we look *at* communication rather than *through* it, what do we see it *as*? If Steiner is right, we'll see what we already know how to see, and this has to do with our theories, whether implicit or explicit.

I've had any number of experiences in which I've been looking at "the same thing" as someone who knew far more about it than me and been struck by how much more, and what different things they see. I'm thinking about my tennis coach, whom I pay good money to see things in my game that I can't see, and my *aikido sensei* who told me for years about particular techniques that occurred right in front of me but I couldn't see.

A similar thing happens when we watch (or participate in) patterns of communication. As part of my research, I've spent far too many years sitting behind one-way mirrors with my professional colleagues, watching other human beings communicating about important and/or difficult matters. When we close the curtain and talk among ourselves, I'm struck by what different stories my colleagues and I have about what we've just seen and heard. Many of them have different professional languages than I and, because we believe different things, we see different things happening. Our conversations prove the wisdom of philosopher Ludwig Wittgenstein's (1922: section 5.6, p. 149) aphorism "The limits of my language mean the limits of my world" and novelist Carlos Fuentes's (1985) observation that "nothing is seen until the writer names it. Language permits us to see. Without the word, we are all blind."

This chapter offers a specific language for naming and participating in the process of communication. I call this "the coordinated management of meaning" or "CMM." Although an awkward phrase, I used it in print 30 years ago and seem to be stuck with it (Pearce 1976).

There's a sense in which theory-building is far more like painting a picture than solving a puzzle. Like a painter's first brush stroke, the concepts initially selected by the theorist shatter the mute unity within the frame and prefigure all else that we do. Any number of theories can be built on the canvas of the communication perspective, and while the artist/theorist's choice of brush and stroke are under-determined, they have consequences. As we assess those consequences, we revisit those initial choices. Not for nothing do artists purchase far more canvases than they will produce finished paintings, and my overflowing paper-recycle container attests to the fact that theory-building flows "backward" (from some successes and far more failures in application) as well as "forward" (from concepts and purposes to applications). But over the years, I've found CMM useful because it names the two essential parts of the process of communication: coordinating actions and making/ managing meaning.

Coordinating Actions

A few years ago, I was in a long meeting of the "governance team" at the university in which I work. In this particular moment, I was not particularly engaged with the topic being discussed and frustrated by what I perceived as the poor quality of the discussion. It seemed as if many people had unspoken agendas and were using the topic as a surrogate for achieving other purposes, were not listening to each other very well, and otherwise were failing to discern and/or act wisely into the bifurcation points of the discussion. One of my colleagues who was just beginning to study CMM was part of the group, and we moved our chairs so that we could take an observer's perspective. Perceiving my frustration with the quality of the process, she good-naturedly challenged me to do a CMM analysis of what was happening. I took it as a welcome opportunity to distract myself and said, "Forget what they are talking about. Think of the people in the group as trees blowing in the wind, or as dancers on a dance floor. Look at how the conversation ebbs and flows, picking up and losing speed. Now, let's start looking at some of the patterns . . ." We noted the staccato pattern in which sequential turns took the form of emphatic statements, rather than more fluid patterns in which one turn flows gently into another; we noted that certain voices always followed other voices while many voices were completely silent. And on and on . . .

That's what I mean by "coordination." I include this story here because my colleague told me that she had not picked that up from any of the things I had written, and that it was a turning point for her in understanding CMM.

The term coordination has not been a major topic in philosophy or social theory and, until recently, few practitioners used it in the name of their work. And when people have used the term, they've usually used it to describe a goal, for example, differentiating between a well coordinated conference and one that is not coordinated or poorly run (Malone and Crowston 1994).

I propose that we think of coordination as a "sensitizing concept" that, as sociologist Herbert Blumer (1954: 7) said, does not try to identify any stable part of our social worlds (because our social worlds aren't sufficiently stable for that kind of work) but instead "merely suggest directions along which to look." That is, "coordination" doesn't tell us what are the necessary criteria to distinguish between coordinated and uncoordinated actions. Rather, it says "look at the way people put their actions together, regardless of whether they are well coordinated or not." Rather than describing coordinated behavior, as used here, the term jiggles our elbow and says, "Look here, look here."

But, mindful that we see what we already know, I want to say a bit more about coordination so that we will have a sufficiently rich understanding that we can recognize its complexity and subtlety. To do this, let me compare three things: piles of sand, packs of wolves, and conversations among people.

If you start dropping grains of sand on top of each other on a flat surface, those grains of sand are not responsive to each other except as physical objects. And yet, if you drop enough, the *pile* will begin to take an orderly shape. In fact, if each new grain of sand falls precisely at the same place as the preceding, very regular things will occur. The pile will reach a precise ratio between its height and the slope of its sides, and when a certain critical ratio is reached, the next grain of sand will precipitate a catastrophic restructuring of the pile. (That's a term of art among those who study such things; what it means is that there will be a "landslide" and the pile will get broader at the base with a lower slope, and the process will continue.)

Imagine a pile of sand on which an infinite amount of sand continues to fall at a regular rate. If we were to watch this pile over a long period of time, it would appear that the relationships among the grains of sand in the pile were coordinated, because the shape of the whole fluctuates regularly between an upper and lower ratio of slope to height (Bak 1999).

If you introduce a number of individual wolves into an area in which there are none (as has recently been done at Yellowstone National Park in the United States), they will form packs, social groups ranging from 6 to 8 (but sometimes many more) wolves. These packs have a clearly marked structure, marking the hierarchy of status within the pack and the differentiation between those in and outside the pack.

One of the biggest differences between a pile of sand and a pack of wolves has to do with coordination. Piles of sand are clear examples of self-organizing systems, but individual grains of sand do nothing to place themselves within the pile. There is no repair mechanism if someone comes along and flattens the pile. Wolves, however, are preoccupied with coordinating their actions with each other. They fight or use dominance displays to create and maintain their positions in the pack and they use elaborate communication systems involving scent, tails, ears, teeth, and voice to mark their place in the pack. A wolf that challenges the structure of the pack may be disciplined or killed . . . unless their challenge is successful, in which case the structure of the pack changes and the dance of coordination continues.

Human conversations are even more complicated than the social structure of wolves. In a manner that wolves find unthinkably scandalous,[1] human beings belong to multiple packs simultaneously. Our actions in any given moment can be seen through the lens of coordinating with our families, professions, religions, sports club, friendships, etc. Like wolves, we often challenge our place in the various packs of which we are a part, but unlike wolves, we also sometimes explicitly try to redefine the meaning of, or limits of, standardized practices in our packs. Any account of "coordination" in human social interaction must include such things as heroism and betrayal, honesty and deceit, loneliness and excessive conformity. In short, coordination for human beings isn't just a matter of "fitting in" or "compliance." It is more complex than that.

I believe that using the lens of "coordination" to look at some aspects of the process by which we make our social worlds achieves three things. First, it liberates us from an assumption about communication that is dysfunctional in the contemporary world and enables us to find new ways of relating to each other. Second, it gives us a way of finding openings for understanding and acting into the contingencies of our social worlds. Third, it provides a basis for discerning the differences among several forms of communication and for taking steps to call into being those forms of communication that better meet our needs.

Choosing "coordination" as a sensitizing concept for understanding communication

"Coordination" is probably not the first word that leaps to your mind when someone says "communication." Perhaps it should be. Let me tell the story of how I came to give it such a prominent place in my understanding of communication.

Like most of us, when I started studying communication, I thought of it as a means of gaining understanding or agreement. To the extent that I thought of coordination at all, it was as a consequence of mutual understanding or having achieved common ground. I found Theodore Newcomb's (1953) article, "An approach to the study of communicative acts," useful as a way of conceptualizing communication. Newcomb's model envisioned two persons (A and B), each having an "orientation" toward some object (X) in the environment. The social psychologist (who was not "in" the picture but for whom the model was drawn) could compare the extent to which the orientations of persons A and B were similar. If similar, persons A and B were said to be cooriented. If A and B disagreed about object X, supposedly they would communicate about it and come to greater coorientation. Despite its title, Newcomb's model did not include communicative acts; it functioned as a before-and-after snapshot of people's co-orientation about the events and objects in their social worlds.

By now, you can probably already name many of my discontents with this model, but it took me a long time to work them through. My colleagues Keith Stamm and Herbert Strentz and I spent several years doing research on this model, and some other models that we and Jack McLeod and Steve Chaffee derived from it. Those studies were successful from the perspective of a social scientist – we accounted for a lot of the variance in the data and they were published. But they really didn't move me along toward the kind of answers that I wanted, and I ultimately concluded that what was wrong involved the basic, underlying assumptions about communication and that no amount of further tinkering with the model or the research design would move us forward. If you want to follow along my learning curve, take a look at Chaffee and McLeod (1968), Stamm and Pearce (1971), and Pearce and Stamm (1973).

Because of the disconnect between the findings of these studies and the questions that I wanted to answer, I examined my own basic assumptions about communication. I concluded that, of course, agreement is important, but probably not as important as some other things. As a result, I stepped back and started rethinking what is going on when communication occurs. This led to a very different type of research.

Instead of starting with particular conditions ("coorientational states") and trying to determine what forms of communication occurred in them, my new colleagues and I moved from experiments to case studies in our preferred research designs. We identified particularly interesting patterns of communication and studied them to see what we could learn about them. Specifically, we set ourselves to describe these patterns and understand why, out of all of the many possible ways that people might coordinate their behavior, this is the one that occurred (Pearce and Cronen 1980: ch. 7).

A close analysis of the patterns of communication in a family (we called the adults Donna and Ray Flynn) was the turning point for our group (Harris 1980). We deliberately selected the Flynns from an initial screening of many families because they were "normal" (that is, had no reported or observable pathologies), the parents in the family were both articulate and reciprocally affectionate, and they described their family as doing well. This was our first study of this type and we didn't know if we were prepared for the complexities of a "sick" family. The method for the study included general interviews, specific follow-up interviews in which the family members were asked to describe – on a turn-by-turn basis – some of the key episodes that gave shape to their family, and finally a role-playing exercise in which the couple (enthusiastically) re-enacted their most challenging episode while our team observed them.

We were surprised to find that this "normal" family had paradoxical rules and misunderstandings in their communication patterns. Even more perplexing, it seemed as if these paradoxes and misunderstandings were integral parts of the family's ability to do the things that they cited as their strengths. They described a pattern of escalating conflict, in which Ray withdrew and Donna nagged. "About three or four times a year," they told us, they would reach a point where they could not continue this pattern and initiated a different episode in which they confronted their conflict. Insulating themselves from the children, they engaged in several hours of accusations, apologies, defensiveness, support, emotional displays, concessions, acceptance, and constructive discussions, leading to lovemaking and promises to do less withdrawing and less nagging.

The primary analyst in this study, Linda Harris, identified three elements that seemed as if they should prevent this family from coordinating their actions. First, the relationship had to get "bad" before it could be "good." That is, to initiate the episode that renewed and deepened their relationship, they had to engage in behaviors (nagging and withdrawing) that both disliked.

Second, their ability to engage in the relationship-renewing confrontation episode depended on a patterned misunderstanding/disagreement about who initiated it. For the episode to work, both needed to be able to take credit for being the initiator. Each saw it as something that they – not their partner – had chosen:

(1) *Ray:*   Finally you will intensify your nagging. I will decide I've had enough of this.
(2) *Donna:*   Yeah, but you would never bring it up. I think it would continue to go on unless I eventually brought it to a head.

Third, multiple episodes were being enacted simultaneously. At least to an observer, it wasn't clear what various acts meant, and there seemed to be patterned, intentional shifts in the way Donna and Ray interpreted what they did. Actions that at one time are taken as initiating the confrontation episode are at other times seen as the nagging/withdrawing that make it necessary. Harris interpreted it this way: when the conflict is going on, Donna's attempt to confront the conflict is perceived by Ray as just more nagging, and Ray's refusal to confront the conflict is perceived by Donna as just more withdrawing. It wasn't clear to the observers when an action perceived at one time as "more of the same" would be dramatically re-interpreted as the breakthrough that leads to the healing confrontation episode.

What surprised us so much was that this normal – even exemplary – couple had such convoluted patterns of communication. While trying to make sense of this, we were struck by how well people seem to coordinate their actions even though they don't agree about their meanings or even understand what the other means.

Another study led us even further in the direction of celebrating the complex ways in which people coordinate their actions. Dave and Jan (not their real names, of course) were living together but not married. They described their primary relational difficulty as involving "dominance."

For Dave, the issue was relatively straightforward: he wanted them to live as equals, sharing major responsibilities and decision-making. His own story about himself was not consistent with being a dominating person in a relationship.

Jan's story was much more complicated; we saw it as a paradoxical loop. She described herself as "lazy" and wanted a dominant other to push her to do what she needed to do. She saw her relational task as that of controlling Dave sufficiently so that, despite his reluctance, he would take the controlling role in the relationship and tell her what to do. She said that Dave "sets the rules a lot of the time. It takes a lot of work from me, but he pushes me around a lot to make me do something . . . he really does it for a positive reason . . . he encourages me to do lots of things to become more independent and in touch with my own power."

We wanted to know how two people with such incompatible expectations for the relationship could coordinate their actions. We asked them to recall two specific episodes in which "dominance" was an issue. We interviewed them together, co-constructing with them an act-by-act text of these episodes that we then used as the basis for an interview about how they understood what was happening in each turn. One of the episodes involved Jan's failure, once again, to apply for a job. In the episode below CETA is an employment assistance organization in the nearby city of Northampton.

(Dave comes home from work)
(1) *Dave:*   Did you go to CETA today?
(2) *Jan:*   No.
(3) *Dave:*   *(silence)*
(4) *Jan:*   I called and there wasn't anything in today.
(5) *Dave:*   Did you leave the house?
(6) *Jan:*   I fed the cats.
(7) *Dave:*   You should have gone to Northampton. You're never going to get a job by laying around. The only way to do it is to start.
(8) *Jan:*   I know, I know . . .
(9) *Dave:*   Well, why aren't you doing anything about it?
(10) *Jan:*   *(silence)*
(11) *Dave:*   You have to do something about it. You're just being lazy. It can't go on like this.
(12) *Jan:*   *(silence)*
(13) *Dave:*   Look, we have to get $200 for May rent; we're already overdue on the phone bill. I don't know where we'll get May food money . . .
(14) *Jan:*   I know . . .
(15) *Dave:*   So why didn't you go to Northampton?
(16) *Jan:*   I was up and ready at nine, but I just couldn't do it.
(17) *Dave:*   Well, you're getting up at eight o'clock and we're leaving the house at nine.
(18) *Jan:*   All right.

When they had finished writing the text of the episode, Dave told the interviewer "What we're really fighting is the dependency thing" and that it is "a much bigger issue than finding a job" (Pearce and Cronen 1980: 277).

In our interview of how they understood each of the turns in this conversation, we found a critical moment in turn (17). Jan and Dave misunderstood each other about what happened in this turn, and the structure of this unrecognized disagreement was necessary for the episode to serve the needs of their relationship. In turn (17), Dave gave Jan explicit *instructions* about what to do. Jan interpreted this as just the *ultimatum* (do this or our relationship is over) that she had been working to solicit from Dave. In fact, she told the interviewer that she would have re-initiated the episode at another time if Dave had not delivered such an ultimatum. Dave, however, interpreted what he said in turn (17) as *backing down*. In his words, "I'm telling her everything will be OK; what's past doesn't matter, she can just start out fresh tomorrow." From his perspective, he was moving out of the dominating position that he took in turns (1–15). He interpreted Jan's comment in turn (18) as confirming that they have achieved equality in their relationship (Pearce and Cronen 1980: 276).

We had to be clear about our role in this study. We were doing research on volunteers, not therapy on clients. We were still learning to be sufficiently playful with the complexities that we encountered. Still working in the shadow of the idea that good communication leads to understanding, we were struck by the way this episode "succeeded" because of a misunderstanding of a key turn (17). Jan did, in fact, go for an interview on the following day and was hired. But we wondered if the relationship might have been better served if the episode had failed. Dave and Jan were doing paradoxical dances with each other in a way described by Watzalawick, Beavin, and Jackson (1967: 199). In our way of putting things, Jan was controlling Dave so that he would control her; Dave's response might be described as "in order to make you my equal, I must be dominant."

Using the text of the two episodes that Dave and Jan helped us write, we compared what Dave and Jan told us in our interviews about the meanings of those conversations to the interpretations of a panel of competent, trained observers. We used a standard technique for doing research of this kind: a panel of six people, each trained to use a clearly written coding procedure and who had achieved a very high inter-rater reliability coded each turn in the episode. All six raters interpreted turn (17) as an ultimatum and (18) as "giving in to pressure," thus missing the key feature that made this episode work for the participants (Pearce and Cronen 1980: 279). This finding contributed to our confidence in concluding that "understanding" is more elusive than it seems and not necessarily a reliable basis for coordination. The whole panel of well-trained raters missed the key factor in the coordination of this episode because they failed to understand Jan's paradoxical position of *controlling the episode* so that Dave will control her *in the episode.*

Other studies of coordinated interactions followed. Among the most significant were long-term projects studying unwanted repetitive patterns, family therapy, mediation, domestic violence, and the "culture wars" between the religious "right" and secularists (Barge and Pearce 2004). All of these convinced me that coordination is a complex process, requiring a much richer set of tools than I would have imagined, and that it is a fruitful lens through which to look at communication.

Understanding how patterns of communication develop and discerning critical moments

I suspect we've all had the experience of seeing someone we love or respect engage in actions that are self-destructive, and we ask, "Why do they do that?" Or we may see a corporation or a nation persist in a pattern of behavior that betrays its purpose and character, and we ask, "Why are they doing that?" Or, to turn the example, we see people and organizations suddenly perform more competently than ever before and we ask, "What happened to them that allows that?"

One paradigm would pose those questions, and hear the answers to them, in a vocabulary of meanings. Don't they *know* better than to act that way? What *beliefs* do corporations or nations have that cause them to act this way? What have they *learned* that enables them to act differently? These questions make sense within the paradigm that I described in chapter 2 as supporting the transmission model of communication. Those who use this perspective look for relationships between what people do and what meanings (beliefs, attitudes, values) they have in their heads.

This is the paradigm that I was taught, both in the informal school of my culture and in the formal education I had in college and graduate school, and, like a recovering alcoholic, I'll never be "cured" of it, but I'm trying and I'm grateful for the help of my friends as I do.

Using the term "coordination" as a way of understanding these experiences is part of the paradigm that I called in chapter 2 the "social construction" approach to communication. It suggests that, instead of a correspondence between mental state and action, we pose questions and look for answers in the flow of actions themselves. That is, we understand what people say and do as taking "turns" in patterns of communication, not as "signs" pointing to something else. If someone we love is engaged in self-destructive behavior (staying with an abusive partner; substance abuse), we would to look to see how that behavior fits into ongoing patterns of interaction with other people rather than inquire about what's wrong with him or her (Sundarajan and Spano 2004).

This social construction paradigm has many roots and intellectual supports (Burr 2003; Gergen and Gergen 2003). I think CMM's distinctive contribution is to focus on turn-by-turn coordinations. Among other things, this provides us with a template that sharpens our ability to discern critical moments. The template is a simulation game that I call "coordination."

A professor at another university gave a lecture at the University of Massachusetts at Amherst. His argument was that if we knew enough about the individuals who were communicating, we could predict the pattern of communication. As hosts and respondents to his presentation, Vern Cronen and I countered with the argument that the social world is contingent and that the pattern of interaction itself was its own best explanation. The argument dragged on with little chance that anyone would change his or her mind.

To break the pattern of assertion and counter-assertion, I invented a game[2] that would prove that the pattern of interaction is more closely related to contingencies (what people do in critical moments) than to the beliefs, values, or personality traits of the participants. That is, "simple" people can participate in complex patterns, "complex" people can get locked into simple patterns, and the patterns of communication that occur depend on particular features of the pattern itself – for example, who speaks first – rather than characteristics of the persons communicating.

For the purposes of the game, the social world consists of three persons, Pat, Mike, and Ellswood, who use a simple language in their interactions with each other. Unlike the rest of us, the three people in this make-believe world have only a few rules and must follow them. They are incapable of either creativity or rule-breaking; everything not explicitly permitted is forbidden.

There are two sets of rules in this game. Think of these as "cultural rules" that apply to everyone, all the time.

- There are only four messages in the language: circle, square, star and triangle.
- All conversations consist of a sequence of turns; each turn is taken by "saying" only one of the messages in the language.
- All speakers intend to produce a "good" conversation; one in which all four messages in the language are used in as few turns as possible.
- The first turn in any conversation must be "circle."

As shown in figure 4.1, each person also has a set of "personal rules" that describe what he or she must and may do in specific circumstances. These rules take the form: if the other person does X, then I should do Y. Some rules specify that the person can do only one thing in the next turn. For example, if Mike or Ellswood says "square," Pat must respond with "circle." Other rules give the person options. For example, if Mike or Ellswood says "circle," Pat must respond in the next turn with one of three possible messages: "square," "star," or "triangle."

In real life, we would not know all of the rules; we would only know what each person does in response to our actions. I want to come back to

Pat's rules:

If Mike or Ellswood says:	Then Pat must respond with:
circle	square, star, or triangle
star	circle, triangle, or star
triangle	circle, triangle, star or square
square	circle

Mike's rules:

If Pat or Ellswood says:	Then Mike must respond with:
circle	square
square	star, square, or triangle
star	circle, triangle, or square
triangle	circle, triangle, star, or square

Ellswood's rules:

If Pat or Mike says:	Then Ellswood must respond with:
circle	circle
square	circle
star	triangle
triangle	square

Figure 4.1 Rules for Pat, Mike, and Ellswood in the simulation game "coordination"

that topic later, but let's start with the unreal but useful situation in which all of us know all the rules that govern everyone involved.

Just looking at the rules in figure 4.1, we might observe that Pat and Mike are similarly complex individuals, while Ellswood is a simpleton. If the guest speaker were right in his argument that knowing about persons individually is sufficient to understand coordinated patterns, we would expect that Pat and Mike would be able to have good conversations (according to the rule: using all four messages in the fewest number of turns) with each other, but that each would have difficulty communicating with Ellswood.

In my workshops, I assign individuals to take the roles of Pat, Mike, and Ellswood and engage in conversations. The demonstration works best if you can see it unfolding in real time. As you read, try not to see the conversation as a whole; see it as a series of turns, following each other in sequence, in which what happens next is unknown until it happens.

Let's start with a conversation between Pat and Mike. Mike speaks first:

(1) *Mike:*   circle
(2) *Pat:*   square
(3) *Mike:*   star
(4) *Pat:*   triangle

There you have it! A well-coordinated, good conversation. We can imagine Pat and Mike feeling good about the conversation, thinking well of each other, and looking forward to seeing each other again. So they meet again the next day, and this time, for no special reason, Pat speaks first and says:

(1) *Pat:*   circle
(2) *Mike:*   square
(3) *Pat:*   circle
(4) *Mike:*   square
(5) *Pat:*   circle
(6) *Mike:*   square

And so on, until either Pat or Mike gets tired, bored, or mad and leaves.

Refer back to the rules. In every turn, including the first, both Pat and Mike are doing what they have to do. As individuals, they haven't changed, but they are producing a very different conversation, and not a good one this time. We can imagine each being frustrated with the other and with the conversation, wondering what the heck is wrong with the other person, and wondering what changed since yesterday. From our vantage point, we can tell them that precisely nothing has changed – except who spoke first, and that this apparently trivial, arbitrary difference was a sufficient reason for a surprisingly frustrating conversation.

A couple of days pass during which Pat and Mike avoid each other. Pat gets so lonely that he finally strikes up a conversation with Ellswood. It goes like this:

(1) *Pat:* circle
(2) *Ellswood:* circle
(3) *Pat:* star
(4) *Ellswood:* triangle
(5) *Pat:* square

This was a surprisingly good conversation! It met the criterion (all four messages used) in only one more turn than Pat and Mike's first conversation.

Let's assume that Mike is lonely, too, and notices how well Pat's conversation with Ellswood has gone. He seeks out Ellswood, and says:

(1) *Mike:* circle
(2) *Ellswood:* circle
(3) *Mike:* square
(4) *Ellswood:* circle
(5) *Mike:* square
(6) *Ellswood:* circle
(7) *Mike:* square

You can play with other possible combinations of conversations among these persons, but all show that the social world (the conversations produced) is contingent on the hook-up between the rules of one person and the those of the other, on capricious things such as who speaks first, and the choices that people make in critical moments. In some turns, players in this game have the ability to choose which of several responses are possible, and their choice determines the pattern that emerges.

As I've used this game in research, I've found that people begin to learn the contingencies within their rules and to make strategic choices.

For example, in my workshops, I've often asked two people to play the role of Pat and Mike with twenty or more other participants watching. If Mike says, "star," this creates a critical moment. The rules *allow* Pat to say "circle," but the people in the room groan if the role-player makes this choice, because it sets off the unbreakable "circle–square–circle–square" pattern. If I allow the others to coach the role players, they begin to identify the messages that are "safe" and those that fall into this trap – staying within the rules.

One of the unrealistic aspects of this game is that people have such simple rules and have to follow them. In real life, we often change the rules; people are creative and sometimes adapt to each other.

Acting wisely in critical moments

The artificiality of the game "coordination" is both its strength and weakness. Some participants in my workshops find it hard to relate to disembodied people and conversations composed of sequences of geometrical shapes. But the fact that they have little emotional or meaningful connection to these people and shapes enables them to discern the bifurcation points more easily and to identify strategically wise courses of action. Sometimes we have trouble recognizing and acting wisely into bifurcation points because we are so caught up in the meaning of what is going on that we lose sight of the possibilities of changing the shape of the pattern. For example, can we see the bifurcation points if we are in the midst of a process involving gangs, a bereaved mother, and political considerations?

Chicago has always been a violent city, and, like most American cities, it has problems with gangs and guns. While I was living there in the early 1990s, Mayor Richard Daley was presented with what seemed to me an opening to change the social world by acting in a way that would have been a bifurcation point.

> *First turn:*   There was a tragic incident, so horrible that it disturbed the civic conscience even in this violence-habituated city. A mother was frightened of the gang violence in her neighborhood. She refused to let her children play outside unsupervised and insisted on walking with them to and from school – just a few blocks from their home. She was holding her seven-year-old son's hand, walking him to school one day when he was hit and killed by a "stray bullet" from a gang fight.

Second turn: Film of the bereaved mother's grief was broadcast on all the local news media, capturing her crying and asking "What more could I have done? What more could I have done?" This question resonated throughout the city. Even the members of gangs were affected. Some of the leaders of rival gangs began to talk to each other.

Third turn: The leaders of several gangs, without admitting guilt in this particular incident, approached the Mayor's office, asking the Mayor to convene a meeting in which they could talk about ways of reducing the violence in their communities.

Fourth turn: The Mayor refused to convene the meeting or to talk with the gang leaders. Instead, he called a press conference, informed the media of the request, and said that he refused it because he did not think the gang leaders were sincere.

Fifth turn: Gang-related violence continued. There have been many other tragic incidents.

As I interpret this sequence, there had been a stable pattern of violence among the gangs. Every attempt to change it – community policing, sting operations, harsher sentences for those convicted of crimes – had only reinforced the pattern. Call this circle–square–circle–square. The events described in the first to fourth turns created a critical moment. As an analogy, star–triangle–triangle. The Mayor was confronted with (1) the requirement to do something; and (2) in my judgment, a wonderful opportunity to call into being a different stable pattern. Instead, in the fourth turn, he went back to what had been happening before, and reintroduced the original pattern. It is as if he said "circle" and reinstated the circle–square pattern. Many of us in Chicago at that time had a visceral sense of narrowed possibilities and of being trapped in the same old pattern.

I believe that the Mayor missed an opportunity to change the pattern because he was working in the transmission model of communication. He identified the meaning of the gang leaders' request (in the third turn) in terms of its correspondence with their mental states (that is, he questioned their *sincerity*). From the communication perspective, one might respond by saying "Who cares if they are sincere?" The more interesting question is "What can we make in this situation?" That question directs our attention to what these turns mean in terms of the pattern itself, and toward the direction in which it might go depending on what, in this case, the Mayor does in the fourth turn. I think the Mayor's political concerns and his beliefs about gangs prevented him from seeing a bifurcation point that would have been obvious if the conversation had used circles, squares, and triangles.

Are there concepts and tools that can help us discern bifurcation points and possibilities for acting wisely even in situations fraught with meaning? The concepts and tools of CMM presented in chapters 5, 6, and 7 are responses to that question.

Making/Managing Meaning

The process of communication has two faces: coordinating actions and making/managing meaning. These should not be seen as different, because there can be no meaning without action and no action without meaning. But they can be differentiated, and doing so sometimes helps us discern critical moments and make decisions about how to act into them.

In my discussion of coordinating actions, I pushed back against giving too much attention to meaning. I did so not because meaning isn't important. To the contrary, meaning is so important to what it means to be a human being and in the making of our social worlds that it has distracted us from the other half of the process of communication. My push back was a plea that both sides of this process be given full consideration.

Making meaning is as fundamental to being human as forming packs is to wolves. We do not have to teach infants to make meanings of their environment; we just need to make sure that their environments contain enough nurture and stimulation. In addition, we don't have to teach infants to make meaning linguistically or in the form of stories. They will learn and begin to use whatever language they hear and encode their experience in the form of stories. I particularly like book reviewer Kate Morton's (1984: 1–2) way of putting this:

> The first sign that a baby is going to be a human being and not a noisy pet comes when he begins naming the world and demanding the stories that connect its parts. Once he knows the first of these he will instruct his teddy bear, enforce his worldview on victims in the sandlot, tell himself stories of what he is doing as he plays, and forecast stories of what he will do when he grows up. He will keep track of the actions of others and relate deviation to the person in charge. He will want a story at bedtime.

> Nothing passes but the mind grabs it and looks for a way to fit it into a story, or into a variety of possible scripts: he's late – maybe he was in an accident. Maybe he ran off to Tahiti with a blonde. Maybe he stopped on the way here to buy flowers. She will keep writing these "novels" until he shows up or till she finds one story in which all elements, emotional and circumstantial, blend. Then, whatever he says later she will know what she "knows."

When we take the communication perspective, we assume that people make and manage meaning. The interesting and useful questions have to do with what specific meanings they are making in given situations, how they are making those meanings, and how these meanings affect the social worlds that they are making.

Philosopher Martin Heidegger (1996) developed a concept that any parent contemplating the opportunities and constraints placed on their newborn child can understand. We are "thrown," he said, into a world of relationships and things that have already been named and interpreted. These things include ourselves. We are born into families that we did not choose, are of a gender that we did not select, and thrust into a cultural, economic, racial milieu that will shape our lives but which we had no part in making.

The prepackaged meanings in this world bring marvelous gifts, but at a price.

Coherence: the gift of meaning and purpose

Human beings cannot live with facts alone, and whatever language we learn already includes a social world. "To create a sentence is to constitute reality; to put two sentences together is to create the world" (Peckham 1962).

If we want to understand our social worlds, we can choose either of two paths. One is to look at the complexity of meanings in specific situations, using tools and models that help identify the untold stories, the unknown connections among things, and the multiple levels of meaning embedded in even such apparently mundane things as Jan and Dave's discussion about her going for a job interview. The other strategy is to get behind or beneath meanings to "the facts." CMM wholeheartedly takes the first approach.

In deciding to explore the complexity of meanings, CMM is aligned with Clifford Geertz's "interpretative anthropology." Geertz (1980: 3) reviewed a book on sociobiology that tried to explain the differences between men and women by the "mere facts" of existence without bringing culture into it. His devastating critique consisted of listing things that, he said, figure rather predominantly in male–female relationships but that are not mentioned in this sociobiological analysis: guilt, wonder, ideology, humor, obligation, despair, trust, malice, ritual, madness, forgiveness, sublimation, pity, ecstasy, obsession, discourse, and sentimentality.

Geertz's list of events and objects in human relationships reminds us that many features in our social worlds don't have a physical equivalent. Rather, they are made in our social worlds by our actions. Literary critic Kenneth Burke (1970: 274–5) eloquently described how this works in his analysis of "purpose."

> Insofar as men "cannot live by bread alone" . . . they derive purposes from language, which tells them what they "ought" to want to do, tells them how to do it, and in the telling goads them with great threats and promises, even unto the gates of heaven and hell.
>
> With language, a whole new realm of purpose arises, endless in scope, as contrasted with the few rudimentary purposes we derive from our bodies, the needs of food, drink, shelter, and sex in their physical simplicity.
>
> Language can even build purpose out of the ability to comment on the nature of purpose. However, the purposes that arise through the tangles made possible by language are not merely the old bodily appetites in a new form. They are appetites differing not just in degree but in kind. . . .
>
> In any case, obviously, the talking animals' way of life in a civilization *invents* purposes. Rationalized by money (which is a language, a kind of purpose-in-the-absolute, a universal wishing-well), empires arise. Such networks of production and distribution, made *possible* by language, become *necessary*. So, they raise problems – and many purposes are but attempts to solve those problems, plus the vexing fact that each "solution" raises further problems. (Confidentially, that's the dialectic.)
>
> But the very resources of language to which such quandaries owe their rise also goad men to further questioning. For language makes questioning easy. Given language, you can never be sure where quest ends and questions begin. Hence, the search for some Grand Over-All Purpose, as with philosophers, metaphysicians, theologians.

If we are to understand our social worlds, we will need tools capable of coming to grips with the complexities of meaning such as Burke described.

Subjugation: the cost of fitting into prefigured molds

The exercise of power always seems to cut in two ways, both liberating and constraining. And so it is with the power of language and culture that enables us to move into a world of meaning and purpose that we did not create. On one hand, it supports and sustains us in having identities, motives, and opportunities for sophisticated lives beyond our own capacity to create. At the same time, it programs us to fit predetermined niches within these societies, and prefigures problems as well as opportunities.

In his report of work on human development, Nigel Calder (1976: 13, 10) described society as a conspiracy to make our children to be like us. The family, school, policeman on the corner, and images we choose as literature and subjects for bronze statues in the park function "to encourage proper behavior and to check what is improper. . . . People make people, not just by breeding them but by shaping one another's behavior."

Moving from the metaphor of "conspiracy" to "computer programming," Clifford Geertz (1973: 44, 35) summarized the findings of ethnography as showing that human beings are "cultural artifacts."

> Culture is best seen . . . as a set of control mechanisms – plans, recipes, rules, instructions (what computer engineers call "programs") – for the governing of behavior . . . [and] man is precisely the animal most desperately dependent upon such extragenetic, outside-the-skin control mechanisms, such cultural programs, for ordering his behavior.
>
> Whatever else modern anthropology asserts – and it seems to have asserted almost everything at one time or another – it is firm in the conviction that men unmodified by the customs of particular places do not in fact exist, have never existed, and most important, could not in the very nature of the case exist.

As we work with tools based on the communication perspective, we will need to account for the experience of people as being subjugated by their culture. Our tools need to be able to tease out the sometimes-delicate ratio of subjugation and independence.

Mystery: the gift of wonder and openings for exploration

From a distance, a culture seems coherent, consistent, and complete. But the closer one gets to it, the more we see that there are fractures and fissures, open-ended escape valves, and internal contradictions and paradoxes in any culture. Although we find ourselves thrown in a "web of signification we ourselves have spun," there is room for us to move.

> Culture, the shared meanings, practices, and symbols that constitute the human world, does not present itself neutrally or with one voice. It is always mul-tivocal and overdetermined, and both the observer and the observed are always enmeshed in it; that is our situation. There is no privileged position, no abso-lute perspective, no final recounting. (Rabinow and Sullivan 1979: 6)

Among other things, these features provide opportunities for us to escape subjugation, to avoid simply repeating the cultural patterns by identifying bifurcation points and acting wisely in ways that are some-times culturally inappropriate. It is, using Geertz's metaphor, as if the com-puter is running several programs simultaneously, written by different programmers for different functions. The gaps and contradictions among these enable us to find spaces in which we can develop ourselves as autonomous, act wisely into still-unfolding patterns of action, and free ourselves from acting out the problems and neuroses of our culture.

Some cultural forms call attention to these opportunities. Virtually all cultures include a reference to the "mystery" that lies beyond the ordinary aspects of life. Sometimes this takes the form of myths. When a storyteller says "Once upon a time . . ." this is serious business. It is an invitation to enter a quality of experience, not a historical fact, a thesis for debate, or a scientific hypothesis. This is even more serious when the mechanics of storytelling are not so obvious, as in the stories embedded in your family, organization, or culture.

> No human society has yet been found in which . . . mythological motifs have not been rehearsed in liturgies, interpreted by seers, poets, theologians, or philosophers; presented in art; magnified in song; and ecstatically experi-enced in life-empowering visions. . . . Man apparently, cannot maintain himself in the universe without belief in some arrangement of the general inheritance of myth. In fact, the fullness of his life would even seem to stand in a direct ratio to the depth and range not of his rational thought but of his local mythology. (Campbell 1959: 3–4)

It seems that there is a human ability to look beyond the mechanics of storytelling and to respond to the story *as* a story, even though you know full well that you're in a theater, that the demonstration has been choreographed, or that the political speech was pretested on focus groups before being given. In his life-long study of the myths of all cultures, Joseph Campbell (1959: 21) noted the important use of masks in tribal societies. At crucial points in their rituals, members of the tribe put on masks and enact the roles of the gods. At one level, everyone knows that these are their parents, cousins, and neighbors wearing masks, but for the story to "work" there must be something mysterious, and the neighbors-wearing-masks become god-with-us.

As we become more sophisticated about what we are doing when we communicate, we can see that every naming is also a not-naming; that every affirmation is a denial of alternatives. With this evidence of human fingerprints on our social worlds, we can discover mystery in every moment of communication, not just when the masks come out. Literary critic Philip Wheelwright (1962: 177–8) invited us to have this playful attitude in our consideration of what we read, from newspapers to novels.

> The nature of reality is intrinsically and ultimately hidden from any finite exploration. . . . Reality is ultimately problematical, not contingently so, for to grasp and formulate it, even as a set of questions is to fragmentize it. The best we can hope to do is catch partisan glimpses. . . . If we cannot hope ever to be perfectly right we can perhaps find both enlightenment and refreshment by changing, from time to time, our ways of being wrong.

It was in this sense, I think, that Joseph Campbell (1968: 84) said: "The best things cannot be told; the second best are misunderstood. After that comes civilized conversation." If I understand them, Wheelwright and Campbell are not dismissing literature and conversation; rather, they are inviting us to a fullness of spirit in which we see even the most eloquent of these as partial strivings, streaks of fireworks in the sky to be relished for what they are but with the full awareness that they will fall back to earth.

If we can develop some tools and concepts that expose the openings in our culture and enhance our awareness of mystery, they will help us find bifurcation points and act wisely into them.

Communication as the Site where Social Worlds are Made

Our social worlds are made in the dance between the two faces of the communication process: coordinating actions and making/managing meaning. This is the site where speech acts, episodes and forms of communication, selves and forms of consciousness, and relationships and minds are made.

This brings us to the middle of the model shown in figure P.1. You now have the rough outline of the argument of this book, and it is time to turn to the specifics. In the following chapters, I'll argue that the glittering array of events and objects in our social worlds all are made in the performance of speech acts – that is, by what real people in real situations do and say in response to and in anticipation of what other real people will do and say.

This emphasis on the smallest unit of social interaction may seem contradictory to the comments in chapter 3 about thinking systemically, but it is not. I do not believe that "larger" units of social interaction are simply aggregates of speech acts. In fact, as shown in figure P.1, I propose that we think of a two-step emergent process.

Think of speech acts as comprising a field. Each speech act is unfinished; its meaning is contingent on its relation to all the other speech acts, particularly those adjacent to its immediate temporal and spatial location within the field. In addition, the configuration of speech acts is not uniform across this field. There are clumps where certain types of speech acts proliferate and others where they are rare. Finally, this field is held together by a sense of "oughtness" that I call "logical force" in chapter 5. That is, in this social world, the equivalent of mass and motion is some moral sense that can be rendered in the form "if this happens, I should/must/must not do X and if I do, then Y should/should not/must/must not happen."

Because this field is complex, we should expect entities to emerge that are more sophisticated than speech acts themselves. In this sense, "sophisticated" means that they have abilities and properties of their own; no matter how much you know about speech acts, you cannot understand these emergent entities without learning something about them as wholes. In chapters 6, 7, and 8, I call these first-stage emergent entities episodes, selves, and relationships.

So imagine a second field, superimposed on the first, in which episodes, selves, and relationships exist. All of these are made by and include speech acts, in a complex interdependency that I call "contextualization." That is, once these first-stage emergent entities are formed, they function as contexts for the speech acts that formed them, and redefine their meaning.

Stay with me, because the image needs yet another level of complexity. There are second-stage emergent entities. In chapters 6, 7, and 8, I call these patterns of communication, forms of consciousness, and relational minds. They, too, comprise a field superimposed on the field of episodes, selves, and relationships, just as that field is superimposed on the more simple field of speech acts. These forms of communication, consciousness, and minds have a similar contextual relationship to episodes, selves, and relationships as these first-stage emergent entities have to speech acts.

In the next four chapters, I'll describe these events, objects, and emergent entities in our social worlds more fully. In doing so, I'll present some models and concepts that are useful for understanding them, describe how these models and concepts can be used in specific situations, and show how doing so can make better social worlds.

Notes

1   Perhaps I'm engaging in anthropomorphism, but for nearly ten years, I've lived with a canine companion whom I believe to be a full-blooded timber wolf. We've had many discussions about these things, and I think I'm representing his views accurately. He is clearly outraged when I spend time in social groups that do not include him.
2   This was a game in the tradition of game theory in economics, which studies the choice of optimal behaviors when the outcomes of those behaviors are not fixed, but are contingent on the choices made by others. The movie *A Beautiful Mind* is a biography of John Nash, one of the developers of game theory.

References

Bak, P. (1999), *How Nature Works: The Science of Self-organized Criticality*, New York: Copernicus.

Barge, K. J. and Pearce, W. B. (2004), A reconnaissance of CMM research, *Human Systems*, 14: 13–22.

Blumer, H. (1954), What is wrong with social theory, *American Sociological Review*, 18: 3–10.

Burke, K. (1970), *The Rhetoric of Religion: Studies in Logology*, Berkeley: University of California Press.

Burr, V. (2003), *Social Constructionism*, 2nd edn., London: Routledge.

Calder, N. (1976), *The Human Conspiracy*, London: Penguin.

Campbell, J. (1959), *The Masks of God: Primitive Mythology*, New York: Viking.

Campbell, J. (1968), *The Masks of God: Creative Mythology*, New York: Viking.

Chaffee, S. and McLeod, J. (1968), Sensitization in panel design: a coorientational experiment, *Journalism Quarterly*, 45: 661–9.

Fuentes, C. (1985), *Old Gringo*, tr. Margaret Sayers Peden and Carlos Fuentes, New York: Harper and Row.

Geertz, C. (1973), *The Interpretation of Cultures*, New York: Basic Books.

Geertz, C. (1980), Donald Symon's "The Evolution of Human Sexuality", *New York Times Review of Books* (January 24).

Gergen, M. and Gergen, K. (2003), *Social Construction: A Reader*, Thousand Oaks, CA: Sage.

Harris, L. M. (1980), The maintenance of a social reality, *Family Process*, 19: 19–33.

Heidegger, M. (1996), *Being and Time: A Translation of Sein and Zeit*, tr. Joan Stambaugh, Albany: State University of New York Press.

Malone, T. W. and Crowston, K. (1994), The interdisciplinary study of coordination, *ACM Computing Surveys*, 26: 87–119.

Morton, K. (1984), The story-telling animal, *New York Times Review of Books* (December 23).

Newcomb, T. M. (1953), An approach to the study of communicative acts, *Psychological Review*, 60: 393–404.

Pearce, W. B. (1976), The coordinated management of meaning: a rules-based theory of interpersonal communication. In G. R. Miller (ed.), *Explorations in Interpersonal Communication*, Newbury Park, CA: Sage, pp. 17–36.

Pearce, W. B. and Cronen, V. E. (1980), *Communication, Action and Meaning: The Creation of Social Realities*, New York: Praeger. (Available online at http://www.cios.org/www/opentext.htm, retrieved December 22, 2005.)

Pearce, W. B. and Stamm, K. (1973), Coorientational states and interpersonal communication. In P. Clarke (ed.), *New Models for Communication Research*, Beverly Hills, CA: Sage, pp. 177–204.

Peckham, M. (1962), *Beyond the Tragic Vision: The Quest for Identity in the Nineteenth Century*, New York: Braziller.

Rabinow, P. and Sullivan, W. M. (1979), The interpretive turn: emergence of an approach. In P. Rabinow and W. M. Sullivan (eds.), *Interpretive Social Science: A Reader*, Berkeley: University of California Press, pp. 1–24.

Stamm, K. and Pearce, W. B. (1971), Communication behavior and coorientational relations, *Journal of Communication*, 21: 208–20.

Steiner, R. J. (1992), Believing is seeing, *Art Times Journal*. Retrieved on December 22, 2005, from http://www.arttimesjournal.com/peeks/believingisseeing.htm

Sundarajan, N. and Spano, S. (2004), CMM and the co-construction of domestic violence, *Human Systems*, 15: 45–58.

Watzlawick, P., Beavin, J., and Jackson, D. D. (1967), *Pragmatics of Human Communication: A Study of Interactional Patterns, Pathologies, and Paradoxes*, New York: W. W. Norton.

Wheelwright, P. (1962), *Metaphor and Reality*, Bloomington: Indiana University Press.

Wittgenstein, L. (1922), *Tractatus Logico-Philosophicus*, London: Routledge and Kegan Paul.

Chapter 5

Doing Things in Communication: Speech Acts

Preview

The communication perspective suggests that we ask questions like "What are we making together?" "How are we making it?" and "How can we make it better?" The theory of the coordinated management of meaning points to the dynamic dance between coordinating actions and making/managing meanings as the site where we might find answers to those questions. The two faces of communication come together in what we say and do when we take a turn in unfinished, ongoing patterns of communication; one name for this is "speech acts." Speech acts include compliments, insults, threats, promises, etc.

This chapter begins a series of examples of how CMM concepts can be used to understand specific situations, discern critical moments, and decide how to act wisely into them. The concepts presented in this chapter include conversational implicature, the conversational triplet, logical force, and ante-narrative. The chapter concludes with three ways in which you can make better social worlds using your knowledge of speech acts.

Speech Acts and the Quality of Our Lives

The term "speech acts" names a class of very familiar things, such as *promises*, *threats*, *insults*, *speculations*, *guesses*, and *compliments*. Your ability to recognize and perform speech acts is important to the quality of your life. It makes some difference whether your spouse interprets what you've just said as an *insult* or as a *compliment*; whether what your employer or client just said is a *promise* or a *threat*; and, if you are steering a sailboat in a fog and ask your navigator which way you should turn to avoid running aground, you'd want to know whether her reply is a *guess*, a *calculation* ("dead reckoning"), or a *fix* (GPS reading or triangulated bearings on at least two known points).

In addition, the quality of our lives varies in direct relation to the number and ratio of various speech acts in which we participate. That is, the quality of life for a child is different if surrounded by speech acts of nurture, love, appreciation, and encouragement rather than by their opposites. The quality of life for an adult is seriously diminished if, for whatever reason, he or she is no longer allowed to participate in speech acts involving making decisions for him or herself. Your ability to accomplish your objectives is enhanced if you can somehow get those who "oppose" you to "collaborate" with you – but how can you transform speech acts intended as "opposition" into "collaboration"?

Is it possible for us to develop the ability to change the quality of our lives through attention to speech acts? I think so. To act wisely in the critical moments that shape the worlds in which we live, we need to perform and/or enable or entice others to perform certain speech acts. From the perspective of the speech act, there are three ways of making better social worlds. First, we can change the situation in which we find ourselves so that a different ratio of desirable and undesirable speech acts will occur. I'll give an example of how this happened with a most unlikely organization – the United States Navy. Second, we can prevent or resist the performance of undesirable speech acts. I'll describe a teaching demonstration and then show how the principle behind it can help us in designing meetings that inhibit the production of undesired speech acts. Third, we can facilitate the performance of desirable speech acts. I'll tell a story about a personal experience that perhaps points to an important leverage point in making better social worlds.

Our Social Worlds are Made of Speech Acts

Let me start with an extended analogy. In a sense, speech acts are like the pixels on a television screen. If you look at your television screen from a sufficient distance, you can't see any single pixel. What you see are images created by ratios of various kinds of pixels. To keep it simple, let's assume a black-and-white picture. The picture (Grandma? a news report? whatever . . .) is really composed of many black pixels on a white background (or is it the other way around?) arranged in just the right way so that your eye will see Grandma, or a news reporter, or whatever . . . If you move closer to the screen, and if you use a microscope, you can see the individual pixels.

In much the same way, every event and object in our social worlds is made up of ratios of various speech acts, sometimes arranged in specific sequences. "Church," we suppose, has more speech acts of "worship" and fewer of "ribald joking" than a bar or a classroom. If we look sufficiently closely at any institution, personality, or event, we can identify what speech acts occur, in what ratio, and perhaps in what sequence. We might even be able to identify speech acts that may not occur in particular spaces in our social worlds, or what difference it would make if they did.

OK, we *can* take a pixel-eye view of our social worlds, but why would we *want* to? Well, this is where the analogy breaks down. In the social world, we are not just observers; we are participants who are agents in the making of the social worlds that we create. We need to know what speech act we are making and how to make it.

But for the moment, stay with the notion that the events and objects of the social world can be seen as the range and ratios of various types of speech acts. Here are six short stories. In each, imagine the range, ratios, and distribution of the speech acts involved in them.

- (In a cartoon, where dogs can talk) Two dogs greet each other, tails wagging. One says, "Hi! My name is 'No! No! Stop that!' What's yours?"
- A group of researchers were interested in the linguistic worlds in which children live. They put voice-activated tape recorders in little backpacks and then analyzed the recordings of what adults said to the children. They found that over 90 percent of the messages addressed to these children were negative; that is, they dealt with what *not* to do, how *bad* things are, what *wrong* thing was done or good thing done *wrongly*, who is to *blame*, etc. (David Cooperrider, personal communication, 2001).
- Athletes spend a lot of time focusing on their performance and seeking to improve it. But what helps them improve? A study compared the amount of improvement achieved from coaching sessions that focused on their mistakes and coaching sessions focused on what they did well. Their improvement was greater when they focused on what they did well (David Cooperrider, personal communication, 2001).

- A group of male graduate students decided to test the hypothesis that our selves are created in social interaction with others. They identified the least attractive female graduate student in their class and began treating her as if she were the most attractive. Using a random procedure, they organized themselves in a sequence to ask her out on dates; the "loser" had to go first. Over the course of the following weeks, this unattractive woman was the object of much flattering male attention, and she began to take more care of her appearance and became more outgoing and cheerful. The experiment had to be terminated because she began to be asked out for dates by people not involved in the study, and preferred to spend time with people more attractive and interesting than her male graduate student colleagues.
- Two men were asked their names. One said, "My name is Bill"; the other said, "My name is Alexander the Great." Bill was welcomed to visit the hospital and given a report on "Alexander's" progress; "Alexander" was confined to the hospital and given drugs and therapy for his delusions of identity.
- A family went into a restaurant. The father said, "I'm not hungry" and did not order anything. His three-year-old son said, in the same tone of voice as his father, "I'm not hungry either" and his mother ordered for him and forced him to eat.

As the three-year-old and "Alexander" discovered, not everyone is allowed to perform every speech act; this has to do with the distribution of speech acts in specific spaces in our social worlds. Stories of power and privilege may explain why. As the unattractive graduate student, the athletes, and the children know very well, the quality of their lives is directly related to the nature of the speech acts that those around them perform. And as "No! No! Stop that!" doesn't quite understand, sometimes speech acts are poorly performed, and what is "done" is something other than what was intended. As we go on, I'll show how this is not necessarily a bad thing; used intentionally, the gap between intention and accomplishment can be an opening for making better social worlds.

Why call them "speech acts"?

The term "speech acts" is not a part of ordinary language, and I hesitated to use it here. I decided to use it because it is as good a term as any *if* you understand that speech acts don't necessarily involve speech; they may be accomplished nonverbally. In addition, if I didn't use this term, I'd have to invent another that would be equally as bad but disconnected from the literature from which I've learned.

How many speech acts are there?

I know a tennis coach who begins working with a student by saying that there are only – strokes in tennis, and that he will teach them all. Sorry, I've forgotten the number of shots, because I chose not to hire him as my coach. There were other reasons as well, but I have this crazy notion that a cross-court forehand is a different stroke depending on where I am on the court, where (and, at my age, how far) I'm coming from to make it, how the point has been orchestrated so far, what my opponent is expecting based on what I've done the last several times in this situation, whether the ball is coming to me flat, with top spin or with back spin, etc. Calling it "one" stroke loses some important information.

It's the same with speech acts. Philosopher John Searle (1969) is undoubtedly the person most would associate with speech acts. His project is to describe the categories in which the mind works by analyzing types of speech acts. He claims that

> there are five and only five basic things we can do with propositions: We tell people how things are (*assertives*), we try to get them to do things (*directives*), we commit ourselves to doing things (*commissives*), we express our feelings and attitudes (*expressives*), and we bring about changes in the world so that the world matches the proposition just in virtue of the utterance (*declarations*). This is a strong claim in the sense that it is not just an empirical sociolinguistic claim about this or that speech community, but is intended to delimit the possibilities of human communication in speech acts. (Searle 1990)

Well, that's one story. The approach that I find more convincing is grounded in Ludwig Wittgenstein's analysis of communication. Where Searle said that there are "five and only five" kinds of speech act, Wittgenstein (1953/2001: 11e) said that the number is "countless . . . and this multiplicity is not something fixed, given once for all; but new types of language, new language-games, as we may say, come into existence, and others become obsolete and get forgotten. . . . Here the term 'language game' is meant to bring into prominence the fact that the *speaking* of language is part of an activity, or of a form of life." Using a series of homely examples, he showed that we are social artists, capable of using language to do many things, including:

> Giving orders, and obeying them –
> Describing the appearance of an object, or giving its measurements –
> Constructing an object from a description (a drawing) –
> Reporting an event –
> Speculating about an event –
> Forming and testing a hypothesis –
> Presenting the results of an experiment in tables and diagrams –
> Making up a story, and reading it –
> Play-acting –
> Guessing riddles –
> Making a joke; telling it –
> Solving a problem in practical arithmetic –
> Asking, thanking, cursing, greeting, praying. (Wittgenstein 1953/2001: 12e)

"Commanding, questioning, recounting, chatting" and other nonreferential uses of language, Wittgenstein noted, "are as much a part of our natural history as walking, eating, drinking, playing" (Wittgenstein 1953/2001: 12e).

Speech acts are also more complicated than something that can be crammed into simple lists. For example, Lars pretended to reduce the time he spent drinking in bars in order to convince his father that he was a responsible young man so that his father would not cut him out of his will. To do this, he phoned his father at 11 P.M. every night to wish him a good night's sleep. But he realized that if he went to the bars at his usual time and left temporarily to make the call, his speech would be slurred by all the drinking he had done and his father would know that he really was spending too much time in bars, so he decided not to go to the bar until after he called his father each night. So he wound up reducing the time he spent in bars in order to pretend that he was reducing the time he spent in bars . . .

Pardon me, which of Searle's five types of speech acts did Lars perform?

Where do speech acts come from?

Psychologist Marga Kreckel (1981) observed infants in various families, and saw them learning to recognize and perform speech acts by joining in the language games that these families played. She was particularly interested in how speech acts varied among families. She found that what would be recognized as a successful accomplishment of *warning* in one family simply would not be heard the same way in another. Complicating the matter still more, she found that there were differences among the members of the same family in the way they connected actions and speech acts.

Dictionaries are histories of the use of language. Communication professor Ray Gozzi, Jr. (1990/1991: 449–50) noted that the 1986 version of a standard English dictionary published in the United States included 12,000 words not found in the previous edition published in 1961. Gozzi argued that changes in language are a "cultural indicator" of what is going on in society. These new words, he said, have "caught on" well enough "to find their way into print, more than once, over a period of time. . . . The very fact of its presence in a dictionary certifies, to some extent, that the new word has been more than a passing fancy, and many people have paid attention to it – enough to remember it, use it, and perpetuate it."

Of these 12,000 new words, 75 named speech acts. So, if a woman were to take a nap in 1961 and wake up in 1986, she would be living in a social world containing 75 speech acts which she does not know the names for or how to perform. My guess is that the period from 1986 until now has been at least equally productive of new speech acts. In fact, to test this hypothesis, I just *googled* "speech acts" and got about 19,700,000 hits in 0.31 seconds, but I didn't *surf* them.[1]

Anthropologist Michelle Rosaldo (1990) argued that the social worlds of different cultures contain speech acts not known in other cultures. This is a controversial claim and one that, if true, is fascinating. This seems an important aspect of the heteroglossia of our social worlds. Is it possible that the Ilongot (the people Rosaldo studied in the Philippines) perform speech act that we simply don't know? Is it possible that what Wittgenstein would call their form of life is sufficiently different from our "form of life" that, even if we were to speak their language perfectly, we wouldn't be able to perform the conversational implicature necessary to understand what they were doing? As Wittgenstein is said to have remarked, if we could talk to the animals . . . we wouldn't have a thing to say to them, because our forms of life are so different! Is this true among cultures as well?

Speech Acts are Made in Coordinated Actions

How do we know what speech act is being made in a specific instance of communication? Some early speech act theorists thought that they could identify a set of criteria by which to identify speech acts. For example, to accomplish the speech act "promise" one must declare an intention to do something and be perceived as having the ability to do it. While this seems reasonable, as a method, it is grounded in the same paradigm as the "transmission model" of communication: it identifies the meaning of the speech act by its correspondence with the mental states of the people involved.

If the process of communication has two faces, as I argued in chapter 4, we need to look at both the meanings people have for what they say and do and at coordinated action. If we do this, we quickly see that the reason why many speech acts don't come off as intended has little to do with criteria such as "capable of performing the relevant action" and much to do with coordination.

In a conversation that he says that he doesn't remember, my friend John Shotter advised: "If someone stops you in the middle of a conversation and asks, 'what did you mean by that?' your answer should be, 'I don't know yet; we haven't finished our conversation.'" Is what we are doing in communication so fluid?

In the example below, I want to show you that the accomplishment of a speech act – even in a relatively low-intensity, small slice of our social worlds – flows back and forth and evolves as the pattern of coordinated actions unfolds. I invite you to join me in a sense of mystery and wonder that we ever achieve good communication!

Sonia and Luis have just watched a movie together; Luis is driving them home. They are riding in companionable silence when the following conversation occurs:

(1) *Sonia:*   Are you hungry?
(2) *Luis:*   No.
(3) *(Pause)*
(4) *Sonia:*   You are so selfish!
(5) *Luis:*   What? What are you talking about?
(6) *Sonia:*   I'm hungry and you don't even care!
(7) *Luis:*   Of course I care! I didn't know you were hungry! If you want something to eat, why didn't you say so?

(8) *Sonia:* I did say so! Why don't you listen better?
(9) *Luis:* There's a good Italian restaurant in the next block. I'll stop there.
(10) *Sonia:* Don't bother! I'm not hungry any more. Take me home.

I've used this conversation in trainings on three continents and find that it captures something about gender-inflected differences in communication styles (I adapted it from Tannen 1990: 26–7). Even though it plays on stereotypes, men often laugh in rueful recognition of Luis's no-win situation, and women usually identify with Sonia's frustration with Luis's cluelessness. But I want to focus on the accomplishment of speech acts, not gender differences.

Look at Sonia's first turn: she asks "Are you hungry?" This looks like a straightforward speech act of "question" and Luis treats it that way; he answers "No." But the interaction – and the speech act – isn't over. Sonia's silence (turn (3)), followed by "You are so selfish" affects the meaning of Luis's response. When Rom Harré and I offered a course together, he taught me to say that responses like this "move the meaning of the speech act toward completion." It's a good phrase. Turns (3) and (4) allow us to see that Sonia's question in turn (1) was intended to mean something other than an inquiry about whether Luis is hungry. Because he misjudged what Sonia was doing when she asked that question (Luis foolishly focused on the content of the question rather than its "use" in a conversational sequence), his response in turn (2) became a statement of his failure to understand her – which Sonia perhaps unfairly attributes to his "care" for her.

Hmm. Is Sonia using this whole sequence as a means to get Luis to do something that she wants him to do? That is, does the block of turns (1) through (7) function as a single speech act, something like "get him to declare how much he cares for me"? Stranger things have happened – remember the real example of Jan and Dave that I reported in chapter 4 – but that's not my preferred interpretation. In the eighth turn ("I did say so! Why don't you listen better?"), Sonia clearly expresses her sense that what she said in the first turn should have been heard as a statement about her own hunger, neither a question about Luis nor a gambit in the evolution of their relationship.

In the first turn of this conversation, Sonia was *doing* something a bit different than the literal meaning of her question indicated – and assuming that Luis not only *could* but *should* understand her intention. Specifically, she says that their poor coordination was *his* fault for not inferring correctly what she intended, not *her* fault for saying something other than she intended to be heard as having said. If this interpretation is correct, an alternative form of the conversation might have gone like this:

(1) *Sonia:*   Are you hungry?
(2) *Luis:*   No, but are you?
(3) *Sonia:*   Now that you mention it, I am. Let's stop at a good restaurant
     – I'll treat!

In this three-turn sequence, Sonia's intended speech act is quickly and gracefully accomplished. Luis's turn (the second in the pattern) confirms Sonia's intention and moves the speech act toward completion; Sonia's final turn (the third in the pattern) completes it.

Of course, Luis and Sonia could achieve a well-coordinated interaction if Sonia would say something with a literal meaning that is closer to the speech act that she wants to perform. For example:

(1) *Sonia:*   I'm hungry. How about you?
(2) *Luis:*   Yes, I'm hungry, too. I know a good Italian restaurant a couple
     of blocks ahead. How does that sound to you?
(3) *Sonia:*   Sounds great!

This short, comparatively simple example shows that speech acts are accomplished in coordinated action, not just in the minds of either or both of the participants. What is done in any given conversational turn isn't finished in that turn; its meaning derives from what happened before and from what happens subsequently. The analysis of this little example also shows that the relationship between what is said and what is done in any given turn is sometimes quite slippery. Well-formed grammatical sentences may be clumsy and equivocal speech acts, and vice versa. Here's a good summary:

> in everyday life, words do not in themselves have a meaning, but a *use*, and furthermore, a *use only in a context*; they are best thought of, not as having already determined meanings, but as *means*, as tools, or as instruments for us in the "making" of meanings. . . . For, like tools in a tool-box, the significance of our words remains open, vague, ambiguous, until they are used in different particular ways in different particular circumstances. (Shotter 1991: 200)

Performing Speech Acts

If Sonia and Luis were to read this book, would they be more likely to perform the speech acts they intended in their conversations with each other? I think so, not only because they would be more mindful of the fluid nature of speech acts and aware of how their meanings float through sequences of coordinated actions, but also because they would be more careful in shaping the speech acts that they perform. I think they could create a more life-giving and mutually supportive social world in their home if they did.

In this section, I lay out four useful aspects of the performance of speech acts. To aid the presentation of these four aspects, I want to introduce Tina, Rolf, and Dennis, all part of the management team in a large corporation. I'll use their experience throughout the following chapters.

Tina received an email marked "urgent" from Dennis, the assistant managing director. The message instructed her and the other division managers to come to a meeting the following day in which Rolf, the manager of another division in her company, would roll out the new Strategic Initiative for her company. The email ended by saying, "I know that we all are very grateful to Rolf for his leadership of this project, and will cheer him on as he describes the part that your division will play in this important initiative."

Even with this instruction, Tina did not feel "grateful" toward Rolf and she certainly did not look forward to being "told" what part her division "will play in this important initiative." She resented Dennis's decision to give Rolf the responsibility for the Strategic Initiative. She believed that there were several other division managers, including herself, who would have done a better job. In part because Dennis seemed to pick the least able division manager, she was suspicious that the "Strategic Initiative" was simply a smokescreen for other purposes that would further the careers of some high-level people in the company but not necessarily be good for the company or for her division. These suspicions were deepened by the way Rolf managed the planning process. She thought he had been unnecessarily secretive and knew that he had spent what seemed to her an enormous amount of money during the planning process. This process had already taken away some of the resources that her division needed, and she feared that the Initiative itself would divert so much that her division would be unable to make needed changes so that it could respond to a changing market. Like everyone else, she had noticed how Dennis had started to use terms like "increasing profit margins," "eliminating sites of unprofitability," and "assured return-on-investment" in his official memos, and she imagined a situation in which the investment of fewer resources in her division would cause it to become unprofitable and vulnerable.

This thin slice of Tina's day at work is filled with speech acts, some of which are even more ambiguous than Sonia's "Are you hungry." What speech act is Dennis performing by sending this email? He is clearly calling for Tina and the others to perform the speech act of "being grateful" to Rolf. But how can she perform that speech act? Should she even try, given the way she feels? What else can she do?

I hope that you will find this situation sufficiently familiar that you can empathize with Tina; it is a compilation of situations I know from my own experience, research, and my work with clients. As I wrote it, I tried to portray Tina in a bifurcation point in which multiple things are happening, and having to make difficult decisions about how to act wisely. And, as is always the case, there is more to the story than meets the eye or than she would tell you in an initial meeting.

How can Tina act wisely into this situation? And, even if she knows what speech act she'd like to perform, how can she make sure that this is the speech act that is actually performed?

The performance of any speech act involves four things. They are known in the scholarly and professional literatures as conversational implicature, the conversational triplet, logical force, and ante-narrative.

What is being done by what is said? Conversational implicature

"Conversational implicature" is a term of art among those who study conversation closely. For our purposes, it serves as a reminder to differentiate what is said from what is being done in any given turn in a conversation. It calls for a kind of double consciousness. In addition to just noting that someone has picked up a big stick, we have to infer that this is a *threat*, not an intention to build up the campfire; if someone says "the door is open" we have to infer whether that is a *warning* to speak in a whisper because others might overhear what is said, a *request* to close the door because the room is cold and the speaker wants it to retain the heat from the fire, or a *command* to go through the door and leave the premises.

How should Tina understand Dennis's email? Is it a straightforward message thanking Rolf for his work? Is it an indirect way of telling everyone in the corporation that he, Dennis, has already approved what Rolf has done and that he will not welcome any criticism of it? Is it a warning that Tina should stop complaining about the initiative? Whatever answer she gives, she is performing conversational implicature.

To what is that a response? The conversational triplet

I invited you to think of the meaning of speech acts as floating through the sequence of coordinated actions. Now let's put a structure on that fluid process.

I don't think there are, or can be, any single-turn speech acts; they are co-constructed in a sequence of interactive "turns." The ideal or prototypical structure of a speech act is a three-turn sequence, or "conversational triplet" (Xi 1991). For example, we might see the situation above like this:

(1) *Dennis says:* _____
(2) *Tina says:* _____
(3) *Dennis says:* _____

In this simplest-case example, the meaning of Dennis's email in turn (1) depends in part on how Tina replies. That is, Dennis might well have been giving Rolf a sincere compliment AND suggesting that this is not a time for other division managers to complain. But IF Tina's reply in turn (2) is an email broadcast to every employee in the corporation saying that the Strategic Initiative is a waste of resources, that Rolf is incompetent, and that Dennis is a poor manager for not giving her division the resources it needs – well, will that response affect the meaning of Dennis's first statement? I think so. If we take Dennis's email in turn (1) as having a range of potential meanings, Tina's response in turn (2) – no matter what it is – will crystallize the meaning of turn (1) in some of the ways in which it might have had its meaning, but not in others. And in the same way, Dennis's response in turn (3) will affect both the meaning of his turn (1) and Tina's turn (2).

At a very practical level, Tina might be well advised to be seriously playful in her conversational implicature of Dennis's email in turn (1). She might ask, what range of possible meanings are there in this turn, and of them, which do I want to help realize and which to I want to help fade away? Now, how might I act in turn (2) that would help perform the speech act in turn (1) that I prefer most?

There are a couple of other things to say about the conversational triplet. First, the turns that are chronologically adjacent aren't necessarily the turns that comprise the triplet. We often engage in complex patterns of coordination, so when we think about how our actions in the present turn will move other actions toward completion, we should be open to the possibility that what we do "now" will have greatest effect on actions that happened some turns ago, not necessarily the most recent turn. Just as an example of two triplets, neither fully enacted, embedded within each other:

(1) *Secretary:*   Hello.

(2) *Unidentified female voice on the telephone:*   Where is Bill?

(3) *Secretary:*   Who's calling, please?

(4) *Female voice:*   This is his mother. His wife has been injured and he's not answering his cell phone.

(5) *Secretary:*   Sorry, he's in a meeting and asked me to hold his calls. Stay on the line, please, and I'll get him for you.

Note that the third turn is not actually responsive to the second. The second turn is a *request* for information; the third is a *challenge* to the legitimacy of the request but not the answer requested. The nature of this challenge is masked by the civility of the comment ("Who's calling, please?"); a more bald challenge might be "Who wants to know?" The fourth turn is responsive to the third, and *establishes* (a) her personal right to contact Bill (she's his mother), (b) the situational importance of doing so (his wife has been injured); (c) the fact that Bill has authorized her to contact him directly (she has his cell phone number); and (d) the fact that she has taken appropriate steps on her own (he's not answering). The fifth turn is responsive to the second.

So even though we can't limit our attention to three consecutive turns, the principle remains that what speech act has been performed depends on its relationship with preceding and subsequent acts.

Finally, it isn't necessarily obvious what is a "first" and what is a "second" turn in the conversational triplet, and this can be important. Perhaps you already took note of the fact that Dennis's email had a history and a context. To treat it as the "first" turn in a conversational triplet is to make the assumption that it can best be understood by subsequent rather than preceding events. But it could also be seen as a "second" or a "third" turn in conversational triplets.

Imagine that Tina's first response to the email was to feel . . . well, the complex set of responses that I described above. Her second response was to create a space for reflection using the conversational triplet as a template. Perhaps she sketched a conversation triplet like this:

(1) _____
(2) Dennis's email
(3) What I should do now

and asked: to what is Dennis's email a response? That is, if Dennis's email was a "second turn" in a conversational triplet, what was the first?

After imagining a number of possibilities, she might then develop a sketch like this:

(1) _____
(2) _____
(3) Dennis's email

and ask: to what was that a response? That is, if Dennis's email is a "third turn" in a conversational triplet, to what was the turn before it a response?

Tina may never know what the previous turns were, but the exercise of imagining them is a useful way of enriching her own understanding of the situation in which she finds herself, and thus of choosing wisely how to act into it.

What can/must/should I do? Logical force

Tina was outraged by the email message in which Dennis told her not only what to think but how to feel. If she were to articulate this hot flush of anger, she might have said something like this: in a situation like this, a person like me can't let something like this go. I have to act in a way that will set Dennis straight about what he can and cannot do, and that will express my resentments and concerns.

And I can imagine all of us saying, "Hold on, Tina! Think before you act."

Tina's feeling that she must act out of her outrage is a specific instance of what I believe is the glue that holds our social worlds together: our sense of "oughtness"; our sense that, if he, she, or it has done "this," then we may, must, or must not do "that." For reasons best confined to a footnote, I call this "logical force."[2] Twenty-five years later, I might have chosen a different term, such as "moral force" or simply "perceived oughtness."

Each speech act performed by others elicits a response from us. If someone threatens your children, what should you do? If you go to work and the boss stops by and compliments you, how should you respond? If someone asks for your bank account number or wants to know how much money you earned in the previous year, what do you do?

I hope you felt a visceral "pull" toward acting in one way or another as I posed these questions. If so, that's "logical force." Over the years, I've been struck by how powerful logical force is. Two examples: moral conflict and family violence.

In moral conflict, I've found that people who do things that others find loathsome are, in their own minds, doing exactly what they feel that they should and must do. To denounce one side or the other is only to perpetuate the conflict; the possibility for moving forward together begins when each side can acknowledge – not necessarily approvingly – that the other is acting, within their own social world, out of a sense of duty and honor equivalent to their own.

What could bring a husband to hit his wife or a parent their child? Studies of family violence guided by the concept of logical force found that family members who hit others in their family usually did not have good stories about why they acted as they did. In reply to gentle questioning, they said things like "I don't know" or "she asked for it." When the researchers changed the way they asked questions, they got more useful answers. Treating "violence" as a speech act and looking at it in a sequence of turns, they found that those who hit their family members reported feeling an overwhelming sense of obligation to do something and that anything except a physical attack would not count as a sufficient response (Harris et al. 1984).

The concept of logical force has at least two contributions to make to Tina's situation. First, she would be well advised not to act unthinkingly on the basis of what she feels she ought to do in this situation. In general, whatever the logical force of a situation impels us to do will perpetuate whatever pattern is occurring. If she is unhappy with the way things are going, Tina might want to consider other options than the most immediate and obvious.

Second, Tina might want to explore the logical force in which Dennis and Rolf are working. Again, she might not be able to know for sure, but to explore her best perceptions on the basis of the best evidence available might well enrich her assessment of the situation and thus position her to act wisely into the situation.

What is the wisest course of action? Ante-narrative

Tina has been in her office for some time now. Dennis's email is still on her computer screen but she's covered a couple of sheets of paper with conversational triplets and notions about what logical forces are working in this situation. Now she has to decide what to do. She sits up straight, pulls her computer keyboard to her and . . .

I'll come back to Tina and the decision she makes in the next chapter. For the moment, I want to focus attention on what she's doing. Management and organization theorist David Boje calls it "ante-narrative."

Like many of us, Boje has come to think of organizations from a narrative perspective. That is, instead of (or in addition to) asking to see the chart describing who reports to whom, many people think that we can understand organizations best by learning the stories that they tell about who they are and how they function (see Czarniawska 2004). For example, all organizations have to make decisions, like whether to have a Strategic Initiative, to appoint Rolf rather than Tina as its project manager, etc. These decisions can be understood and critiqued rationally by examining the good reasons for and against making them. But they can also be understood by listening to the stories told about them.

> In organizations, storytelling is the preferred sense-making currency of human relationships. . . . People engage in a dynamic process of incremental refinement of their stories of new events as well as ongoing interpretations of culturally sacred story lines. When a decision is at hand, the old stories are recounted and compared to an unfolding story line to keep the organizations from repeating historically bad choices and to invite the repetition of past successes. . . . Each performance is never the completed story; it is an unraveling process of confirming new data and new interpretations as these become part of an unfolding story line. (Boje 1991: 106)

Most of the research on organizational narratives focuses on fully-formed, well-told stories. Boje asks: Where did these stories come from? How did these stories, rather than all the others, become the ones that everybody tells? With a turn of mind similar to the communication perspective, Boje says that the most interesting part of the analysis of organizational narratives comes from the time *before* the narrative is formed, or "ante-narrative."

> Every once in a while, someone interrupts the flow of experience and asks you to give an ACCOUNT of WHAT IS GOING ON? Your mind races, experiences come to mind, a plot thickens, and you begin to speak, and a story is told. You are living experience before narrating it, before someone requires you to provide a story with the coherence of beginning, middle, or ending. And then it is out there, but you know it is only ONE WAY to tell the story. Others will have their ways. You never know the WHOLE story (there is none). The Story never finishes, it keeps unraveling, keeps coming undone, and keeps getting RESTORIED. (Boje n.d.)

In her office, Tina is engaged in "ante-narrative." She is living experience in her mind before constructing a story about it. She is in the middle of an unfolding sequence of actions and trying to act as wisely as she can, knowing full well that she can't predict or control what will happen next.

This moment of ante-narrative is the key moment for acting wisely. It is a moment in which we need to bring the best that we are into contact with the best understanding of the situation that we can get. And then we act, and hope that it is enough.

Making Better Social Worlds

We find ourselves bobbing along in the white-water rapids of logical force, pulled and pushed this way and that, and at each moment required to act in the ways that we should or must. It seems more than enough just to float with the current, trying to keep our canoe afloat. But, impetuous and determined as we are, we also want to steer in a predetermined direction. Sometimes we want to go upstream. How can we purposively alter the configuration of speech acts in our social worlds?

Change the situation so that there will be a different ratio of speech acts

If we could look at the whole of our social worlds all at once, one thing we might notice is that the array of speech acts is not equally distributed. There are parts of these social worlds in which there is an unusually high concentration of acts of kindness, generosity, and hope, and there are parts with unusually high concentrations of evil, selfishness, and pessimism. Whatever the reason for these unequal distributions in those local configurations, I think it legitimate to assume that the quality of life for people in them is also uneven. We might also note that the array of speech acts differs from place to place. Some local configurations include a wider diversity of speech acts than others.

One way of improving your social world is to move to a different place, one that has a higher ratio of the kinds of speech acts in which you want to participate. I wonder about people who seek out or stay in local social worlds in which there is an abnormally high ratio of undesirable speech acts. I suspect that they don't see that they have alternatives, and I hope that a better understanding of how speech acts are made – of their role in the making of the speech acts in which they are surrounded – will suggest some ways for them to avoid or change these patterns.

Another strategy is to change the place that you are in so that the kind of speech acts you want will increase. Here's an example. Many organizations are characterized by "command and report" patterns of communication. In these organizations, many people are treated like the three-year-old who told his parents that he wasn't hungry – and learned that he was not allowed to participate in the speech acts involving decisions about when and what he would eat. In command-and-report structures, people with higher ranks have a high ratio of speech acts involving giving orders and making evaluations; people of lower rank are expected to have a high ratio of speech acts involving receiving orders and evaluations and submitting reports. There is little or no place in the organization for speech acts of deep listening, deliberation, or dialogue.

The United States Navy is a large, dispersed organization that has a formal command and report structure. This communication pattern is assumed to be good, even necessary, for some of the Navy's functions. However, the limitations of this pattern of communication have also been noted. In December 2001, the Navy experimented with an Appreciative

Inquiry (AI) Summit to see if it were possible to create a space in the organization for a different form of communication – specifically, dialogic democratic communication – and, if so, what would be the consequences. I was invited to be a participant/observer of the process.

The formal assessment of the impact of the Summit stressed the different relationships among participants and the changed perspectives and sense of involvement in the whole by the participants.

> The use of the AI Summit approach in an environment with a strong command and control structure is an especially powerful illustration of the potential of democracy in the workplace. Though the structure of a Summit is decentralized, the intent is not to permanently alter formal organization structure. Rather, the Summit creates and strengthens informal ties across organizations. The use of dialogue and inquiry as an organizing form invites ownership and commitment by drawing in multiple stakeholder groups to transform strategically chosen aspects of the organization. Thus, the AI Summit represents a communal atmosphere where the temporary suspension of normal organization structure allows for the accomplishment of significant, empowered strategic work. (Powley et al. 2004)

Those writing this assessment might have equally well described the Summit as providing a site in which speech acts usually prohibited from the hierarchical command and report structure could occur, and in which people usually disallowed to engage in certain speech acts were enabled and encouraged to do so.

As an observer, I found this experience remarkable both for its objectives and its accomplishment. If an organization as constrained by mission and by tradition as the Navy can create spaces for dialogic communication, surely other organizations can do the same, and this has the potential for making better social worlds. One of my favorite moments came when an admiral (the top of the command structure) listened to an impassioned complaint (already an unfamiliar speech act) by an enlisted woman (near the bottom of the chain of command) about an unnecessary separation of families and replied, "You are absolutely right. I'll cut orders to deal with this situation when I return to my desk on Monday."

Resist or prevent the performance of undesired speech acts

There are many ways of doing this, of course. The one I want to focus on is based on the structure of the conversational triplet.

When I'm teaching in face-to-face contexts, I sometimes tell the participants that I can make it impossible for them to perform the speech act "insult." "Go ahead," I challenge them, "insult me!" After a bit of hesitation, this activity usually generates a lot of energy as people say terrible things about my clothes, nationality, Southern accent, dull training sessions, and terrible writing skills. After each attempted insult, I thank the participant and sometimes say something worse about myself or taunt them for not coming up with worse things to say.

After a while, the participants get frustrated because the things they are saying – which meet the normal definition of "insults" – aren't working as insults. Clearly, something is going on here, but what?

This demonstration involves a trick, of course. It takes advantage of the structure of the conversational triplet. I make it appear that the terrible things that the participants are saying about me are the first turn in a conversation. In fact, they are the second turn. The first turn was my request for them to insult me; the second is the terrible things that they said; and the third is my expression of gratitude *for helping me with this demonstration*. The triplet looks like this:

(1) *Me:* Please help me with this demonstration by trying to insult me.
(2) *Participant:* You write terribly, have a funny accent, use obscure scholarly words, etc.
(3) *Me:* Those are good ones! It hits me where it hurts when you talk about my writing, since I've worked so hard on that. Thank you! Anyone else?

If I work this demonstration well, the meaning of the second turn changes right in front of everyone's eyes depending on what I say in the third turn. For example, "you write terribly" changes from an *insult* to *compliance* or even *help with a classroom exercise*.

Think how you can use this "trick" in designing meetings in which you know that there will be great controversy. Can you design the meeting so that the "first" turn in the conversational triplet takes the opposition and transforms it into collaboration or cooperation? Sure! Well . . . sometimes!

Dennis surely knew that Tina resented Rolf, felt that her budget had been cut, etc. etc. One explanation for his email is that it was an attempt to stifle Tina's resentments and worries; he might have thought (as have many managers with whom I've worked!) that the best thing that could happen in the meeting is that Rolf could make his presentation, he (Dennis) could keep everyone's emotions under control, and that they would escape without an ugly confrontation.

What if Dennis's email had created a different frame for the meeting? He might have said "I know that many of you have legitimate concerns about ... I want us to deal with those issues in this meeting as well as looking at the plan that Rolf is going to roll out for your comments. So please write me your concerns so that I can put them on the agenda."

This email from Dennis would have performed a different "first" turn in the conversational triplet. This turn transforms Tina's expression of outrage, resentment, and concern about her division from *rebellion* to *cooperation*. If done well, it might have made a very different and more productive meeting.

Facilitating or enabling the performance of desired speech acts

During the past twenty years, in addition to my work as a teacher, my professional practice has focused on creating conditions conducive to dialogic communication. I often say that dialogic communication is learnable, teachable, and contagious. By "contagious," I mean that the speech acts experienced in dialogue are unusual and unusually satisfying, so much so that if someone is enabled to participate in them, they want more.

Kim Pearce invited me to come to her class in Interpersonal Communication at De Anza College. She was teaching her students about dialogic listening, and wanted them to see a demonstration of it, not just read about it in their textbooks. She picked a topic that was concerning her and I listened, using what I've come to consider standard procedures for good communication. These include asking questions and responding in ways designed to help her explore the topic and to feel absolutely supported in all of her doubts and certainties. I picked up on the metaphors that she offered and invited her to elaborate on them until they seemed to run out of steam, and then I offered other metaphors until I got to one that resonated with her. I avoided introducing my own interests or thoughts, but I did express my curiosity, particularly about those parts of her story that sounded inconsistent with other parts or were less well developed than others.

That is, I was acting strategically as well as genuinely, to provide the context in which whatever she said was OK and counted as the speech act "exploring a topic." I consciously thought of the conversational triplet, and chose to react in ways that would bracket what she said in ways that invited her to explore more deeply or broadly. This wasn't always easy, because she's my wife and some of the things she said had implications for me and for our relationship, but I was clear about what was going on in this situation and that it wasn't about me.

We couldn't finish the conversation. The students interrupted us with comments about how unusual they found the pattern of conversation and how much they wished that this were part of their interactions in their families. They wanted to know the techniques that I was using. My reply was that while I was drawing on the concepts and models of communication theory, the most important thing was that I was genuinely involved in supporting Kim's exploration of the topic. That is, the techniques were in service to my personal commitment, not just a set of tools that can be used insincerely. In their final evaluation of the course, several students said that witnessing this demonstration was the most significant moment of the course for them.

The students' response to this demonstration both pleased and saddened me. I was pleased that they got the point and actually saw an example of dialogic listening, but I was saddened that this was so foreign to their experience. What a pity that something as simple and as desirable as dialogic listening is so rare.

Kim and I have spent a lot of time designing public events so that they encourage and enable the speech acts of dialogic communication. Such events need to invite people to act in ways that simultaneously hold their own ground while being profoundly open to the experiences of people who disagree with them. The participants need to find ways to express their deepest commitments in ways that make others want to listen, and to listen in ways that make the others want to speak honestly about their most precious ideas.

Using the idea of the conversational triplet, we think that the best way of enabling people to engage in dialogue is for a trained facilitator to provide the first and third turns in the speech act. The first turn might be, for example, a question asked out of genuine curiosity (rather than, for example, to find the flaw in the other's reasoning). The third turn might be:

- a summarizing paraphrase (letting the speaker know that she was heard and understood);
- a question for clarity or inviting the speaker to elaborate (again letting the speaker know that she was heard and understood and that the listener is operating from the perspective of curiosity); or,

- an appreciative reframe (both affirming the speaker and recasting what the speaker said in terms that are inviting rather than offensive to the others present who do not share the speaker's opinions).

We've found that it is possible, with good planning and hard work, to create opportunities for people to engage in speech acts that they ordinarily would not be willing or able to perform, at least in the presence of the others in the meeting. When this works, it changes the range, ratio, and distribution of speech acts in the social worlds of the participants and, in the best instances, stimulates the personal growth of the participants while enhancing their interpersonal relationships (Pearce 2002).

For me, the cutting edge of this work is figuring out how to make permanent (or at least "lasting") the changes in the local range, ratio, and distribution of speech acts. Things are different after people have engaged in dialogue, but those differences are hard to name, measure, document, or see. And, being largely unnamed and undocumented, they tend to disappear when others are brought into the group, the group disbands, or the group separates and comes together again. If we are to find ways to make these changes sustainable, it will probably require developments at the level of episodes, selves, and relationships – the topics of the following three chapters.

Notes

1 Just to make sure: "google" and "surf" – at least used as I did – name speech acts that (I'm fairly confident) were not in the 1986 dictionary (at least with these meanings) but will be in a forthcoming dictionary.

2 When Vern Cronen and I were developing CMM, we needed to name this sense of "oughtness" (Cronen and Pearce 1981). We realized that our sense of what was going on differed a good bit from the very rational models being developed in the work of other social theorists with whom we were talking. These theorists assumed that people acted logically. But what they meant by "logic" was Aristotelian logic, and we knew that those who studied logic had come a long way. In our reading of modal logics, we found an article by Finnish philosopher Georg von Wright (1951) that developed a complete logical system based on the relationships of "prohibited; obligatory; permitted; and irrelevant." He called it "deontic logic," and we began to use it for our own purposes that were quite different from von Wright's. His model gave us a vocabulary for describing the way people feel, not just relationships among

propositions in a logical form. We even went so far as to use traditional seven-point scales to quantify the degree to which someone felt "obligated" to act in certain ways.

References

Boje, D. (1991), The story-telling organization: a study of story performance in an office-supply firm, *Administrative Science Quarterly*, 36: 106–26.

Boje, D. (n.d.), What is antenarrative. Retrieved, from http://cbae.nmsu.edu/~dboje/papers/what_is_antenarrative.htm on January 28, 2003.

Cronen, V. E. and Pearce, W. B. (1981), Logical force in interpersonal communication: a new concept of the "necessity" in social behavior, *Communication*, 6: 5–67.

Czarniawska, B. (2004), *Narratives in Social Science Research*, Thousand Oaks, CA: Sage.

Gozzi, R., Jr. (1990/1991), New speech act verbs in American English, *Research on Language and Social Interaction*, 24: 449–59.

Harris, L. M., Alexander, A., McNamee, S., Stanback, M. H., and Kang, K.-W. (1984), Forced cooperation: violence as a communicative act. In S. Thomas (ed.), *Communication Theory and Interpersonal Interaction*, Norwood, NJ: Ablex, pp. 20–32.

Kreckel, M. (1981), *Communicative Acts and Shared Knowledge in Natural Discourse*, New York: Academic Press.

Pearce, K. A. (2002), *Making Better Social Worlds: Engaging in and Facilitating Dialogic Communication*, Redwood City, CA: Pearce Associates.

Powley, E. H., Fry, R. E., Barrett, F. J., and Bright, D. S. (2004), Dialogic democracy meets command and control: transformation through the Appreciative Inquiry Summit, *Academy of Management Executive*, 18: 67–80.

Rosaldo, M. (1990), The things we do with words: Ilongot speech acts and speech act theory in philosophy. In D. Carbaugh (ed.), *Cultural Communication and Intercultural Contact*, Hillsdale, NJ: Lawrence Erlbaum Associates, pp. 373–408.

Searle, J. (1969), *Speech Acts: An Essay in the Philosophy of Language*, Cambridge: Cambridge University Press.

Searle, J. (1990), Epilogue to the taxonomy of illocutionary acts. In D. Carbaugh (ed.), *Cultural Communication and Intercultural Contact*, Hillsdale, NJ: Lawrence Erlbaum Associates, pp. 409–18.

Shotter, J. (1991), Wittgenstein and psychology: on our "hook-up" to reality. In A. Phillips-Griffiths (ed.), *The Wittgenstein Centenary Lectures*, Cambridge: Cambridge University Press, pp. 193–208.

Tannen, D. (1990), *You Just Don't Understand: Women and Men in Conversation*, New York: Morrow.

Von Wright, G. (1951), Deontic logic, *Mind*, 60: 1–15.

Wittgenstein, L. (1953/2001), *Philosophical Investigations*, tr. Elizabeth Anscombe, Oxford: Blackwell Publishing, section 23, p. 11e.

Xi, C. (1991), Communication in China: a case study of Chinese collectivist and self-interest talk in social action from the CMM perspective. PhD dissertation, University of Massachusetts at Amherst.

Chapter 6

Episodes and Patterns of Communication

Preview

This chapter describes episodes and forms of communication as complex entities that emerge from the field of speech acts. Episodes may be thought of as sequences of speech acts, punctuated with a beginning and an end, and united by a story. Close attention to the way episodes are made provides us with tools for making better social worlds. Continuing what was started in chapter 5, this chapter describes how consultants, managers, and others can use CMM concepts to meet the challenges they face. To help understand episodes, this chapter presents the concepts of framing, punctuation, emplotment, and contextualization, and begins the introduction of CMM's hierarchy model. "Episode-work" names the processes we use to define or change whatever episode is occurring. Three forms of episode-work are presented: casting or chaotic emergence, realizing through planning and/or rituals, and improvisation. To understand these processes, the chapter describes CMM's concept of emergent interactional logics, introduces some parts of the serpentine model, and further develops the concept of logical force introduced in chapter 5.

Forms of communication may be thought of as clusters of episodes sharing a deep grammar. Best seen as wholes, forms of communication establish the cultural frames in which we live. The chapter ends with three suggestions for using these ideas to make better social worlds.

Social Life is Episodic

Episodes include such things as having dinner with friends; having an annual physical examination with your doctor; and doing a performance review of an employee. They include fights, friendly competition, and collaborative teamwork. If you look at them with a fuzzy focus, all episodes have a common structure. They may be described as sequences of speech acts, punctuated as having a beginning and an end, linked together as a story.

If we are to be competent members of any social group, we have to know how that group punctuates sequences of speech acts and what stories they tell to make these sequences coherent. Take the episodic structure of ordering dinner in a restaurant as an example. In some restaurants, the episode begins when the greeter escorts you to a reserved table. It proceeds through a sequence in which a waiter takes your order, serves your food, brings you a bill, takes your credit card to the cashier, and returns the card and receipt to you. The episode ends when you leave. Perhaps the greeter thanks you for your patronage and asks you to come again soon.

Not all restaurants have the same episodic pattern. There are restaurants in which the preferred episode begins when you enter and take a tray from a stack conveniently provided near a long table bearing a wide variety of dishes. You select the food yourself, find a cashier, pay, find a table and, when you are finished eating, perhaps clean the table yourself and leave.

You are probably familiar with both of these, and the easily achieved challenge is to determine which of these episodes is preferred in the restaurant that you have entered. But there are other possible episodes – as I learned, much to my embarrassment, in what might be called "The Tale of the Angry Waiter."

Twenty years ago, I was invited to dinner at the prestigious and elegant Automobile Club in Buenos Aires. I saw a long table bearing many dishes and looked for a stack of trays. A smiling waiter walked up to me carrying a tray. I thanked him and tried to take it from him. He pulled it back. I tried again to take it . . . and before we had gotten too far in this tug-of-war, my Argentine friends explained to me that I was taking the waiter's job from him. I learned that, in this restaurant, I was supposed to walk along the buffet table and indicate what food I wanted so that the waiter could take it and put it on the tray that he was carrying. When I had all I wanted, I would find an unoccupied table, sit at it, and wait for the waiter to bring the food and serve it. I'm sure that the waiter said some uncomplimentary things about this crazy American who didn't even know how to act in a classy restaurant.

Can some of the more important areas of our lives be understood as variations of this problem in knowing and performing the appropriate episode? Of course! And these are some of the social skills we need to be a competent member of any human social group. And as we learn and perform these skills, we are shaped by them, becoming the kind of person who belongs to the human social group in which we are participating.

But we are not limited to becoming the person made by the episodes of a particular social group. Sometimes we don't want to "fit in" to whatever is going on. There are times when we want to, and should, set ourselves to oppose the enactment of a particular episode or to change the episode that is occurring. For example, how can you transform a fight into collaborative teamwork, or a performance evaluation into a constructive mentoring session? Such transformations – I'll call them "episode work" later in this chapter – require a different order of social skills . . . and the practice of these social skills makes us more sophisticated persons.

Like speech acts, episodes come in clusters. Although the specific content of these episodes might differ – some having to do with work, some play, some entertainment, etc. – there are "family resemblances" among the episodes that adhere to each other. Drawing on some of the concepts introduced in chapter 3, I suggest that we think of these clusters not simply as aggregates (that is, heaps or piles) but as emergent entities. Names for these entities might include national, ethnic, or organizational "cultures," "society," "community," "discursive structures," "social systems," or "institutions." Consistent with my intention to explore what we might gain by taking a communication perspective, I'll call them "forms of communication."

Our Social Worlds are Made of Episodes

I first started thinking about episodes in 1972. Valeri Borzov was being interviewed after winning the Olympic gold medals in the 100- and 200-meter sprints. Borzov surprised me when he said that he had written a doctoral dissertation about the 100-meter race – I had never imagined focusing that much attention on something that is apparently so simple. Describing his strategy for the race, he said that he calculated the number of steps he would take between start and finish-line, and divided the race up into several segments. Again, I had never thought of counting the steps in a race – I just assumed that one started running and kept on running until reaching the finish line. Each of the segments, Borzov told us, presents a specific challenge and requires a different style of running. Without using the term, I realized that Borzov was thinking of the 100-meter race episodically and that this gave him a level of mindfulness and control over his performance that I can only admire from a distance.

At about the same time, I read a remarkable book co-authored by philosopher Rom Harré and psychologist Paul Secord (1973), in which they claimed that "human life" consists of, and can productively be analyzed in terms of, episodes. Their definition of episode seemed to fit Borzov's description of the 100-meter race, but to be sufficiently general to include other things as well. Episodes, they said, are "any sequence of happenings in which human beings engage which has some principle of unity" (1973: 154). They offered these examples: "buying a chocolate bar in a small shop; bumping into a passer-by, apologizing and going on; reading a book and discussing it with several other people, some of whom have not read it and one of whom pretends to have read it but has not; a change of attitude; the emergence of a leader; a trial; a strike; a playground game, and so on" (1973: 154–5). Another way of defining episodes was given by sociolinguist John Gumperz (1975: 17), who suggested that we look at "communicative routines which [people] view as distinct wholes, separate from other types of discourse, characterized by special rules of speech and nonverbal behavior and often distinguished by clearly recognizable opening or closing sequences."

Making Episodes

If we want to live in better social worlds, we will have to make them. So how can we make episodes that serve us well?

I want to use the two faces of the process of communication to structure my answer to this question. One part of making episodes has to do with meaning making and management. That is, how do we perceive what episode is happening? Our perceptions of what is happening are underdetermined by the facts themselves. It is always possible to interpret the same event or sequence of events as making up a different episode – or many different episodes. The other part of making episodes has to do with coordinating actions. That is, how can we call into being desirable episodes and/or block the enactment of episodes that are undesirable?

Making/managing meaning: perceiving
the flow of experience as episodes

One way of thinking about life is that it is a flow of experience: an unbroken stream of events. Using this metaphor, perceiving episodes is a process in which we mark some points as the "beginning" and "end" of an episode and wrap the speech acts between these points in a story.

The metaphor of the "stream of experience" is very attractive. It sounds so calm, orderly, and peaceful. I wish that life as I know it was so gentle and linear as to constitute a stream. More often, my experience is more like a waterfall or a white-water river furiously crashing down among rocks. Even this metaphor is too one-dimensional. I believe that there are multiple levels of episodes and that even in apparently placid social situations, the act of interpreting what is happening is fateful.

Let me show you what I mean. You met Tina in chapter 5. She's a frustrated and worried division manager. Among other things, she's trying to decide how to respond to an email sent by her supervisor, Dennis, telling her both that she must attend a meeting and how to respond to Rolf's presentation about the new corporate Strategic Initiative. She can't bring herself to feel, as Dennis told her that she should, "grateful" for what Rolf has done.

Start by trying to give a name to the episode in which Tina finds herself. Do you find a well-developed cultural repertoire of names for this episode? How obvious is it what episode is occurring? In chapter 5, I described some tools for analyzing situations like this; I think that those tools have the potential to enrich Tina's understanding of what is going on. In this chapter, I'll provide some more tools. But does understanding the situation in a richer way make the episode easier or more difficult to name and act into?

Any moment in our social worlds can be seen as a part of numerous episodes based on what we know and on what we choose to focus on. The technical name for this is polysemy, or literally, many meanings. It isn't that one definition is right and the other wrong, but that everything has multiple meanings depending on what you have in view.

Here's a bit more information about Tina, Dennis, and Rolf. If I've written this well, your interpretation of what episode Tina is in as she sits behind the closed doors of her office will change as you read each new bullet point.

- Rolf and Tina had planned to marry when they finished college. Both sets of parents adamantly opposed their marriage on the basis that Rolf and Tina are of different races, religions, and social classes. Shortly after they finished college, Rolf broke off their engagement, saying that he could not bear the disapproval of his parents. Three days later, Rolf announced his engagement to another woman, the daughter of his parents' friends whom Rolf had known all his life. They now have three children, but Rolf doesn't seem very happy. Tina was broken-hearted, has no significant romantic relationship, and scarcely dates. Although both are division managers in the same company, they avoid talking to each other as much as possible.

- When Tina and Rolf were engaged, Dennis was their best friend. Tina has always wondered what role he played in Rolf's decision to break off their engagement. She suspects that Rolf confided in him and that all along he knew what Rolf was planning to do but did not tell her. She has never asked him about his role in their breakup and carefully avoids talking about this part of their history in her interactions with him. While she is friendly with Dennis, she doesn't fully trust him and seeks to keep a bit of distance from him.

- After graduating from college, Tina, Rolf, and Dennis began working for three different organizations. However, in the spate of acquisitions and mergers brought about by globalized markets, the company in which Dennis worked bought the companies in which Rolf and Tina worked. Both Rolf and Tina believe that Dennis used his influence to make sure that they did not lose their jobs during the acquisition.

- Tina is the first and only female division manager in this company, and feels a sense of obligation to other women to succeed. She believes that the senior managers, some of whom expect that she will fail, are watching her very closely.

- Tina's division works in one of the fastest-changing sectors of the global market, and has been profitable until last year. To continue to be profitable, Tina believes that they need a major reorganization, including setting up production and distribution facilities in emerging markets. She is disappointed that senior management has turned down her requests for a transitional budget to make these changes and fears that the new Strategic Initiative will further divert corporate resources away from her division.

To help understand how Tina – or any of us – can make sense of our social worlds, I suggest four ideas: framing, punctuation, emplotment, and contextualization.

Framing

Alone in her office, Tina might well feel overwhelmed by the task of figuring out just what episode is being played out in Dennis's email. Or, perhaps she thinks that there are many episodes being played out simultaneously, and Dennis's email plays a different role in each. Here are some of the possibilities:

- Dennis is asserting his supervisory responsibility for the strategic initiative;
- Dennis is telling Tina and Rolf that they need to get over their history and start working together;
- Dennis is – again! – siding with Rolf against Tina;
- etc.

For Tina to avoid being overwhelmed, she needs to be able to place the events within an interpretive frame. Frames make "what would otherwise be a meaningless aspect of the scene into something that is meaningful" by arraying it within a meaningful structure (Goffman 1974: 21). The frame selected "allows its user to locate, perceive, identify and label a seemingly infinite number of concrete occurrences defined in its terms. . . . It seems that we can hardly glance at anything without applying a primary framework, thereby forming conjectures as to what occurred before and expectations of what is likely to happen now" (1974: 21, 38).

But how do we make or select among these frames? Sociologist Erving Goffman proposes that they "render" – in the sense of "cut" or "tear into pieces" – our social worlds. If we don't push the metaphor too hard, it is a good one. We cannot perceive all of what is going on even in a specific moment. Not only is there just too much happening, but everything that happens has multiple meanings. The only way we can make sense of it is to focus on some things and not others, to foreground some things and not others, and to see some sequential patterns and not others – in short, to tear out a hunk of it and ignore the rest.

My point is that we never perceive our social worlds completely or as they are. The work we do to perceive episodes is always a process of selection, and involves the act of tearing as well as stitching things together again.

Punctuation

Punctuation refers to the process of dividing and organizing interactions into meaningful patterns. It is a specific way of framing, involving identifying the beginnings and the end of an episode (Watzlawick, Beavin, and Jackson 1967).

Choosing from among all the available possibilities what you will take as the "beginning" of an episode is fateful, as I was recently reminded. My colleague Frank Barrett and I were preparing to teach a graduate seminar on the intellectual development of social constructionism for the students at Fielding Graduate University. We knew how we wanted to end the story, but were very aware that the meaning of the ending depends, in part, on where the story began. Some of the possible starting points that we considered were the publication of Berger and Luckmann's *The Social Construction of Reality* in 1966, John Locke and the Enlightenment in the seventeenth century, and Plato and Aristotle in classical Greece. Depending on this choice, our story would be like Cronen's (1998) "Cleaning up the wreckage of the psychology project" or "Building on Berger and Luckmann." In this case, Frank graciously allowed me to start the seminar with a presentation about the pre-Socratic Greeks; the story I told might be named "Extending some ideas from the Sophists into the era of globalization."

I felt pretty good about this way of punctuating the story for a week or two, until one of the students in the seminar asked me how the story would be different if it had started even earlier. The Sophists, she said (with enough footnotes to warm any teacher's heart), borrowed many ideas that had been in circulation in Egyptian culture, which was already ancient at the time of the Sophists, and many of these ideas were borrowed from even older sub-Saharan African cultures.

She was absolutely right, of course, and this created a critical moment for me. I had to decide whether to search for the "true beginning" of the story of the intellectual development of social constructionism, or to say that there is no "real" beginning.[1] I chose the latter, and would like to believe that it was because I don't believe that this or any other story has a "true beginning" and not that I'm just too lazy to continue my research. At any rate, if you hear me lecture in the future about the development of social constructionism, I will begin with "In one way of telling this story . . ."

I've become very sensitive to the fictitiousness of the terms "in the beginning . . ." and "the end." To say that these are "fictitious" is not to say that they are wrong, only that they are made. "Making by shaping, feigning" is, after all, the etymological root of "fiction." My point is that perceptions of beginnings and ends of any episode are matters of responsibility, not epistemology. If we take responsibility for the way we punctuate episodes, we can create opportunities for unusually productive discussions.

The study of the Flynn family reported in chapter 4 found a pattern of interaction so common that it has become a stereotype: the husband withdraws and the wife nags. Or is it that the wife nags and the husband withdraws? That's the point: the couple (and any sentient observer) agree about the sequence of actions. They disagree about which initiates the pattern; that is, which act is "first" and which is the "response." As a result, unproductive quarrels happen in which each asserts his or her punctuation and describes the legitimacy of his or her response: "I withdraw because you nag" or "I nag because you withdraw." Both are right and little is gained by successive repetitions. A critical moment is achieved if the couple can call their punctuation into question, and if they can see the pattern as a whole, the logical force compelling them to do more of the same can change.

I learned this lesson in a conversation with a Laotian young man who had immigrated to the United States in the 1960s. When I asked him why he chose to leave Laos for the US, he replied, "It was my duty to kill a man." That wasn't quite the answer I was expecting. As he explained, his culture had a strong ethic of retribution and vengeance. If there were a murder, it was the ethical duty of the oldest male in the family of the victim to kill the murderer. Of course, the family of the man most recently killed perceived this as the murder of an innocent man who had only done his ethical duty, and this placed the burden of retribution and vengeance on the eldest male . . . and so on.[2] "A man from the other village," he said, "killed my father. My father had killed his father. It was my turn and I saw the pattern going on and on, involving my son and his son and his son after him. And I said, 'No! Enough! It ends with me!'"[3]

Note that the story and the sense of "oughtness" in it changes depending on what is selected as the beginning and the ending. If the episode starts with "a man from the other village killed my father," then there is a powerful logical force to retaliate. In this context, his refusal to kill and his choice to leave the area show irresponsible cowardice. However, if the episode is perceived as starting in the unremembered past and continuing into the unforeseeable future, his actions are wise and courageous, an example for us all.

Emplotment

Punctuation defines where an episode begins and ends; between those points is a story. One of the tasks in making an episode is to convert the sequence of events into a plot; to transmute a string of sheer happenings into a meaningful narrative.

I'm borrowing the term "emplotment" from philosopher Paul Ricoeur, who makes a distinction between *cosmological* time (temporal sequence) and *phenomenological* time (time experienced as past, present, and future). These combine in *human time* through the process of emplotment, or storytelling. In Ricoeur's view (*Internet Encyclopedia of Philosophy* 2005), narrative emplotment "configures events, agents and objects and renders those individual elements meaningful as part of a larger whole in which each takes a place in the network that constitutes the narrative's response to why, how, who, where, when, etc." Emplotment often involves changing the sequence of what happened first and next, selecting what to include and exclude, etc.

> What is depicted as the "past" and the "present" within the plot does not necessarily correspond to the "before" and "after" of its linear, episodic structure. For example, a narrative may begin with a culminating event, or it may devote long passages to events depicted as occurring within relatively short periods of time. Dates and times can be disconnected from their denotative function; grammatical tenses can be changed, and changes in the tempo and duration of scenes create a temporality that is "lived" in the story that does not coincide with either the time of the world in which the story is read, nor the time that the unfolding events are said to depict. (*Internet Encyclopedia of Philosophy* 2005)

"What story do you have about that?" is a question often heard in the CMM tradition of practice. This question contains the embedded suggestions that, however the other perceives a part of the social world, it is a *story*, it is *one* story, and it is *their* story. The question calls attention to the narrative emplotment done by the other.

Contextualization: the hierarchy model

We can render the social world by tearing it into stories, but this isn't enough to clarify what episodes are being performed. Many times, there are stories within stories, or multiple stories all being enacted simultaneously. CMM's concept of the hierarchy model provides a way of coming to grips with the fact that we never only mean one thing at a time in our actions.

The hierarchy model builds on Gregory Bateson's (1972) idea of meta-communication. Bateson noted that communication ordinarily occurs at different levels of abstraction, such that the higher modifies the meaning of the lower. He illustrated this idea by analyzing monkeys at play in San Francisco's Fleishhacker Zoo. Bateson described them engaged in an episode in which the actions were identical or similar to those of combat, but actually meant something other than they would if the episode were "combat." The monkeys were whooping, beating their chests, and biting each other, but they did not respond to each other as they would if the context had been "fight." How do monkeys (and puppies and other primates) know the difference between the speech acts of a *playful nip* and an *aggressive bite* – and know the difference *before* sensing how deeply the teeth sink into skin?

Bateson suggested that they are metacommunicating, which he defined as "exchanging signals which would carry the message, 'this is play'" (Bateson 1972: 179). Messages about what episode we are performing – play, fights, games, debates, etc. – are not "in" the episode, but "about" the episode; they are at a different level of abstraction. Building on Bateson's ideas, Watzlawick, Beavin, and Jackson (1967) developed five "axioms" of communication, one of which states that all messages have both a content and a relationship meaning such that the relational meanings provide a context for the content.

All of this indicates that communication occurs at several levels simultaneously, and that some of these stories function as contexts for other stories. Because humans are more sophisticated than monkeys and puppies, there is more room for error in our metacommunication about what episode we are making together. At our best, we treat what others do as symbols rather than things, and symbols can be distrusted, falsified, denied, amplified, corrected, and so on. We sometimes make our metacommunication explicit rather than depend on winks and nudges by asking "what are we making together?" and giving complete descriptions of the episodes we are creating and that we want to call into being.

I've spent more time observing puppies playing than monkeys, and it is a delight to watch them play the game that I call "you chase me and then I'll chase you." But there is a certain repetitiveness to this game. Humans create more sophisticated contexts, such as mystery, fantasy, horror, irony, and drama, in which we differentiate between what is said and what is meant on the basis of the context in which it occurs. As Bateson (1972) noted, any normally sophisticated person knows that the monster in a horror film does not denote what it seems to; that is, the film is not a scientific report that "monsters exist." Rather, the image denotes what the monster would denote *if* the monster existed.

CMM put these ideas together in the hierarchy model of meanings (Pearce, Cronen, and Conklin 1979; Pearce, Harris, and Cronen 1981). Assume a chronological sequence of speech acts. The meaning of each speech act is determined, in part, by its relationship to the speech acts that come before it and after it (that's the conversational triplet discussed in chapter 5). But the meaning of each speech act is also partly determined by the episode in which it occurs.

As shown in figure 6.1, we borrowed the symbol for a context-marker from Brown (1969/1994; further developed by Varela 1979) and used it to mean "*x* is in the context *y*." This context-marker invites you to make explicit a particular kind of distinction that we are all too familiar with, but sometimes forget to make or make only implicitly.

If we know "*x*," we can use this model as a heuristic, pointing us to identify the context. If "*x*" is Dennis's email summoning Tina to a meeting, then she needs to make some trained judgments about what is the episode of which this email is a part; then she can better judge its meaning and decide how to respond.

A city in California experienced a rapid change in its ethnic composition. Within 15 years, the percentage of Asian residents increased from less

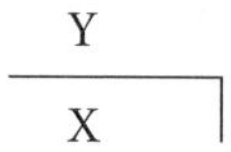

$$\frac{Y}{X} \quad \rceil$$

Figure 6.1   A way of representing a contextual relationship

than 15 percent to over 40 percent. Newly arrived immigrants accounted for most of the increase, and most of them were challenged to adapt to the new language and culture. The following is my transcription of an impromptu speech given toward the end of a large (about 150 persons) public meeting in which the races were proportionally represented. Although I've changed both names, the "David Lee" to whom Chang Lee referred was present in the meeting and was at the time serving as the first Asian Mayor of the city.

Yes, my name is Chang Lee. I am not David Lee's brother, OK? It just so happens to be the same last name.

I think there's a cultural gap in between, between when we're talking about the diversity here. For example, in my business, I went out door-to-door knocking a lot. I heard a lot of comments that Asian community or Asian owner doesn't participate. They are the takers. They are not the givers. And then, they don't take care of their yard. And when I went back and think about it, where I came from, Taipei, Taiwan, I mean barely you don't have a yard to take care of at all. So we have no custom, no tradition, no habit to take care of the yard. Now we end up here with a big yard and what are you going to do? If you don't do anything in summer, within two weeks, it die already. So a lot of those differences, a lot of people don't understand.

And then when I came out running for city School Board, last year, when David and I won, and the local newspaper want to have an article after they interviewed me and David, they say they would have an article wrote it in this way. Heading says, "Lee Dynasty Taking over the City!" I mean when we're accused not coming to serve, to help, to participate, and then when we come out then they will say you are taking over the city, which is not, you know, doesn't feel quite well from my feeling, so I have to protest.

And also when I started a couple of years ago when I was helping in the school with my wife. Then the other parents asked me "Why don't you help out in the PTA?" and I said, "What's the PTA?" and they say, "It's Parent Teacher Association is helping the school a lot." I went to the PTA meeting and as you men know, most PTA were attended by mothers. So when I went over there, I was one of the few fathers in there. And added up with when every organization have their ongoing business going on, and when you cut in the middle, you really got lost. Then second, when I sit in there, I heard the mother said "I move this, I move that." I was very puzzled because I thought she was sitting there, she was not moving anywhere. Why is she keep saying "I move this, I move that?" And then someone follow would say "I second" and I was even more puzzled because I feel you don't have to be so humble, no one claim to be the first, why you have to be second. And that's the cultural difference.

　　Maybe I let you know back in the country where I came from, the government at the time wasn't purposely try to give you the democratic because they know if they give you the democratic, the people will ask for power. So we never been trained that way. So let alone coming here, you get all this different language barrier, and all this format, all this democratic process. So I thought it was someone inside the door waving to people outside "Why don't you come in and help?" and then the people outside couldn't find the door. So that's a situation we have to understand and I think the most important, we have to understand the cultural gap and also the tolerance between each other. And that's my comment.

If you look at the content of what Chang said, it is pretty harsh. He "protests." He describes the dominant culture as not understanding cultural differences and not acknowledging the lived experiences of people who have immigrated from other social and political systems. He accuses the city of setting the immigrants up to fail: they demand that people like him participate in local governance but then make it difficult to do so and finally find fault with them – for different reasons – whether they succeed ("you're trying to take over") or fail ("you take but you don't give").

　　Ouch!

You already know that the literal meaning of what Chang said may or may not resemble what he is doing and making. To understand what's being made, you need to know to what it is a response, and what response it elicits. As it happened, Chang's speech was frequently interrupted by laughter and followed by thunderous applause from both the Asians and Caucasians in the audience. From that, you get the idea that something special is going on. But what? One way to answer that question is to describe the episode of which it is a part. Chang's speech was a part of a public dialogue meeting in which the community was trying to develop ways of talking productively about the issues generated by the rapid change in the ethnicity of the residents (Spano 2001). As shown in figure 6.2, a statement that might have been an "accusation" if delivered in another context was an "acceptance of an invitation" in this one.

Sometimes we know that a given action has at least two contexts, and we want to know their relative importance. That is, which is the context for what? This story appeared in the *New York Times* (Falk 2005):

Public dialogue about ethnic relationships

| (1) Invitation to describe ⟶ (2) Chang Lee's ⟶ (3) Laughter and |
| experiences   speech   applause |

Figure 6.2   Chang Lee's speech in context

FORBIDDEN IDEAS: With more than 100 million users, the Internet is boom-ing in China. The American Web giants Microsoft, Yahoo and Google have all grabbed a piece of the lucrative Chinese market – but only after agreeing to help the government censor speech on the Web. In providing portals or search engines, all three companies are abiding by the government's censorship of certain ideas and keywords, like "Tiananmen massacre," "Taiwanese independence," "corruption" and "democracy." Most foreign news sites are blocked. This year, Yahoo even supplied information that helped the government track and convict a political dissident who sent an e-mail message with forbidden thoughts from a Yahoo account; he was sentenced to 10 years in jail. "Business is business," said Jack Ma, Yahoo's chief in China. "It's not politics."

On the basis of this information, we can draw some conclusions about the social world according to Mr. Ma and Yahoo, the corporation that employs him. Let's assume that in the context of politics, Mr. Ma and Yahoo are committed to individual liberties and would not reveal personal informa-tion about a client to a hostile government. This commitment runs into the reality that, in order to do business in China, Yahoo is required to pro-vide personal information about its users to the government. So: business or politics? Which is more important? That is, which is the "higher level" of context in the hierarchy model?

Based on what we know, it is easy to see that "business" is more import-ant than "politics." When the two conflict, Mr. Ma and Yahoo, appar-ently without suffering much regret or stress, put business first (this is depicted in figure 6.3). As Mr. Ma said clearly, "Business is business. It's not politics."

Even though Mr. Ma's world sorts out easily into a stable hierarchical relationship between business and politics, there might be a tension between what Mr. Ma thinks he should do in these two realms of business

Business

Politics

Disclose client's personal information if the government requests it

Figure 6.3　A hierarchical model of business and politics in Yahoo's China division

and politics. As long as he has a very stable hierarchy – that is, that the ordinal relationship between business and politics remains unchallenged – he can deal with this tension without uncertainty. However, we might imagine any number of things, including a conversation with a consultant or an experience in which one of his own family members was involved, that might threaten his ability to manage the relationships among levels in his hierarchy of meanings. If politics (or family or personal integrity or some other story) took over the role of the highest level of contextualization, his behavior would have to change.

Let's use the same hierarchy model to depict what is going on in another situation.

> FORBIDDEN VACCINE: Every year, about 500,000 women throughout the world develop cervical cancer. In the United States alone, the disease kills about 3,700 women annually. This year, scientists developed a vaccine against human papillomavirus, a sexually transmitted disease that is the primary cause of cervical cancer. The vaccine produced 100 percent immunity in the 6,000 women who received it as part of a multinational trial. As soon as the vaccine is licensed, some health officials say, it should be administered to all girls at age 12. But the Family Research Council and other socially conservative groups vowed to fight that plan, even though it could virtually eliminate cervical cancer. Vaccinating girls against a sexually transmitted disease, they say, would reduce their incentive to abstain from premarital sex. (Falk 2005)

Using the hierarchy model, I'd describe the situation as shown in figure 6.4. Both groups, "some health officials" and "the Family Research Council," have stable hierarchies but place different stories as the most important level of context. Both are committed to preventing unnecessary deaths due to cervical cancer, but this commitment is at different levels

	Health officials:	*Family Research Council:*
Ideology:	Preventing unnecessary deaths from cervical cancer	Preventing immoral behavior (premarital sex)
Programmatic goal:	Encouraging safe sex	Preventing unnecessary deaths from cervical cancer
Specific policy proposals:	Vaccinate all girls at an early age; teach safe sexual practices	Preach sexual abstinence; don't vaccinate them

Figure 6.4   Different patterns of contextualization about vaccinations

in the pattern in which they contextualize various stories. For the "health officials," it is the highest level of context; for the Family Research Council, it is secondary to "preventing immoral behavior."

In the public discourse about this topic, the two groups will clash about their specific policy proposals. In order to understand why they see each other as obstacles, we can articulate their pattern of contextualization. Noting that the two groups have different concerns as their highest level of contextualization might help us discern critical moments in the noise and clamor of conflict between these groups, but even if not, it helps us understand why they are opposed to each other in this way.

If we are sufficiently aware of our pattern of contextualization, we can better manage our meanings. Sometimes that means deliberately not responding to the content of what someone says because it is more important to maintain a particular definition of the episode. Here's an example involving mature parenting in a difficult situation. This brief, highly emotional exchange occurred between a teenaged girl who had gotten into trouble and her mother.

(1) *Mother:*   [unknown]
(2) *Daughter:*   I hope you burn in hell!
(3) *Mother:*   Listen, I've done plenty on my own to get there, but the one thing that is getting me to heaven is you. (Carpenter 2006)

The hierarchy model in figure 6.5 is one way of understanding this interaction. Mother and daughter have different concepts of what episode is the context for this conversation, "good parenting" or "getting my own

	Mother:	*Daughter:*
Definition of episode:	Good parenting	Getting my own way
Form of action:	Envisioning consequences; acting so as to create a long-term good relationship with daughter; accepting daughter's anger in the moment	Search for immediate gratification; little concern for long-term relationship with mother

Figure 6.5   Differing high-level contexts in a conversation between mother and daughter

way." Daughter's turn (2) is clearly meant to be offensive and to end the episode. Mother's statement in turn (3) responds in content to the second turn, but refuses to accept the implications of the statement for the change in context. To the contrary, mother's turn (3) can be heard as a powerful, eloquent assertion that nothing that the daughter can do or say can change the highest-level context of her love and commitment to being a good mother. On one level, this denies the daughter the power to perform certain speech acts; on another, it accomplishes some quite different things.

Realizing episodes in coordinated action

Episodes are not made only by perceiving them in particular ways. They have to be realized in coordinated actions. To what extent can we call into being those episodes that are good for us; that we love or find useful? And to what extent can we act in ways that prevent realization of episodes that we hate or fear, that are dangerous, toxic, or obnoxious?

Episode-work[4] describes what people do to make sure that the desired episode takes place. As a way of making some useful distinctions, and *not* as an attempt to provide a list of all and only ways in which this is done, I suggest three ways in which episodes develop: casting/chaos; planned; and improvised.

Realizing episodes through dramatic "casting" or chaotic emergence

Chaos theory describes complex patterns that result when a system follows relatively simple rules through many iterations. Remember the example of "boids" in chapter 3: the complex movements of a flock of birds can be simulated if each boid follows three simple, hierarchically organized rules (Reynolds 2001).

I think some episodes develop something like the movements of flocks of birds. They are made when two or more people follow their own rules for action and these actions intermesh in ways not intended by any of the participants, who are often surprised, dismayed, or delighted by the results. This is perhaps the most capricious and unsophisticated way in which episodes can be realized. It "works" because so many of us draw from the same well of rules for meaning and action and, if I may be so bold as to suggest, because we have such low community standards of "quality control" for the episodes that we realize. There are better ways of making episodes.

Before chaos theory was developed, Vern Cronen and I used the metaphor of the theater. The idea is that we are in a play, but there is no director. Each of us knows some scripts, but not necessarily the same ones as the other actors know. Each of us wants to play certain roles, but not necessarily the complements to the roles that other people want to play. This metaphor imagines us all wandering around an immense stage, blurting out our favorite lines in the hopes that we will meet others who will take our lines as their cues and reply in a manner that "realizes" the play that we want to perform. That is, each of us has a play in mind and is looking to "cast" other people into the supporting roles (Pearce and Cronen 1980: 120–1).

Sometimes this works, I guess, but seems awfully inefficient and appears to ignore many useful critical moments. Here's an example of what happened when an outraged youth and an unresponsive government official realized an episode by "casting" each other into their own scripts for the episodic sequence.

The young man had a grievance against the local government. He armed himself, went to the City Hall, took hostages, and threatened to kill them if the government did not comply with his demands. The local governor immediately surrounded the City Hall with armed soldiers and pledged that there would be no negotiations as long as the young man was threatening hostages. A perfect stalemate was reached when the young man said that he would not release his hostages until there had been negotiations. Neither was willing to *back down* (I italicized this phrase just to remind us that this is a speech act).

In his analysis of this situation, anthropologist Edward Hall (1977) noted that both the governor and the young man were willing to *negotiate* (another speech act), but they had very different stories about where the speech act *negotiation* fit into the episodic sequence of resolving grievances against government. The young man actually wanted to negotiate, but he envisioned a sequence in which he took dramatic actions that showed how serious he was, elicited a response that acknowledged the depth of his emotion, and that turned into negotiation. However, the governor saw hostage-taking and occupying a government building as the last step of a desperate man who was not likely to be a responsible partner in negotiations. He envisioned a process in which the negotiation came very early in an episode and certainly before rather than after actions as provocative as hostage-taking. Because they had different ideas about the proper sequence of speech acts – specifically whether hostage-taking comes before or after negotiation – they could find no way of moving forward together without violence.

I was involved in an intercultural communication situation that began as "casting" but – fortunately – turned into something else. The episode was ultimately realized through metacommunication (see! I told you that there were more than three ways of realizing episodes!).

The Jesuit leaders of the University of Central America (UCA) were sharply divided about the civil war that had been going on in El Salvador during the 1980s. Some sided with the American-backed government; others had become open supporters of the peasants, supported by the guerrilla FMLN (*Farabundo Martí para la Liberación Nacional*). In fact, the Jesuits referred to themselves as having created two schools at the same University – they called them "UCA-one" and "UCA-two" – and, against the tradition of their Order, lived in separate residences.

Shortly before dawn on November 16, 1989, soldiers went to the house where the Jesuits supporting the peasants were sleeping and murdered all six professors, their housekeeper, and her daughter. They dragged the bodies on to the lawn and left them as a blatant statement of the fate awaiting those who opposed them.

This act of government-sponsored terrorism failed. Within hours, the nongovernmental human rights group Americas Watch brought lawyers and criminal investigators to the scene. These investigators were able to identify the perpetrators and distributed a full account both in El Salvador and in Washington, DC. Within days, other Jesuits, equally strong in their support for the poor and oppressed, had replaced those who had been murdered. These new university teachers and administrators began by introducing themselves to the military leaders who had ordered the murder of their predecessors. One of them told me that he did this "so that, if they come for me, they'll know who I am." Among other consequences of these events, American support of the government diminished. In 1991, the officers involved were found guilty of murder; peace accords between the government and the FMLN were signed in 1992.

I was one of three department chairs at Loyola University Chicago sent to El Salvador to participate in the commemoration of the third anniversary of the murders and to work with our counterparts at UCA to help them recover from the effects of the war. All of us in the Loyola group appreciated the cultural differences between the United States and El Salvador and were particularly sensitive to the possibility of reproducing patterns of cultural imperialism. In a planning session before our first meeting with our Salvadoran colleagues, we reminded ourselves that the episodes for such events would be different in El Salvador than in Chicago. We knew that the Salvadoran scripts dictated that we spend the whole of the first meeting establishing relationships and enjoying each other's company. We should have no agenda to push; the real work would come in subsequent meetings. When we arrived for our meeting, we were relaxed, prepared to enjoy good Salvadoran coffee with our new friends and to end the meeting without having had substantive discussions.

To our surprise, the Salvadorans were hardly through the door before they began to discuss specific proposals for collaboration. They had a specific agenda and were determined to get down to business.

It took only a few minutes before we all realized that both groups had had similar planning sessions in which we rehearsed the episodes that the other would expect and committed ourselves to adapt to them. As a result, the first few minutes of our meeting reproduced the common pattern of cross-cultural coordination problems, but with each of us – with the best of intentions – playing the role of the other group. When we recognized what had happened, mixed in with all the laughter and joking, we were able to negotiate a new episodic structure for our meetings that had some of the best of both cultures (for a fuller analysis of this incident, see Pearce 2004).

Realizing episodes through planning and/or rituals

Many episodes are fully planned. From a participant's perspective, there are no hard choices or moments of uncertainty. Think of a church service or inauguration of a new CEO in which the liturgy or program is printed and distributed. In church, people are told when to stand, kneel, or sit; when to pray and what to say when they do; and when to sing and when to listen. The only challenge for realizing such episodes is knowing what to do and organizing others to follow the script.

Other episodes are planned in general, but the participants are given some flexibility in terms of how to achieve them. Athletic events provide an example. Much of what will happen is fully specified before the game begins and referees are on hand to enforce the rules. The number of teams, number of players on the team, time allowed, and activities permitted are fully described, but teams are encouraged to invent winning strategies or perform mandated actions with uncommon skill.

More common are general agreements about the desired episode and considerable latitude about how it will be achieved. The public discourse about political issues in the United States is so polarized as I write that it resembles casting/chaos, and it isn't working well. In an attempt to show that alternative conversation forms are possible, Cal Thomas and Bob Beckel set themselves to have public, printed "civil conversations" about the hot-button items in the national newspaper *USA Today* (Common Ground n.d.). What makes this exercise interesting is that Thomas is a conservative newspaper and television commentator and Beckel is a liberal campaign strategist and that they have a long friendship despite their political differences.

Episode-work is clearly evident in their conversations. Each person works to ensure that, no matter what the other says, they co-construct an episode with the desired "civility." Sometimes this means treating fairly sharp comments as jokes rather than being offended at them; often it means admitting the limitations of one's position; and almost always it means moving to an agreement (the promised "common ground") that includes the best of the positions initially staked out by both of them.

Realizing episodes through improvisation

Improvised episodes occur when we, as participants, keep one eye on the emerging sequence of actions and the other on the episode we are making. At times, this means that we will act as others expect; at other times, we may act unexpectedly. In improvised episodes, we may start out not knowing what episode we want to enact but, at some point, work very hard to realize, or prevent the enactment of, a particular episode. We may switch between one episode and other.

CMM has developed three concepts to help understand the realization of episodes: emergent interactional logics, the serpentine model, and logical force. I think these concepts are best presented in a discussion of episodes realized through improvisation.

Emergent interactional logics: A study of "aggression rituals" described a dynamic process in which episodes seemed to develop a life of their own, evolving along paths independent of the intentions of the people involved in them. Harris, Gergen, and Lannamann (1986) wrote vignettes of an episode and showed them, one turn at a time, to a group of research participants. After each turn, the participants were asked to describe the *probability*, *desirability*, and *advisability* of what the other person should do in the next turn. These options ranged from "highly conciliatory" to "violent." After rating these possible next turns, the research participants were shown what the person in the story actually did, and the process was repeated for all subsequent turns in the story. The vignettes were written to show an interaction in which the people involved became increasingly aggressive toward each other, including – toward the end of the episode – acts of violence.

As the researchers expected, as the episode moved along through the turns, the participants described aggressive responses as more likely to occur. The surprising finding, however, was that they also described escalating hostility as more desirable and advisable. They approved and would advise actions at the end of the episode that they certainly would not have at the beginning.

This study shows the emergent logic of interaction in improvised episodes. One speech act elicits another, that one yet another, and after three or more turns, the participants in the episode are engaging in actions that no one expected. While most studies have been done of negative or conflict-filled episodes, the same dynamic can sometimes produce episodes of surprising joy and beauty. But improvisation is not limited to being pushed by preceding acts into unexpected places. As Frank Barrett (1998) has shown, there is much more to improvisation than that.

Skillful improvisation involves creativity within a structure. We learn basic patterns of episodes as part of becoming a member of a family, an organization, or a culture. Our personalities can be described as those patterns that we have taken on board from the larger array of patterns provided by our society, as well as the unique blendings and tweakings that we have put upon them.

The serpentine model: As a way of showing what this model does, let's return to the story of Tina, Dennis, and Rolf (see figure 6.6). Tina has decided that she has no choice but to attend the meeting that Dennis has announced, but she thinks she might have some options about what to do in the meeting. In one way of punctuating the episode, the first turn is Rolf's presentation at the meeting. At this moment, Tina is willing to frame the meeting as a consultation between Rolf and the division managers, but she is hoping to find a critical moment in which she can introduce her concerns about her division. As she sees it, if she is able to express her concerns, this will still be within an episode of "consultation."

Rolf doesn't see the episode beginning with his presentation at the meeting. His story is that the episode began nearly a year earlier; that the Strategic Initiative is the most important thing being done in the corporation; that he has the responsibility for making it work and if he fails, the corporation may go bankrupt; that his division, working with senior management, has done months of careful research and planning on the Strategic Initiative; and that this meeting is a courtesy to the other division managers in which he is taking time to explain to them what they will need to do to support the Strategic Initiative. He expects them to have questions about some of the controversial aspects of the plan, and is confident that he and his three assistants, who are with him in the meeting, can answer them satisfactorily by describing the research and scenario-building processes on which those decisions were based.

In what I've called turn (1) but which Rolf would see as very late in the unfolding of the episode, Rolf distributes a glossy bound document and

Rolf's story of the episode

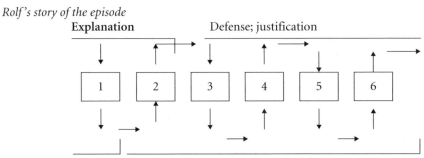

Tina's story of the episode

Figure 6.6 The serpentine model (partial)

uses a combination of video and PowerPoint presentation to lay out his plan for the initiative over the next five years. This turn takes about 45 minutes. The final ten minutes consists of a summary of what each of the other divisions will need to do and ends when he asks, "Are there any questions?"

Tina's division has been struggling with its assignment for the past two years. She and her management team are convinced that the diversion of corporate resources into the Strategic Initiative has crippled their ability to take the necessary steps for them to respond to changing market structures that they face. She has been frustrated because the Senior Management team has turned down her requests for additional resources, and when she has asked about the Strategic Initiative, she has been told that they are not yet ready to consult with other divisions. She is willing to participate in a consultation if it gives her a long-overdue opportunity to present the needs of her division.

But the manner as much as the content of Rolf's presentation offends her so much that she finds it impossible to sustain the framing of the episode as a "consultation." She interprets Rolf's long presentation in turn (1) as inconsistent with a consultation; she sees the plan being presented as a completed whole. She is offended by Rolf's list of things that she and the other division managers will need to do to support the plan, seeing it as his personal attempt to exercise more power than he has in the management structure. And she is enraged that, once again, she is being denied an opportunity to present her division's needs for increased resources; to the contrary, Rolf's plans require her to divert some of her already inadequate resources to support his initiative.

She feels a very strong sense that she "ought" to interrupt the corporation's implementation of this plan in order to create an opportunity for the entire management team to discuss the "costs" of the Strategic Initiative. When Rolf ends turn (1) with an invitation for other division heads to comment, she speaks up. In turn (2), she announces her decision to *refuse to comply* with Rolf's *demands* for her division, *insists* that the entire Strategic Initiative plan be reviewed by the division managers, and *denounces* the assumptions and decisions on which the plan is based. (I've italicized the speech acts.)

Rolf is surprised and offended by what he perceives as Tina's unwarranted *attack* on the plan. He is no longer in a mood of "consultation" but, in turn (3), he angrily *defends* the plan, citing all the research and planning that has gone into it, asking his assistants if they agree, and making clear that the plan is based on research and scenario-building that Tina doesn't know about.

Rolf's claim, in turn (3), that she doesn't know enough about the plan to criticize it infuriates Tina. In the fourth turn, she gives a lengthy description of the many times in which she has sought information about the plan, only to be rebuffed by Dennis, who supervises them both. She characterizes the Strategic Initiative as Rolf's naked power grab with the intention of utilizing the resources of her division for his own purposes.

The episode that is being called into being is far from what either person had in mind when the meeting began. By the fifth turn in this episode, the specifics of the Strategic Initiative are irrelevant; the logical force generated by Rolf and Tina's argument is propelling the episode.

Logical force and contexts: These relationships can be depicted in the manner shown in figure 6.7, where the arrows indicate some sense of "oughtness." For convenience, we can distinguish various parts of logical force. In the second turn in any three-turn sequence, you will probably feel some force to act or not act in certain ways because of what happened in turn (1): that's *prefigurative force (a)*. As you decide what to do in turn (2), you may feel that your choices are shaped by your expectations or hopes for what the other person will do in turn (3). Perhaps you'll act so that the other will respond in a certain way. That's *practical force (b)*. To some extent, what you can and cannot do is guided by the episode you are enacting. Because it is the episode of, for example, asking the bank for a loan, you feel that you must tell them more about your financial circumstances than you otherwise would. This is *contextual force (c)*. Finally, you may decide that you didn't want a loan after all and that you want to change the episode from "ask for a loan" to "get some financial advice." In order to change the episode from what it currently is to something else, you feel that you may refuse to give them your financial information and must do something that calls the new episode into being – for example, offering them a contract for a consultation. This is *implicative force (d)*.

In the situation described above, Tina was prepared to work within an episode of interdivisional consultation. However, Rolf's glossy bound document, PowerPoint presentation and the trio of obsequious assistants had sufficient *implicative force* that it changed her definition of the episode. By changing the meaning, it created a critical incident in which she had to choose how to act. In this situation, she felt a strong *contextual force* to defend her division and resist Rolf's power-play.

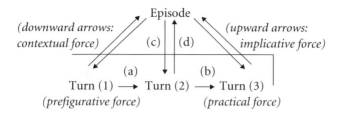

Figure 6.7 Schematic model of logical force

Rolf apparently doesn't interpret Tina's actions in turn (2) as a defense of her division. He is surprised and confronted with a bifurcation point of his own. He has to come up with a story about what's going on, and, on the basis of that story, decide what to do.

Let's assume that Rolf hesitates for just a few seconds before acting in turn (3). He is engaging in "ante-narrative," as we discussed it in chapter 5. He's interpreting what is happening, imagining several possible things he might do, and anticipating the likely consequences of each.

This is what might be going on during this moment. Rolf perceives Tina as performing a petulant attack on him personally, motivated by jealousy at his being chosen for the responsibility of the Strategic Initiative and lingering resentment because he broke off their engagement. But he realizes that if he acts out of this story, it will bring into the open a lot of things that he would prefer the other division managers not to know. So even though he thinks that this is the "real story," he chooses to act as if he interpreted her as attacking the professional competence with which he and his team have developed the Initiative, so he responds in turn (3) with a defense of the data and assumptions on which the planning was based.

Regardless of what he and Tina do, the episode that they realize in that conference room will have an afterlife that will shape the future of the company and their careers.

Patterns of Communication

Episodes cluster with others that are like them. Whatever we call it – and I favor the terms "grammar of action" or "family resemblances" suggested by Ludwig Wittgenstein (*Stanford Encyclopedia of Philosophy* 2002) – there is some connection that makes some episodes virtually substitutable for each other and others strikingly different experiences (Forgas 1976, 1979; Boynton and Pearce 1978). We are only now developing a language that names and makes useful discriminations among episodes that share common characteristics. Some of the names in play among the people with whom I work include dialogue, deliberation, discussion, debate, negotiation, mediation, argument, control-and-report, decide-advocate-defend, public education, seminar, lecture-discussion, and collaboration. I wonder if you share my observation that, when it comes to episodes, like attracts like. That is, you are far more likely to find a second dialogic episode in a family or organization in which you've already found the first one; one argument seems to lead to another; and those who give commands also take them.

Let "patterns of communication" be a general category name for clusters of episodes that have a strong family resemblance. How many patterns of communication are there? I think they are like speech acts in that there can be an infinite number. But, unlike speech acts, I think patterns of communication are emergent functions that, once developed, maintain their boundaries and resist change by actively attracting episodes that share their central characteristics and repelling those that differ or would change them. I'm speaking from the center of my belief but beyond the limits of my data here, so let me share some learnings as support even if I don't have proof.

I spent some time working with a marriage counselor who told me that he was particularly attentive to his clients' use of the words "always" and "never." In the early stages of a relationship, he explained, every moment is new and fresh, and we remember them all. However, after a while, there are so many experiences that we have to "chunk" them, so we emplot them as what the other "always" or "never" does. While this may be cognitively efficient, it also makes it less likely that we will notice when the other does something that they "never" do, so we begin to reinforce our perceptions. And since we act out of our beliefs, we then act in ways that invite the other to respond as we expect, and when they do . . . well, you see the self-confirming and socially-constructing cycle that emerges. Assume that this cycle has dominated a couple's life for many years, but has brought them to a point of unhappiness such that they seek counseling. My friend told me that he observes what hard work it is for these couples to undo the form of communication that has emerged and to replace it with another. This form of communication comprises the family culture.

Once formed, forms of communication invite others like them and resist those that differ from them. As I write, the form of communication in the Federal Government of my country is so polarized that it is difficult to deal with any issue on its merits. One recent example was the nomination of Samuel A. Alito, Jr., to be a member of the Supreme Court. Even those who seemed to be commenting on his qualifications were clearly pushing partisan agendas. I watched this process very carefully to see if anyone would attempt to engage in genuine deliberation about his qualifications, and if so, whether that attempt would be transformed by the form of communication so that it would become just another way of doing the same thing. I didn't find any evidence of effective attempts to go against the grain of the dominant form of communication: what might have been an array of good reasons to support or oppose his nomination was replaced by lists of financial and political forces lined up to support or oppose him. These are quite different forms of communication.

Forms of communication are not neutral; they enable and impede what happens in them. I've argued that there is a direct, reciprocal causal relationship between forms of communication and (the equally abstract concept) ways of being human (Pearce 1989). One way of naming forms of communication uses the terms *monocultural, ethnocentric* (and its modern variant, *neo-traditional*), *modernistic,* and *cosmopolitan.*

Organizational ethicist Marvin Brown (2005: ch. 2) used these forms in his analysis of corporate integrity. I'm going to draw on his striking image of a trade show, where various companies are presenting themselves and their products. The conference hall has four exhibits, each from a different company.

Exhibit A contains a storyboard describing the company; all of the exhibitors are wearing identical company sweaters and are talking to each other.

Exhibit B also has a storyboard describing the sponsoring company and its growth, but this storyboard also includes the story of its competitors. Charts and graphs show that the competitors are inferior companies. Visitors to this booth are welcomed with a guide, showing them exactly how they are to move through it; there seems to be one, right way to do things. The last station on the tour involves a survey, and all of the questions have a "right or wrong" flavor to them.

Exhibit C is filled with the latest gadgets. In fact, we see the original display being taken down and replaced with one even more colorful and with more recent information than the one that was erected only a few hours ago. Everyone seems too busy to welcome visitors to the exhibit and some are engaged in a heated debate about the merits of the new product line. However, there is an interactive computer-projected display on the wall – whups, it was just revised by one of the exhibitors, working on her laptop.

Exhibit D seems at first much more disorderly than the others. There are lots of charts, pamphlets, books, CDs scattered about, and visitors are invited to leaf through them and read or watch what they like. The centerpiece of the display is a circle of chairs in which a number of people are engaged in earnest conversation. It's hard to tell the exhibitors from the visitors, except that the hosts make sure that there is at least one empty chair in the circle, which functions as an invitation to others to join the conversation.

According to Brown, Exhibit A displays monocultural communication; Exhibit B ethnocentric; Exhibit C modernistic; and Exhibit D cosmopolitan communication. Clearly, your experience as a visitor is different in each of these forms of communication. Each structures a social world that has distinctive features and these features make some ways of being and some episodic patterns difficult and others easy. One of the most striking differences among these forms of communication is the way they deal with differences.

Every once in a while – often while watching the antics of actors on televised commercials – my wife and I look at each other and say "we must be aliens." We feel that we have different motivations and different expectations of how to act than the simplistic portrayals of people in this thin slice of popular culture. And we suspect that everyone in contemporary society feels "different" from some of the others.

As a pattern of communication, monocultural communication makes it difficult to perceive or acknowledge differences. Everyone else "should" be a "native" in our culture; they should perceive things in the same way, like the same things, and know the same things. Actions outside the normal pattern are often simply not noticed.

Ethnocentric patterns of communication, on the other hand, are very sensitive to differences. They tend to structure the social world in sharp dichotomies: "us" vs. "them"; "right" vs. "wrong"; and "good" vs. "evil." If you are part of "us," you are expected to agree and conform; if you don't, you are likely to be perceived as part of "them," and "they" are almost always worse than "us."

Modernistic communication celebrates difference – for a while. Like a consumer alert for the new fashion, those engaging in this form of communication quickly tire of new things and look for things even newer. They see disagreements as problems to be solved so that we can "progress." People are seen as virtuous if they "make a difference" or "make things happen," and objects and people are evaluated in terms of where they stand in relation to progress.

Cosmopolitan communication patterns see differences as normal and as sites for exploration. In this form of communication, one would not expect or want to "resolve" differences. Instead, the challenge is to find ways of coordinating with each other in a social world that has in it many different social worlds, and in which people not only are different, but should be different.

This way of naming different forms of communication is useful for some purposes, but surely not for others, and I'm very interested to know how others would sort them out.

The preceding sentence was, of course, appropriate for cosmopolitan communication; it would seem silly or perhaps even evil from the perspective of other forms of communication. And that's the point. These forms of communication are not benign; they are integrally related to the forms of consciousness and relational minds discussed in the following chapters.

Personally, I believe that the world is far too complex and dangerous for us to adopt a laissez-faire approach to forms of communication. The issues confronting us – as individuals, as families, as nations, as a civilization – are too important to stuff them into inadequate forms of communication. My own professional practice as a consultant and facilitator attempts to spur the evolution of forms of communication toward what I'm here calling cosmopolitan communication and sometimes call dialogic communication. As a cosmopolitan communicator, I acknowledge that this choice is not the one that everyone would make, and I seek to coordinate my actions with those who disagree rather than trying to persuade or coerce them into agreeing with me.

But I'm delighted that more and more people seem to be reaching the conclusion that it is useful to distinguish among forms of communication and that these forms are consequential. In my view, learning how to do episode-work is the first step in being able to call into being preferred forms of communication, and being able to call into being preferred forms of communication is a key step in making better social worlds.

Making Better Social Worlds

I believe that the material in his chapter can be used in many ways to help us discern critical moments and to act wisely in them. Let me bring this discussion of episodes and forms of communication to an end by pointing out just two ways of making better social worlds using some of the concepts and models presented in this chapter.

Freeing us up so that we can make wiser choices

The same "glue" that holds episodes together – logical force – limits and shapes what we can do at specific moments during the episode. That is, if I am in an argument, I feel that I have to contradict what you've just said, or if I'm in a negotiation, I feel that there are options on the table that I have to reject or accept. My feeling of oughtness, as studies of family violence have shown, may be so powerful that I may do things that I would never do in other circumstances, or I may deliberately do something (because a person like me in a situation like this *must!*) that is clearly not in my own best interest.

Our social worlds are filled with conditions and patterns of interaction that no one would freely choose. I'm thinking of the desperate poverty in urban slums; the lack of resources in remote villages; and the fear and violence of prolonged war or from state-sponsored terrorism. I believe that these conditions are made, and they persist because those who make them feel that they must act in the way that they do. That is, my chosen hypothesis is that all of us, even those involved in making horrible conditions, are doing what we think we should or must.

This hypothesis implies that it doesn't help us to think of people who do bad things as bad people, or to attempt to correct intolerable conditions by removing the people responsible. A more effective way – if we can forgo our thirst to administer punishment – is to change the logical force that makes them think that they must do what they do. That is, if we think of people as players in the various social games that make up our society, we would do better to change the games so that they have to play by different rules rather than convince them to not to play or to play in such a way that they lose. So how can we change the games or, less metaphorically, free us all from the logical force that compels us to act in ways that have undesirable outcomes?

There are many ways, of course. The one I'll talk about here is a procedure that consultants use in working with clients. For purposes of illustration, let's pick up the story of Tina, Rolf, and Dennis. After the meeting, Rolf goes back to his office, frustrated and angry at what happened. He's not sure what to do, so he calls Ingrid, an internal consultant with the company, and asks her to meet with him.

Ingrid's practice is based on CMM. Her first assumption is that Rolf's social world is organized in such a way that he is experiencing it as a problem. Perhaps he feels blocked; perhaps he feels that he's caught up in an ongoing social pattern that he doesn't like or that has undesirable consequences; perhaps he feels that he's being called upon to play a role he doesn't like. She deliberately takes a position of not knowing what is going on or what Rolf should do. Acting out of that position, she can invite Rolf to become aware of and take appropriate responsibility for the way he's emplotted the episodes of which he is a part. We might call her strategy "de-emplotment" leading to "re-authoring" the story of what is going on. During this process, Ingrid believes, Rolf will identify critical moments that will provide him the opportunity to make a different social world.

Ingrid asks Rolf to meet her in a conference room equipped with a whiteboard and markers. She asks him to start at the beginning and tell her what happened that made him decide that a consultation might be helpful. As he tells the story, she constructs the time-line that is the heart of the serpentine model, first starting with a turn-by-turn sequence of what happened. She helps him tell the story by gently directing his attention away from his interpretations and toward a more objective description of what people actually said and did. She reinforces the notion of sequence – what came before and after other things. Her part of the conversation consists of statements like "and then what happened?" and "you've told me that this . . . and then this . . . did something happen between?" She offers him the marking pen and invites him to help her plot out the story in the chronological sequence in which it occurred. She knows, from her own experience and that of others in this tradition of practice, that Rolf's first telling of the story will leave out many turns and reverse the sequence of many turns. By using the time-line, she has already performed an intervention that causes him to become aware of that part of the way he's emplotted the story. She also inquires about his punctuation. "Is this where you think the story begins?" she asks.

When she and Rolf think they have described the sequence of events well enough, Ingrid begins working with the hierarchy model. With "speech acts" in mind, she asks Rolf to name what was "done" in each turn, knowing that each name that he gives embeds a larger story. She listens carefully while they move through the sequence of turns in the episode, and picks what seems to her one or more turns that might well have been critical moments. She asks Rolf to elaborate on the stories that are embedded in those turns, perhaps prompting him to differentiate among stories about what is going on (episode), about the people involved, and about the relationships among them. She treats these stories as contexts for the actions.

She asks Rolf to articulate the stories embedded in the actions taken by other people in the episode as well as by himself. She doesn't expect him to give very elaborate or rational stories about other people's motivations at first. Rather, she expects him to say that they are "just dumb" or "evil" or perhaps he will even say that he can't imagine what story they would tell. As the consultation goes on, however, she listens carefully to see when his stories about the other people become richer, more human and less dismissive. This is a sign that the logical force that has had him in its grasp is loosening.

To change the story (and the serpentine model they are jointly drawing on the board) from a flat plane to a three-dimensional model, Ingrid invites Rolf to explore the logical force that various people were feeling at specific turns. She doesn't use the term "logical force" of course (unless she knows that Rolf has been in a CMM training session, which makes all of this work much easier!), but she differentiates between feeling that one has to do something "because of" what has already happened (prefigurative and contextual force) and what one has to do "in order to" bring something else about (practical and implicative force). She brings some colored marking pens to indicate the difference, making lighter or darker marks to indicate the strength of the logical force.

When she thinks that Rolf has de-emplotted the episode sufficiently to be able to re-author it, she goes back to the turn(s) that she thinks were the most significant critical moments. "What other things might you (or he or she) have done in this turn?" she asks. She encourages Rolf to be creative and playful, imagining a slightly wider range of possibilities than are likely. Then she asks what story would be embedded in these hypothetical alternative actions. Her purpose is to create a rich range and variety of stories; their content is less important than the activity of developing multiple stories.

At this point, Rolf might start offering revised stories about what happened in the meeting. Ingrid listens politely as he does, but keeps their conversation moving on. When she thinks that Rolf is ready, she invites him to look at the whole serpentine model and comment on it. She might direct his attention to the context markers that show when the episode changed from one thing to another; or to the pattern of logical force.

At this point, Ingrid can make choices about how to continue the conversation with Rolf, but notice that what she's done has been to ask questions that invite him to think about the situation and the patterns of communication in it. She has deliberately avoided anything like "instructing" him or "persuading" him what to do. Using the concepts and tools of CMM, she's enriched his understanding of the episode that he found problematic and she's worked to prevent him from re-authoring his story prematurely. As a result, Rolf is in a position to choose more wisely how to act into the critical moments that will occur "next" in this situation.

Calling better patterns of communication into being

In the description of Ingrid's work with Rolf, I said that this work is made easier if the client knows the concepts and tools of CMM. I think that's true, and that it has two important implications. First, the consultant can and should be totally transparent. There is nothing sneaky about this way of working, and its effect does not depend on doing something out of the awareness of the client. Among other things, that makes life easier for consultants. Second, clients can learn and internalize these concepts and tools, becoming able to use them with less or no help from a consultant. In fact, with some practice, at least some clients will learn to use these tools just-in-time, during the problematic episode, acting wisely into the situation as it develops.

So what happens if many clients learn these tools and use them, just-in-time, in many of the difficult situations in which they find themselves? My joking answer is that consultants will work themselves out of their jobs! It's a joke, because the need is sufficiently great and the learning curve sufficiently slow that we have a good bit of job security. My real answer is that we will start having a greater ratio of better episodes in our social worlds and better forms of communication will emerge. And that's a very good thing.

I believe that practitioners, in their knowledge of how to plan and facilitate meetings and conferences, are far ahead of scholars in their ability to describe and explain what is happening in these more productive and pleasant meetings and conferences. For example, we know that a potentially conflicted episode works better if people discuss their interests before announcing their positions, and that this episodic pattern can occur at the family dinner table, in the corporate boardroom, and in international trade or military negotiations (Spangler 2003). And we know that there is a reciprocal causal relationship between the kinds of communication that occur and the kinds of skills that people develop (Siegel 1999). So we can imagine a spiral in which more and more people are invited into better forms of communication and learn the skills needed for this kind of communication, so they create those forms of communication and invite others into them . . . and so it goes until what I've called "cosmopolitan communication" (others might call it something else, and that's OK) breaks out.

Collectively, we now know a good deal about how to initiate that upward spiral. Here's an example. On September 11, 2001, Reima was part of a surgical team performing an operation in the hospital where she worked. When she left the operating room, someone told her that airplanes had crashed into the World Trade Center in New York. Horrified, she joined other doctors and nurses in the staff lounge to watch the televised news coverage. Some time later, she described her experience this way:

> it is a very big room . . . and it was full of people. And they were showing the Towers coming down and all the people and the confusion and commotion, and for a second . . . everyone turned around and looked at me as though it was my fault. And standing there in that room . . . and these are the people I had worked with for over 20 years . . . I was actually for a moment, and I hate to use this word, I was actually scared . . . I was actually afraid of being there at that moment. . . . Because I could almost feel the hostility . . . And then you know it was either my imagination or it was true . . . I'm not sure but I don't think I could have imagined it all. (Wasserman 2004: 88)

Reima is a Muslim, and wears the distinctive headdress of her Pakistani heritage.

There are some forms of communication in which Reima would not feel comfortable telling this story, and some in which telling it would be perceived as the speech act *accusation*. But Reima joined an interfaith (Muslim, Christian, and Jewish) dialogue group that was dedicated to create – at least among themselves – a different form of communication at a time when the public discourse among these faiths was anything but dialogic.

In fact, Reima told the story in this group twice. Organizational consultant Ilene Wasserman asked the group to allow her to study their attempts to achieve dialogue. One of her findings was that "[r]eflection was a catalyst for storying and restorying dialogic moments" (Wasserman 2004: 160).

> When I asked people to tell me about a dialogic moment in the first individual interview, their first response was: "I don't think there has been one." Within seconds, they began to tell me a story. The very invitation to reflect on dialogic moments called forth a dialogic moment. A dialogic moment was not experienced as such until I asked the question. The question I asked, as well as the contexts in which it was asked, provided the logical force to construct, both individually and collectively, the dialogic moment. (Wasserman 2004: 161)

Having observed and interviewed the group, Ilene selected specific moments for the group to reflect upon. One of these was Reima's story, which she told again. Telling it in this context created an opportunity for an unusual and unusually profound experience of "meeting" among the people present which fit the description of dialogic moments:

> It is the experience of inventive surprise shared by the dialogic partners as each turns toward the other and both mutually perceive the impact of each other's turning. It is a brief interlude of focused awareness and acceptance of otherness and difference that somehow simultaneously transcends the perception of difference itself. (Cissna and Anderson 2002: 186)

The form of communication in this interfaith group encouraged dialogue and created spaces for the members of the group to explore themselves and their relationships with each other in a way strikingly different from the "normal" pattern of communication in the United States during this time. What would it be like if we woke each morning with the calm certainty that this form of communication was normal in our workplace? Would corporate or political decisions be wiser or less wise if those who made them engaged in cosmopolitan communication? If cosmopolitan communication (by whatever name) were normal in bars, on street corners, in schools, and in workplaces, what difference would it make as we read the newspapers each morning?

Notes

1   Technically, to say that "I will begin here, although there is no 'real' beginning" is part of the rhetorical genre of *aporia*. In this form of rhetoric, the speaker dwells on unanswered questions. In its trivial use, it is a way for a speaker to feign ignorance and seek to cajole the audience into "discovering" for themselves what the speaker wants them to believe. In its more serious sense, and the sense in which I suggest its use here, it is a way of clearly signaling the unfinishedness of the thing described, the incompleteness of the description, and the commitment of the speaker to remember that, when all that can be said and done has been, there is still much more to say and do. At least, that's *one* story about *aporia*.

2   This reminds me of the endless pattern of circle–square–circle–square in which we were trapped in the simulation in the chapter on coordination.

3   I don't know this young man's tribal identity and cannot attest to the accuracy of his description of his cultural norms. This was the story he told.

4   I'm patterning the term "episode-work" on Freud's (1990) "joke-work," which in turn was based on his notion of "dream-work." In each instance, it is the "work" that we do to make an episode, joke, or dream. However, I am not drawing further parallels between CMM and psychoanalysis.

References

Barrett, F. J. (1998), Creativity and improvisation in jazz and organizations: implications for organizational learning, *Organization Science*, 9: 605–22.

Bateson, G. (1972), A theory of play and fantasy. In *Steps to an Ecology of Mind*, New York: Ballantine, pp. 177–93.

Berger, P. L. and Luckmann, T. (1966), *The Social Construction of Reality: A Treatise on the Sociology of Knowledge*, Garden City, NY: Anchor Books.

Boynton, K. R. and Pearce, W. B. (1978), Personal transitions and interpersonal communication: a study of navy wives. In E. Hunter and S. Nice (eds.), *Military Families: Adaptation to Change*, New York: Praeger, pp. 130–41.

Brown, G. S. (1969/1994), *Laws of Form*, Portland, OR: Cognizer Press.

Brown, M. T. (2005), *Corporate Integrity: Rethinking Organizational Ethics and Leadership*, Cambridge: Cambridge University Press.

Carpenter, H. (2006), Reconceptualizing communication competence: high performing coordinated communication competence. PhD dissertation, Fielding Graduate University, Santa Barbara, CA.

Cissna, K. and Anderson, M. R. (2002), *Moments of Meeting: Buber, Rogers, and the Potential for Public Dialogue*, Albany: State University of New York Press.

Common Ground: Bridging the Partisan Divide in Washington (n.d.), retrieved from http://www.usatoday.com/news/opinion/common-ground-index.htm on September 6, 2006.

Cronen, V. E. (1998), Communication theory for the twenty-first century: cleaning up the wreckage of the psychology project. In J. S. Trent (ed.), *Communication: Views from the Helm for the 21st Century*, Needham Heights, MA: Allyn and Bacon, pp. 18–38.

Falk, W. (2005), While you were sleeping, *New York Times.* Retrieved from http://www.nytimes.com/2005/12/30/opinion/30falk.html?th&emc=th on December 20, 2005.

Forgas, J. P. (1976), The perception of social episodes: categorical and dimensional representations in two different social milieus, *Journal of Personality and Social Psychology*, 34: 199–209.

Forgas, J. P. (1979), *Social Episodes: The Study of Interaction Routines*, New York: Academic Press.

Freud, S. (1990), *Jokes and Their Relation to the Unconscious*, New York: W. W. Norton.

Goffman, E. (1974), *Frame Analysis*, Cambridge, MA: Harvard University Press.

Gumperz, J. J. (1975), Introduction. In P. Cole and J. L. Morgan (eds.), *Syntax and Semantics.* Vol. 3: *Speech Acts*, New York: Academic Press.

Hall, E. J. (1977), *Beyond Culture*, Garden City, NY: Anchor Press.

Harré, R. and Secord, P. (1973), *The Explanation of Social Behaviour*, Totowa, NJ: Littlefield, Adams.

Harris, L. M., Gergen, K. J., and Lannamann, J. W. (1986), Aggression rituals, *Communication Monographs*, 53: 252–65.

Internet Encyclopedia of Philosophy (2005), Paul Ricoeur: Time and Narrative. Retrieved from http://www.utm.edu/research/iep/r/ricoeur.htm#H5 on October 29, 2005.

Pearce, W. B. (1989), *Communication and the Human Condition*, Carbondale: Southern Illinois University Press.

Pearce, W. B. (2004), The coordinated management of meaning. In W. B. Gudykunst (ed.), *Theorizing about Intercultural Communication*, Thousand Oaks, CA: Sage, pp. 35–54.

Pearce, W. B. and Cronen, V. E. (1980), *Communication, Action and Meaning: The Creation of Social Realities*, New York: Praeger.

Pearce, W. B., Cronen, V. E., and Conklin, R. F. (1979), On what to look at when studying communication: a hierarchical model of actors' meanings, *Communication*, 4: 195–220.

Pearce, W. B., Harris, L. M., and Cronen, V. E. (1981), The coordinated management of meaning: human communication in a new key. In C. Wilder-Mottand and J. Weakland (eds.), *Rigor and Imagination: Essays in Communication from the Interactional View*, New York: Praeger, pp. 149–94.

Reynolds, C. (2001), Boids: background and update. Retrieved from http://www.red3d.com/cwr/boids/ on December 31, 2005.

Siegel, D. J. (1999), *The Developing Mind: How Relationships and the Brain Interact to Shape Who We Are*, New York: Guilford Press.

Spangler, B. (2003), Integrative or interest-based bargaining. In G. Burgess and H. Burgess (eds.), *Beyond Intractability*, Conflict Research Consortium, University of Colorado, Boulder. Retrieved from http://www.beyondintractability.org/essay/interest-based_bargaining/ on September 6, 2006.

Spano, S. (2001), *Public Dialogue and Participatory Democracy: The Cupertino Community Project*, Cresskill, NJ: Hampton Press.

Stanford Encyclopedia of Philosophy (2002), Ludwig Wittgenstein. Retrieved from http://plato.stanford.edu/entries/wittgenstein/#Lan on January 27, 2006.

Varela, F. J. (1979), *Principles of Biological Autonomy*, New York: Elsevier.

Wasserman, I. (2004), Discursive processes that foster dialogic moments: transformation in the engagement of social identity group differences in dialogue. PhD dissertation, Fielding Graduate University, Santa Barbara, CA.

Watzlawick, P., Beavin, J., and Jackson, D. D. (1967), *Pragmatics of Human Communication: A Study of Interactional Patterns, Pathologies, and Paradoxes*, New York: W. W. Norton.

Chapter 7

Selves and Forms of Consciousness

Preview

Our social worlds are polysemic – each part has multiple, often incompatible meanings. The same speech acts that are combined through punctuation and emplotment to form episodes are also, simultaneously, combined in different ways into selves and forms of consciousness. Like episodes, selves and forms of consciousness evolve in the networks of social relationships in which they occur. Unlike episodes, selves and forms of consciousness are embodied.

Selves are seen as emergent entities that have the capacity for continued transformation. Transformative learning is discussed as a particularly desirable form of development, one that supports the evolution of society "upward."

Continuing to describe how CMM concepts and tools can be used by sophisticated practitioners, this chapter extends the descriptions of logical force, speech acts and episodes, it further elaborates the hierarchy model, and introduces the daisy model.

Here I Am!

Pictures of animals were painted on the walls of Lascaux Cave about 35,000 years ago (Clottes 2001). Since the paintings included arrows and spears, it seems that they either recorded or perhaps magically invoked a successful hunt. Beside these pictures, however, is something different. Someone placed his or her hand firmly against the wall of the cave, filled his or her mouth with red-colored paint, and blew the paint against the wall, leaving a clear portrait of a human hand, fingers spread and pointing upward. What statement does this make? Was it a way of saying "here I am!" or "I did this!"?

The plaque attached to Pioneer 10, the first human-made object ever sent out of our solar system, contains a picture eerily similar to this prehistoric painting. A man and woman are sketched along with information the designers think will introduce us to any sentient species that finds the plaque. The man's hand is raised in a gesture identical to the hand painted in the cave. In this case, we know what it was intended to express: "This is me; here we are."[1]

Most of the events and objects of our social worlds don't call themselves "I" and can't recognize their reflection in a mirror as themselves (much less worry that they are losing their hair, decide that they need to lose a few pounds, or congratulate themselves for being so handsome). However, some things in our social worlds do all of these things and more. Some wrestle with questions about "Who am I?" "Where did I come from?" and "What will happen to me when I die?" Some write autobiographies and bore their friends with long stories about themselves. Some bitterly regret past decisions or firmly commit themselves to future objectives. The objects in our social worlds who can do these things are the topic of this chapter; let's call them "selves."

Humans have been preoccupied with understanding themselves, both individually and collectively, for at least as long as we have had written records, and longer, if my interpretation of the hand in the cave is correct. In the first part of this chapter, I don't think I'm adding anything new to this discussion, although I inevitably have to take sides in countless arguments. The discussion serves primarily to indicate some aspects of what we know about selves that are consistent with the communication perspective.

Anthropologists have long known that many cultures have institutionalized respect for elders. As a result of research in education and psychology, we're beginning to learn why that's such a good idea. The process of development in children doesn't stop when the child reaches a certain age – or, at least, it doesn't have to stop. Several lines of research are exploring qualitative changes in adults. Although many of the most important discoveries still lie ahead in this field, it bears directly on the thrust of this book. I believe that the continued development in adulthood passes through discontinuous steps and can be described as the emergence of new forms of consciousness.

Selves are Made in Processes of Communication

When you read the heading of this section, you might have said, "well, of course, they are." But this point of view has been hard-won in many circles, because it contradicts some basic ideas that have been institutionalized in Western society since the Enlightenment. For example, Thomas Hobbes (1651) wrote an essay about government, calling it *Leviathan*. He reflected the sentiment of his times by assuming that the primary entity was a solitary man, coming to knowledge by reflecting on himself and his experiences.[2] From this point of view, society is a device that individual men create and participate in as a "social contract" to stifle and regulate their individual urges. In various forms, this notion of individualism has been inscribed into many of the institutions and practices of Western civilization. Examples include the lyrics of the popular song "I did it my way"; the political principle of "one man, one vote"; and the legal principle that individuals (not families or corporations, for example) are responsible for crimes.

This radically individualist assumption is most powerful when it is taken for granted; once formally stated as a proposition for debate, it has been shown deficient. The Soviet-era psychologist Lev Vygotsky (1978) was one of the first to develop an empirically grounded description of the process by which selves are made in patterns of social interaction. He said:

> Every function in the child's cultural development appears twice: first, on the social level, and later, on the individual level; first, between people (interpsychological) and then inside the child (intrapsychological). This applies equally to voluntary attention, to logical memory, and to the formation of concepts. All the higher functions originate as actual relationships between individuals. (1978: 57)

Vygotsky focused primarily on children's development, and he described a process in which, at any moment, a child has a "zone of proximal development" (ZPD). That is, there are some (less complex) skills that a child can perform without assistance; a set of (more complex) skills that a child cannot – at that level of development – perform even with assistance; and a set of skills (of intermediate complexity) that a child can perform with assistance. This last is the ZPD, and if, for example, an adult helps a child exercise skills within that zone, the child acquires the ability to exercise them without help. That is, the ZPD evolves upward, and at least some of the skills previously unattainable even without help are now within the zone of proximal development.

Development isn't only a function of the presence of a facilitating adult, however. Researchers studying the development of children have noted that there seems to be a biological "readiness" for learning certain things. They've often used grammar in their research. Here's a research design that any of us can use. Ask a child to repeat sentences. Say "the same thing" but using different grammatical forms, such as "Juan hit the ball"; and "the ball was hit by Juan." At a certain level of development, the child will easily repeat the first but be unable to repeat the other. Come back six months later, and try again. It is often the case that now the child will be able to repeat both grammatical forms with no difficulty. I've used a similar strategy for older children. Instead of grammatical forms, I've asked them to explain a proverb, such as "a watched pot never boils." There is a time when such proverbs are simply incomprehensible. However, at some later time when I repeat the exercise, the child gives me a very good explanation – and often a puzzled look, something to the effect of "this is so obvious, Dad! I can't believe that you need me to explain it to you!"

There is every reason to assume that personal development continues in adulthood, and that adults can comprehend – effortlessly – situations that they could not have understood, even with help, at earlier stages of development. I also believe that this kind of development varies among people (that is, it is not linked only to chronological age) and is contextual (that is, we might perform at a very high level of development in one situation but at a much lower one in another). I believe that the level of development in which we are acting has much to do with our abilities to discern and act wisely into bifurcation points. I'll come back to this in the following section.

Because we live in a society that includes contradictory notions of what selves are and where they come from, we have every reason to be confused at times. For example, Eric and Tanya are a young married couple. Both are students in college. On a particular evening, Tanya noticed that Eric was sitting at his desk, ignoring the open textbook and computer in front of him, staring out the window.

Tanya: What's wrong?
Eric: Nothing, really, but . . . Sometimes I just don't understand myself. I worked hard to get to college, and now I'm working hard to support

us while I'm here . . . but sometimes I'm not sure that this is what I want to do.

Tanya: Are you having trouble with your studies?

Eric: No, that's not it. I'm doing well in my courses and I'm very interested in learning . . . but I feel myself changing. I'm not the same person who left home two years ago . . . I'm not the same person who made the decision to come to college . . . I've learned so much that those decisions seem naïve and uninformed. Should I remain committed to the decisions made by that immature and ignorant "me"? But it isn't just that I've learned more "facts"; I think about things differently, and I'm not sure whether I *like* the person I'm becoming. Frankly, it scares me! Who will I be in five years? If I work so hard to get my degree in physics, and then discover that I don't want to be a physicist, won't that be a stupid thing to have done? Five years from now, maybe I'll discover that I want to write poetry or teach literature! How can I make any plans when I feel myself so unstable? What happens to our relationship if I keep changing? Will you love me as a penniless but over-educated poet as much as you would if I were a world-famous physicist? Is it fair to you to ask you to be in a relationship with me if I'm changing as much as I am? Do you see why it's hard for me to focus on these quantum gravity calculations?

How should Tanya reply to Eric? Should she be frightened because he is so unstable? Should she draw back from their relationship so that she won't be so vulnerable? Or should she welcome the opportunity to participate in Eric's exploration and growth? Should she criticize him for being unable to know who he is, or should she bond with him more closely, glad that he is sensitive and open? (The alternatives in these questions that Tanya might ask are intended to express the incompatible paradigms of "self" in our culture.)

Tanya is also a student in college, studying social sciences. Hearing her silence, Eric asks her if there is anything in what she is studying that might help them sort through what is happening to him.

Tanya might tell him that some people think that the cartoon character Popeye summed up one of the most prevalent concepts of self in his enigmatic phrase, "I am what I am and that's all what I am." Clifford Geertz (1975) used a more complex vocabulary to describe this concept: "a bounded, unique, more or less integrated motivational and cognitive universe, a dynamic center of awareness, emotion, judgment, and action organized into a distinctive whole and set contrastively both against other such wholes and against a social and natural background" (1975: 48). One of the ways this concept is institutionalized is in the "Twenty questions test" (Sociology graduate students n.d.). On this basis, Eric would be told, "No worries, mate! We'll figure out who you are in just a minute. Now, take this piece of paper and complete the statement 'I am _____' twenty times."

Based on what he said, I think Eric would fail the "Popeye test" of self. I can imagine him writing, twenty times, "I am confused" and being told by the test administrator that he isn't being sufficiently cooperative.

The semantic differential is another questionnaire that institutionalizes this paradigm about the self (Heise 1970: 235–53). If Tanya brought in one of her friends to administer this test to Eric, he would be asked to rate himself on a series of bi-polar scales (warm–cold; strong–weak; etc.) separated by seven intervals. The test administrator would insert the results into his laptop computer, pull up the appropriate SPSS (Statistical Package for the Social Sciences) subroutine, and generate some numbers indicating the dimensions of Eric's concept of self, and how he scored on each of those dimensions.

I'm sure Eric would be relieved, and assure Tanya that, now that he has increased self-knowledge, she has nothing further to worry about. Sensing his sarcasm, Tanya consoles Eric by telling him that most of the social theorists during the last fifty years agree with him that this concept of self isn't very helpful. Flipping through her notes, she might read him these quotations:

> Poststructuralist authors as various as Roland Barthes, Jacques Lacan, Michel Foucault, and Jacques Derrida argued, not so long ago, that the autonomous subject of the humanist tradition, a subject capable of knowing both the world and itself, was a utopian dream of the European Enlightenment. This view of human subjectivity had to be abandoned in a period that recognized the existence of an unconscious mind, the opacity of language, and the role of discursive practices in the dissemination of social power. (Moxey 1999)

And,

> Traditional assumptions about the nature of identity are now in jeopardy. It is not simply that the present turn of events has altered the emphasis placed on rationality, the emotions, and the like, or that it adds new concepts to the traditional vernacular. Rather . . . the very idea of individual selves

– in possession of mental qualities – is now threatened with eradication. (Gergen 1991: x)

Even though he's not quite sure what these folks are talking about, Eric trusts that Tanya understands them and he feels better, knowing that he is not the only person to wonder who he is, or whether he even "has" a self. However, he's still not quite satisfied with the discussion so far. He asks Tanya, "OK, if the traditional notion of the autonomous self has been discredited, what has replaced it?"

Tanya hesitates, and says, "Yes, that's a good question, and lots of people are working on it." She tells him about Sheila McNamee and Ken Gergen's (1999) project of developing a concept of self as relational. She pulls their book, *Relational Responsibilities*, off her shelf and invites him to read how they are trying to develop a vocabulary that expresses this point of view. When Eric says, "Let's talk more now; maybe I'll read it later," she tells him about Gergen's (1991) *The Saturated Self*, in which he describes "multi-phrenia" – having multiple selves – as normal. This gets Eric interested; it sounds like a description of the way he's feeling. So Tanya opens the book to a passage she marked when she read it earlier and tells him that Gergen describes "multiphrenia" as including:

- *a vertigo of the valued*: the disorientation of what is good and important;
- *the expansion of inadequacy*: a pervasive feeling that you fail to measure up to some standard; and,
- *rationality in recession*: an inability to depend on reason because there are so many potential interlocutors who do not share the same standards for rationality (Gergen 1991: 71–9).

After they discuss this a bit, Tanya refers to the growing literature on adult development. She suggests that Eric think of his predicament as a part of a growth spurt rather than a problem, and reads this statement by psychologist Robert Kegan:

> every adult has a history of a number of extraordinary developmental transformations, and each transformation builds a more complex and elaborated edifice. The process of its undoing – the capacity of the universe to win through these increasingly complex defenses that have better and better ways of deluding us into the belief that we have grasped reality as it actually is – gets harder and harder to do. . . . The great glory within my own

field . . . has been the recognition that there are these qualitatively more complex psychological, mental, and spiritual landscapes that await us and that
we are called to after the first twenty years of life. (Debold 2002)

Eric is beginning to feel that his "problems" are really symptoms of
his strength; he is breaking through the patterns of meaning that might
have been sufficient at one time but are not any more. When he mentions
this, Tanya replies, "Yes, this reminds me of a very exciting group of people
using 'narrative' approaches. They start with the assumption that all of
us are deeply shaped by the stories of our culture, and that some of these
stories put us in situations that we describe as problems. Rather than seeing them as something wrong with us, however, they see us as living out
some – but not all – of the stories in our society. So what we need to do
is to find and 'thicken' our knowledge of some of the other stories in our
society that would lead us in another direction."

"I like that," Eric says. "It's not my fault that I'm confused; it is our
culture that is confused, and I'm just living out that confusion!"

"Well, something like that!" Tanya laughs. "But it is still your responsibility to find those stories that have led to 'unique outcomes' – that
is, people in your situation who were not confused – or to find some
'outsider witnesses' – people who have gone through this confusion and
survived it."

"That makes sense. But where do I find these stories and witnesses?" Eric
asks. "Lots of places," Tanya replies. "Let's see what we can find right now."

Going online, Tanya takes Eric to a website describing "Spiral
Dynamics" (Cowan and Todorovic 2006). This concept describes a series
of ever more complex and sophisticated developmental stages, evolving under
the pressures of the material and social conditions in which we live, and
equipping us to deal more adequately with the challenges we face.

At the very least, Tanya's review of this literature has made Eric feel
less lonely in his uncertainty about what it means to be a self. But it
hasn't helped him decide what he should do about his sense of changing,
and his shifting interests.

One of Tanya's courses taught her how to use some of the tools and
concepts from CMM, so she decides to do a consultation with Eric using
the daisy model. She takes out a large sheet of paper and draws a circle in
the middle of it, and writes "Eric" in the center. "OK, Eric," she says, "let's
talk about the other people in your life. Who's the closest person to you?"
"You are," he says. "Right answer!" she replies, "Now, who are some of

the other people that are close to you?" "Hmm. Well, my parents. Your parents. My friends Johannes and Peter. My professors."

As Eric is talking, Tanya has drawn something like figure 7.1, CMM's daisy model. It assumes that each event or object in the social world is a nexus of many conversations. Those who use this model have found that people seeking counsel usually have under-represented the social complexity of whatever it is that they are interested in, and that this model functions as a heuristic. Each conversation is depicted as a petal on the daisy. At this point in the use of the model, Tanya is only interested in identifying the petals. She'll come back and work with them later, and she expects Eric to remember more petals – some of which might be the most important ones – as they go along. However, she's curious about Eric's naming her parents before he named his friends, and she's struck by the way he identified his professors as a group rather than differentiating among them. Perhaps these aren't important features of his story, but she'll remember and return to them.

Tanya continues asking Eric to identify other people who are important to him until he starts to have difficulty naming them. Drawing in a couple of empty petals, she says, "If you think of any more, tell me and we can add them."

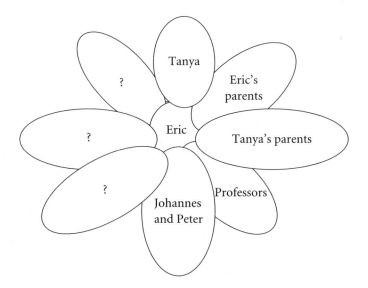

Figure 7.1 The daisy model of Eric's relationships

Depending on the situation and purpose, a CMM-based analyst can work with the daisy model in many different ways. This analysis isn't driven by the need for Eric to make a specific decision or to resolve a particular problem, so Tanya doesn't feel any need to lead him in the conversation. Rather, she decides just to help him enrich his thinking about his situation. She asks, "As you look at the daisy model, how does the number of relationships you have strike you? Does it seem like a lot or not very many?" Eric replies, "Actually, I was thinking about that. It doesn't seem like very many. Between working and going to school, my time is pretty well accounted for, isn't it? I just don't do much with people." "I notice that you didn't identify anybody from work on this model," Tanya says. "Hmm. You're right. For me, working there is just a way of earning money; I don't really have much of a relationship with anyone there," Eric replies. "Are there any other people or activities that you haven't listed?" "Yeah! Now that you mention it, I haven't mentioned anyone that I'm taking classes with."

Tanya knows that some relationships are stronger and more important than others. She suggests that Eric take the pen and darken the shape of those petals that he thinks are most important. She's pleased that he first darkens the petal containing her name, and then notices that he identifies his parents and his professors as the other two important relationships. She thinks about asking him about the ways in which these two groups are alike and different, and thinks that might generate some interesting information.[3] But she chooses to talk about each one separately before comparing them. "Tell me about a typical episode in your relationship with your professors," she asks, and as he replies, she takes out another piece of paper and sketches the serpentine model. When they have finished with that, she repeats the process with a typical episode with his parents. Putting the two serpentine models side by side, she asks him if he sees any similarities between them. Specifically, she inquires about the "self" that he is called to be in these relationships. "What expectations do they have for you? What hopes do they have for you? What demands do they put on you that you don't want to or can't meet?"

When they've finished this conversation, Tanya asks Eric to reflect on it, and, when he is ready, to tell her what he thinks. She then goes back to her homework, but before she can start, Eric says, "Hmm. I've just figured something out," and they continue the conversation.

In this extended example, I wanted to show you one way (repeat: ONE way) of using CMM's daisy model to create an enriched conversation about any event or object in the social world, and to show how it can be used to help a client position himself or herself in the middle of potentially conflicting social pressures. It is based on the assumption that selves are made in communication, and that by bringing those patterns of communication into discourse, we can enable ourselves to understand who we are.

Forms of Consciousness Emerge in Processes of Communication

Every parent knows (or, at times, hopes or prays, or finds consolation in believing!) that selves develop over time, and that, in general, this development is from the simple and undifferentiated toward more complex forms. Sometimes it is easy to identify when such a step in the evolution has occurred. Recently, when our son was 16, he began going to the grocery store and purchasing foods that he likes rather than asking us to do it for him, and words like "responsibility" began to appear in his conversation with us. Just as his body changed dramatically a few years ago (transforming a short, chubby boy into a tall, muscular young man), so the consciousness in which he sees himself and the world around him has evolved – and continues to evolve.

Adults continue to evolve, or at least they can, and I believe that the emergence of more sophisticated forms of consciousness is extremely important if we are to make better social worlds. I am excited to know that there are good people working to describe and study the course of this evolution of consciousness, even if I believe that they are far from having it all figured out. By putting these ideas together with some CMM tools and concepts, we can enhance our ability to act wisely into critical moments.

My certainty about the evolution of consciousness is based more on my life experiences and work as a facilitator and trainer than it is on findings of research done by scholars. When teaching people how to facilitate dialogic communication, for example, it isn't hard to recognize that participants bring different forms of consciousness to the task. In my experience, these differences do not involve age, intelligence, or amount of education. They have more to do with the ability to see around the corners of one's own beliefs, to hold contradictory thoughts in awareness simultaneously without stress, to differentiate between understanding another's point of view and agreeing with it, and to acknowledge that there is something more beyond the limits of one's own ability to perceive and know. I've drawn on the literatures of adult learning and development for a vocabulary of naming some of these differences in forms of consciousness.

I noted the same differences in my research, particularly in my studies of what Stephen Littlejohn and I (Pearce and Littlejohn 1997) called "moral conflict." For example, the conflict between the religious right and those that they call "secular humanists" or, more recently, "liberals" in my country isn't only or even primarily about disagreements about specific policy issues. If it were, they would be able to work out solutions that support the legitimate interests of all sides and, when that work was over, they wouldn't hate, fear, or distrust each other as is the case in the Federal Government at the moment. Instead, the heart of the issue is a clash of two forms of consciousness, one of which can't understand the other (as a preteen can't understand proverbs) and one which remembers the other as having a limited and limiting way of being in the world from which they have gratefully moved on.

I'll continue this analysis of moral conflict after looking at some of the concepts that help us name and differentiate among forms of consciousness. Robert Kegan (Debold 2002) describes a series of transformations in our "epistemology," a technical term that he defines as the dynamic "process by which we *make* reality, the process by which we *create* knowledge." This process involves the way we understand the relation between our selves (the "subject," or the "I" who makes reality) and objects (the happenings and things in our social worlds that we know in our epistemologies, including the "me" that "I" know myself to be). Our epistemologies comprise "the very shape of the window or lens through which one looks at the world. A given subject–object relationship establishes the shape of the window."

As these transformations occur, Kegan said, we don't just add more and more to think *about*, but we experience a shift in *how to think* about them. "Each qualitative move takes a whole mental structure that had been experienced as subject and shifts it so that it becomes seen as object. We feel liberated from the limitations of the earlier epistemology. Perceived as an object, we gain the ability to name our commitments such that we are able to *have* those epistemologies that formerly *had us*." In the early stages of development, Kegan (Debold 2002) says, we confuse the lens for the thing seen; that is, we mistake our epistemology for the world that it reveals. "We take our way of *composing* reality to be *reality*. The great embarrassment or liberation of transformation itself is the recognition that what we have been taking as reality is actually only a *construction* of reality."

Kegan (Debold 2002) describes a rhythm in the development of different subject–object relations, in which the first and last are similar in that the self and object are seen as essentially the same, although they affirm this unity in strikingly different ways. "We start," he said, "from a position, in earliest infancy, where there's absolutely no subject–object distinction at all, because the infant's knowing is entirely subjective. There's no 'not me,' no internal vs. external. There's no distinction, for example, in the source of the discomfort caused by bright light or hunger in the belly. There's no distinction between self and other.... The ultimate state of development would have to do with some way in which the self has become entirely identified with the world. It would be the recognition essentially of the oneness of the universe." Between these epistemologies are several in which subject and object are differentiated. These include:

- *socialized self:* in which we develop the complexity to internalize and identify with the values of our surround; to be a member of the tribe;
- *self-authoring self:* in which we have an internal authority by which we ourselves are able to name what is valuable, or respond to the claims and expectations on us, sort through them, and make decisions about which ones we will and will not follow; we are not just made up by or written on by a culture, but we ourselves become the writer of a reality that we then are faithful to; and,
- *self-transforming self:* in which we come to perceive the limits of self-authoring and the partiality of even our own internal system even though, like any good system, it has the capacity to handle all the "data" and make systematic, rational sense of our experience. This self is much more friendly to contradiction, to oppositeness, to being able to hold on to multiple systems of thinking; it is much more about movement through different forms of consciousness than about defending and identifying with any one form.

For me, it's useful to remember that these are "epistemologies," or ways in which selves understand the world, not a set of propositions describing attributes of objects called selves. That is, a person doing "self-authoring" is not inviting debate about the proposition that we can become a writer of a reality; he or she is living in a particular way. If someone were to formulate that way of life as a proposition and challenge it, the best response would be to "report" how one lives and "invite" the other to try it.

Although I believe that Kegan is on to something very important here, I have a sense that these descriptions of epistemologies and forms of consciousness should be handled gently. Perhaps they are results of an initial reconnaissance rather than the final word about these matters, or perhaps these are things capable of being described, with equal validity, in many different ways. But with this caution, Kegan's descriptions of these epistemologies track very well on to my experience. I've known devout Christians who are best described as "self-transforming" and devout Buddhists who are best described as "socialized," and vice versa, and I've known devout Muslims that use each of these epistemologies. I believe that every major belief system and culture contains sufficient resources to constrict selves into predetermined patterns (socialized self) and to support the evolution of selves into other forms of consciousness.

This takes me back to my studies of the moral conflict between the religious right and liberal humanists in the United States (Pearce, Littlejohn, and Alexander 1987). Moral conflicts are fueled by "emergent interactional logics" (as described in chapter 6). Here's a rather free description of the logic of this conflict as it has played out in the United States since 1980. The claims made by the religious right appear morally simplistic and offensive to the liberals. They feel compelled to *inform* the members of the right about how narrow-minded they are and to *warn* other people not to listen to them. Predictably, the members of the religious right are outraged because the liberal response is personally *insulting* and also *disrespectful* of their religious beliefs. Angered, they believe that the liberals have destroyed any possibility of civil discourse, so they think that anything they want to do is permissible. They are clever and creative in finding ways to *discomfort* and *disempower* the liberals, and take great pride in their ability to *retaliate*. Some of the things they do seem mean-spirited even to members of the movement, but they justify them by remembering what "they" did to "us." Liberals are offended and frightened that the emergence of the religious right will undo hard-won gains in social policies. Often justifying what they are doing as being for the greater good rather than for their own sakes, they lash back as effectively as they can. And so it goes.

Moral conflict can occur between groups at the same level of consciousness. But it is even more likely and more intractable when they are not, because incomprehension occurs, particularly when one or the other side attempts to end the conflict. For example, participants in any conflict have to make the choice to "express" their position or to "suppress" it (Pearce and Littlejohn 1997: 132–46). I put the terms in quotation marks because what this choice entails, and the options that the participants have to choose between, look different depending on the form of consciousness of the participant.

The tension between expression and suppression looks like a clear choice between *fighting* and *surrendering*, with no third position possible, in the form of consciousness that Kegan (1994) described as the third level of cognitive development. In this epistemology, moral choices are expected to be between clear alternatives; the issue is less about knowing what to do than it is about having courage to hold to the decision once it is made. Sincerity, consistency, and simplicity are virtues. The world is divided into two sides, me and mine against all others, and there is a tinge of paranoia in it: those not with me are against me. As an extreme example of actions consistent with this form of consciousness, a person supporting legislation to restrict public services for homosexuals was invited to come to a "community conversation" about the topic. She replied, "In all moral conscience, I cannot agree to come and talk about this with someone who may think differently than I do. I just can't do that" (transcribed from Fort and Skinner-Jones 1993).

The same tension between expression and suppression looks very different in the form of consciousness that Kegan (1994) called the fourth level of cognitive development. In this epistemology, the choice is between *opposing* the other group and *making peace* with them. Peacemaking requires the ability to see that both sides may have excellent reasons for their positions, and that neither side has a corner on truth. Peacemakers are more interested in creating options and making sure that the best is chosen rather than engaging in conflict and seeing who wins. They attempt to create processes (like dialogue or deliberation) in which all sides can participate fully. For example, the person who organized the "community conversation" referred to in the preceding paragraph, Theresa Jensen, explained her purpose like this:

> We did stress that we were asking people to try having a real dialogue, a conversation, with each other in a real way. If you can create a safe atmosphere where they can really be honest and talk about how an issue affects them, how an issue impacts them, their lives, then those two people, I think, can start seeing each other in a new way and some individual empathy can start to happen. (transcribed from Fort and Skinner-Jones 1993)

Theresa Jensen and her colleagues see themselves as acting virtuously and effectively. This makes sense within what Kegan called the fourth level of cognitive development. But their behavior seems weak and/or bad to those who view it from a third-level epistemology, who can see only "fight" or "surrender" as the possibilities. From the perspective of the third level, actions expressing the fourth-level commitment to peacemaking appear to dilute the clarity of the message, give aid and comfort to the enemy by publicizing their views, and perhaps even set the stage for compromising with them.

While (fourth-level) "opposition" is sometimes hard to distinguish from (third level) "fighting," fourth-level "peacemaking" is something quite different from third-level "surrender." Peacemaking is proactively inclusive, based on a principled opposition to one-sided processes that exclude or silence stakeholders in the issue. As such, peacemaking is invisible in an epistemology that has only the categories of "fight or surrender."

I believe that there is a reciprocal relationship between patterns of communication and selves. To some extent, we become the selves that we are because of the patterns of communication in which we are engaged, and the patterns of communication that we are partly responsible for making are shaped by the selves that we have become. We might picture this relationship as a wheel, revolving around and around. But the point that I want to make in this chapter is that the process is not inexorable, and that there are times when higher forms of consciousness emerge from it. Here is a story that describes one person's perception of this reciprocal pattern, and of her decision to step off the wheel.

I noticed that one of the participants in a workshop about CMM – let's call her Elizabeth – was experiencing some strong emotions. When we took our coffee break, I made a point of asking her if she wanted to talk about what was going on with her. She told me a fascinating story of having been involved in a moral conflict and realizing that her participation was making her into a self that she didn't like.

We had been discussing a situation in which a woman had encountered job-related gender discrimination. Elizabeth told me that the discussion brought back strong emotions from a previous point in her history and that this surprised her, because she thought that she had moved on from these experiences long ago.

I thought that I was about to hear a story of how she had been discriminated against, and how she identified with the woman described in the reading material. Instead, she told me that she had been one of the national leaders in the movement advocating for the Equal Rights Amendment (known as the ERA) 20 years previously. She traveled all over the country, speaking to hostile as well as friendly audiences, seeking to persuade state legislatures to ratify an amendment to the United States constitution that said, in its entirety: "Equality of rights under the law shall not be denied or abridged by the United States or by any state on account of sex."

The ERA was first proposed in 1923 (Equal Rights Amendment 2006). To be included in the Constitution, it must be ratified by 38 states. As of January 2006, it has been ratified by 35 states and proposals for ratification have been introduced in three additional states (Arkansas, Florida, and Illinois). The public debate about the ERA was most heated between 1972 and 1982. During this time, all of the confrontational apparatus of modern democracy was trotted out: supporters picketed, engaged in hunger strikes and performed acts of civil disobedience. Supporting organizations refused to do business in states that had not ratified the proposed amendment, and teams of highly sophisticated, articulate spokespersons were sent around the country to advocate for support of the amendment. Their talking points included these:

- Women have been deliberately kept out of American political life. The Constitution itself explicitly refers to "men."
- The Nineteenth Amendment to the Constitution, in 1920, gave women the right to vote. Many women noted that they were still not covered by equal protection under the law in other ways because the Fourteenth and Fifteenth Amendments either did not specify women under their coverage or specifically limited their coverage to men.
- The Equal Rights Amendment would guarantee that women would have no more but no fewer constitutional rights and protections than men.

The efforts of the spokespersons for the ERA were met with equal intensity, of course, by those opposed to it. More to the point, opponents of the ERA usually did not argue about it on its merits. Rather, they dismissed the concerns of supporters as unimportant since no discrimination was happening or argued that the ERA was unnecessary, since women were adequately covered by other legislation prohibiting discrimination.

Elizabeth had been one of the most visible and engaged supporters of the ERA. At some point, however, she reflected on the patterns of communication that she was involved in. Using the CMM serpentine model, she quickly sketched out this turn-by-turn episode, noting the power of the emergent logic of the interaction.

(1) *Pro-ERA speaker:*   She is highly sensitized to past injustices, such as Susan B. Anthony's being arrested and fined for casting a ballot for President before the Nineteenth Amendment was passed. She presents a reasonable argument appealing to the highest sensibilities of all people, regardless of gender.

(2) *Anti-ERA speaker:*   He or she shows little or no awareness of the history of the issue, argues that there is no need for the ERA, and dismisses the pro-ERA speaker's passion and concern as foolish.

(3) *Pro-ERA speaker:*   She is insulted by being dismissed, sees this as a continuation of exactly what she is talking about. She becomes defensive and seeks to demonstrate that the responses of the anti-ERA speaker are "proof" of the rightness of her position.

(4) *Anti-ERA speaker:*   He or she shows no understanding of what the speaker is talking about but notes the heightened emotional state of the pro-ERA speaker and comments on the shrillness of the presentation as evidence that women should not be allowed to meddle in politics.

(5) *Pro-ERA speaker:*   She is angry and lashes out with slogans designed to hurt the other rather than with reasons designed to invite the other to join her position.

(6) *Anti-ERA speaker:*   He or she is insulted and lashes out with slogans and/or dismisses her with laughter.

The pattern continues with many iterations of turns (5) and (6). After this pattern has occurred time and again, the pro-ERA speaker comes to expect it and begins her speech in the next city with turn (5).

Elizabeth said that she noted that her speeches about the issue had shifted from reasonable, balanced presentations to shrill advocacy, and that her relationship with those opposing the ERA had changed from opposition to fighting. She asked, "What am I becoming by being involved in these patterns of communication?" and didn't like the answer. She said that she knew that she had to change the pattern of communication or withdraw, in order to remain and become the self that she wanted to be. To her sorrow, she couldn't find a way to change the pattern of communication, so she withdrew from the pro-ERA movement.

The Role of Selves in Making Social Worlds

Selves are made in processes of communication, and once made, are parts of those processes. Like "episodes," selves may be seen as ways of rendering particular aspects of our social worlds into discernible chunks, and, thus rendered, our selves inform and constrain how we communicate. CMM's hierarchy model is one way of showing how this works.

In chapter 6, I introduced the hierarchy model, showing that "episode" could be seen as a context for other things. Now I want to make the claim that every act we perform has multiple levels of contextualization, and that the ordinal relationship among them – that is, which is the context for which – is significant.

As a way of presenting this idea, let's assume that after the meeting in which she screamed at Rolf, Tina realized that it would help to sort through her own feelings. She really wanted to function as a self-authoring person but felt that she had let her emotions author her. She called Ingrid, the company's internal consultant, and asked for a meeting. Ingrid's secretary said that she was currently meeting with someone else (she didn't say that Rolf was Ingrid's other client!) but would get back to her soon. About an hour later, Ingrid called and invited Tina to meet her in a conference room.

Ingrid began by asking what was going on. Tina explained and then said, "I just want to sort out my own feelings here. I want to make sure that I'm acting under control and not acting out something that I don't want to." Ingrid replied, "Great! I know just a way to do that!" and went to the whiteboard. "Tina, as you told me what was going on, I heard three stories. One is a story about yourself. A title for this story might be 'It should have been me, not Rolf!' Is that how you'd name the story?" Tina chuckled and said, "Yes. Close enough." Ingrid wrote the title on the board. "The other story I heard was about your sense of responsibility to your division. What title might you give for this story?" Ingrid asked. Tina replied, "How about 'If something isn't done, it'll be too late!'" "Good," Ingrid replied, writing it on the board. "And the third story I heard was about the meeting. I don't know how to name that story!" Laughing, Tina said, "I don't either! How about 'I'm going to blow the whole thing up!'" And Ingrid wrote that on the board.

"OK," Ingrid said, "now let's talk about 'contexts.' You know the concept. You have one hour for lunch. Time enough to do any one of these things: go shopping; work out in the gym; or have lunch. But you can't do all three. Which do you do?" Tina said, "It depends. Today, I was very hungry. Probably all the nervous energy anticipating the meeting. So I'd say 'lunch.'" "Good!" Ingrid replied, "so of the three things, the most important was lunch. Using the concept of contexts, we could say that that was the highest-level context for you in deciding how to use the free hour." "That makes sense," Tina replied.

"Now look at the three stories that you told me. Let's play with the possible contextual relationships among them and see which best fits your experience. First, let's put your story about yourself as the highest level of context, your story about your responsibilities to your division as next, and your story about the meeting itself as the least important." As she said this, Tina drew figure 7.2 on the board, and asked, "If this is the pattern of contextualization, how would you act in the meeting?" Tina laughed, "Just like I did. I blew the whole thing up!" "And what might happen that would satisfy you?" Ingrid asked. "Well, on the way out, Dennis and I had a talk. He told me that he gave this assignment to Rolf because it was relatively straightforward, and that they had something else coming down the line that would require a more sensitive touch, and that they wanted to hold me open to take it." "And how did that make you feel?" Tina replied, "Less angry. Still concerned about my division. And foolish, wondering if I had blown my chances by acting the way I did. What do you think?"

Instead of answering Tina's question, Ingrid said, "Let's look at another way of organizing these three stories," and drew the pattern shown in figure 7.3. "If this was the pattern of contextualization, what would you have done in the meeting?" "The same thing!" Tina said. "And how would you have responded to what Dennis told you afterward?" Ingrid asked. "It wouldn't have helped at all. I wouldn't have cared about him admitting

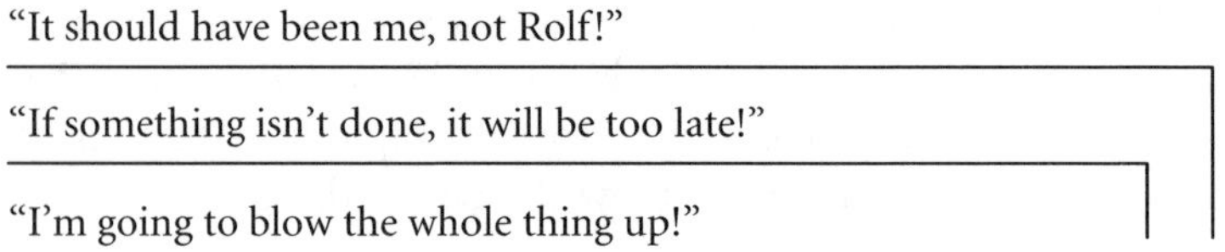

"It should have been me, not Rolf!"

"If something isn't done, it will be too late!"

"I'm going to blow the whole thing up!"

Figure 7.2 Hierarchy model showing Tina's story of her self as the highest context

"If something isn't done, it will be too late!"

"It should have been me, not Rolf!"

"I'm going to blow the whole thing up!"

Figure 7.3 Hierarchy model showing Tina's concern for her division as the highest context

that Rolf's a jerk and that they have big plans for me. I'd probably have blown up the meeting in the hall just like I did in the conference room!"

"So what do you think?" Ingrid asked. "Are you authoring your own self, or are your emotions speaking for you?" "It's pretty clear," Tina said, "that I'm acting out of my own sense of being disrespected and badly treated by Dennis and Rolf . . . Yeah . . . And I've got to take charge of that." "Do you want to talk about it," Ingrid asked. "No. No, thanks, Ingrid," Tina replied. "I know what I have to do."

Among other things, this demonstration shows that both the content of Tina's story about herself (in this situation) and its place as one of several contexts for her actions shape what she chooses and what she is able to do. This is one of the ways in which selves make the social worlds in which they are made in a continual, recurring process.

Making Better Social Worlds

If I'm right about the cave painting, then human beings have been asking about the nature of themselves for nearly 40,000 years. This seems ironic, because I think that this chapter on self, more than any other in this book, refers to scholarly work that is just now getting under way, to topics about which there is heated controversy, and to areas in which I'm more comfortable with the knowledge of experienced practitioners than I am with that produced by disciplined researchers.

In chapter 1, I described three divergent trajectories in which our social worlds are moving. Lacking better terms, I called them backward, forward, and upward. At this point in this book, I'm more ready to specify what I meant by "upward" than I was in chapter 1. Deliberately not trying to be overly specific, the "upward" movement involves the emergence of better patterns of communication as described in chapter 6, higher forms of consciousness as described in this chapter, and more sophisticated relational minds that I'll describe in chapter 8.

Better social worlds can be made more likely if we reduce those factors that inhibit the emergence of higher forms of consciousness and enhance those that facilitate their emergence. What are these factors?

Is there an innate impulse toward evolution of consciousness?

I'm curious about that which impels us to continue evolving our forms of consciousness. Thinking about the misunderstandings that are inevitable as indicated in the analysis of moral conflict, and the effort involved, why does it happen?

This reminds me of a study of childhood development in which the author asked why any of us learns to stand and walk. It seems a step backward, he said, because at the time when we can barely take one or two steps before falling, we can crawl much faster, with more confidence and fewer bruises, and get to where we want to go better than we can by toddling. So why do very young babies have this urge to stand and walk?

I don't know the answer to that question either, but there seems to be some evolutionary push in our forms of consciousness, although it is one that can be resisted or obstructed more easily than our impulse to stand and walk.

Is there a special kind of transformative learning?

Jack Mezirow (1991) started a program to study and foster transformative learning. Three important aspects of this type of learning involve disorienting dilemmas, reflection, and identifying assumptions.

Mezirow describes disorienting dilemmas as situations that are often "emotionally charged" that "fail to fit our expectations and consequently lack meaning for us, or we encounter an anomaly that cannot be given coherence either by learning within existing schemes or by learning new schemes" (1991: 94). Although everyone seems to admit that disorienting dilemmas occur and often prompt transformative learning, critics suggest that the attention to such emotionally charged situations detracts from alternative, more gradual processes that lead to the same end.

However the process of transformative learning is initiated, the key element is reflection. Mezirow differentiates three types of reflection – content, process, and premise.

We may reflect on the content of a problem, the process of our problem solving or the premise upon which the problem is predicated. Content and process reflection can play a role in thoughtful action by allowing us to assess consciously what we know about taking the next step in a series of actions. Premise reflection involves a movement through cognitive structures guided by the identifying and judging of presuppositions. Through content and process reflection we can change our meaning schemes: through premise reflection we can transform our meaning perspectives. Transformative learning pertains to both the transformation of meaning schemes through content and process reflection and the transformation of meaning perspectives through premise reflection. (Mezirow 1991: 117)

The third aspect of transformative learning involves critical reflection on what Mezirow calls epistemic, sociocultural, and psychic assumptions. These assumptions are what have been learned in an earlier stage of development but persist, even though the circumstances in which they were developed have changed. For example, Mezirow (1991: 114) says that "psychic assumptions" are often distorted because they "arise from anxiety generated by parental prohibitions learned under traumatic circumstances in childhood. . . . The distorted assumptions suggest that to feel or act in ways forbidden by the prohibition will result in disaster, even though such an expectation usually is unrealistic in adulthood."

Mezirow's account of transformative learning sounds reasonable – perhaps *too* reasonable. One of the criticisms of this whole approach is that it is, first, too much indebted to a particular culture (Western) and, second, too cognitive. Real life, so the argument goes, is more complex than that.

How can we support each other in our zones of proximal development?

Vygotsky's notion of "zones for proximal development" might be the basis for another way of accounting for the evolution of consciousness. I believe that any one of us may function at different levels of consciousness in different situations. If that's the case, then all of us have an "up-side," or a zone of proximal development in which we can act – even if only temporarily and with help – at a higher level than we could otherwise. And if Vygotsky is right, then repeated opportunities to function at these higher levels will stimulate the evolution of our consciousness.

Executive coach Hilda Carpenter (2006) bases her practice on this concept. As she sees it, her role as coach requires her to discern her client's zones of proximal development and then to act in a way that enables them to function at a higher level than they otherwise would be able to. The same idea lies behind the work that many of us do as facilitators, mediators, mentors, and the like. We become those social supports that enable our clients to function, temporarily, at a higher level than they otherwise would. We have the hope that, in doing so, they will become able to do for themselves that which they previously could only do with help.

In recent years, whole new professions have developed that may be described – even if those who practice them would not accept the description – as supports for others in their zones of proximal development. I'm thinking of mentors, coaches, therapists, consultants, facilitators, mediators, negotiators, teachers, and others.

In fact, this is one way of thinking about the tools and concepts of CMM presented in this book. They function as scaffolds so that people who are "socialized selves" in Kegan's (Debold 2002) term can function, at least in that situation, as "self-authoring selves." I'm not sure I'm altogether comfortable with this characterization, but it seems to have something going for it. And to the extent that it is a useful description, I wonder if CMM also provides useful tools and concepts for the next step – from "self-authoring" to "self-transforming" – in the evolution of consciousness, or whether a different set of social supports is needed.

How can we structure our institutions so that they support the evolution of consciousness?

This question humbles me, and I hope that others will take it as a challenge. But one way of beginning the process is to look at the field of complexity and see if we can find any useful knowledge about "emergence" in general.

I'm intrigued by the seven factors that management consultant Richard Seel (2005) said facilitate the possibility and rate of emergent properties in organizations.

- *Connectivity:* It is not essential that everyone is connected to everyone else – indeed, that is likely to stop emergence. But emergence is less likely if there are disconnected "islands" in the organization or if "silos" exist.

- *Diversity:* If there is not enough diversity in the system, it will be hard for new ideas to emerge; too much diversity will impact negatively on attempts to find sufficient cohesion for emergence. Most organizations tend to have too little diversity.
- *Rate of information flow:* Information overload can inhibit emergence . . . on the other hand, emergence is also unlikely if the free flow of information is blocked.
- *Lack of inhibitors:* There are many factors that can inhibit emergence. Three which seem particularly significant to me are related to power, identity, and anxiety. Emergence is unlikely if power differentials are too great or too small; if a sense of organizational identity is threatened; or if potential change arouses too much uncontained anxiety.
- *Good constraints to action:* Emergence is much more likely if there are some clear constraints to possible action. It is generally more useful to specify what may *not* be done and then give explicit permission for everything else to be attempted.
- *Intention:* Because people have free will and intentionality, their desires can influence the shape of any emergent outcome. A clear sense of shared vision can be very helpful.
- *Watchful anticipation:* Because emergence is unpredictable, it may be necessary to wait. This is a skill that is not common among business people, particularly in the West. It is best if this is not a passive waiting but is filled with an expectancy and openness to potentiality.

Is it possible to use these characteristics, or something like this, as an architectural guide for constructing social institutions that facilitate the evolution of higher forms of consciousness?

Can we take proactive steps to structure better forms of communication?

In chapter 2, I quoted Flemming Rose, culture editor of *Jyllands-Posten*, who said that one effect of publishing the controversial cartoons depicting the prophet Muhammad was the beginning of a "constructive debate in Denmark and Europe about freedom of expression, freedom of religion and respect for immigrants and people's beliefs." He cited both the number of Danish Muslims who have participated in that debate ("Never before have so many Danish Muslims participated in a public dialogue – in town hall meetings, letters to editors, opinion columns and debates on radio and TV") and the fact that it has occurred without burnings or bombings.

I was not a participant in that debate, so I can pose the following questions from the privileged position of ignorance. In what pattern of communication (as described in chapter 6) did that debate take place? What kinds of selves were made in that debate? Remembering Elizabeth's story of her experience as an advocate in the ERA debate in the United States, is participation in this debate moving people toward less highly evolved forms of consciousness where they see only the options of fighting or surrender, or to more highly evolved forms of consciousness where they see peacemaking or even more sophisticated forms of engagement as possibilities? In the United States, the ideal of public deliberation has been supplanted by rancorous attack ads, false dichotomies, conversation stoppers, and wedge issues. We are making political parties that are more polarized than the electorate and members of the electorate who are turned off from politics. Is this what happened in the public discourse in Denmark, or did it stimulate "upward" evolution of selves and society? If so, what made those better forms of communication possible?

Moving from this specific issue to the general question: is it possible for us to design meetings that support the evolution of our consciousness? Imagine leaders in corporations or political systems who see their roles as custodians of the quality of the forms of communication that occur about controversial issues such as the new Strategic Initiative in Tina's organization or the place of Muslims in Europe. What form of consciousness would serve these leaders best? What forms of consciousness would these patterns of communication elicit?

Notes

1 To see a picture of this plaque go to http://spaceprojects.arc.nasa.gov/Space_Projects/pioneer/PNimgs/Plaque.gif (accessed March 9, 2006).

2 My use of gender-specific references in this paragraph is deliberate. In anticipation of the extended example later in this chapter of the woman advocating the Equal Rights Amendment, I want to call attention to the sexism of the documents to which I am referring.

3 If she were to ask these questions, she would be using what is known as circular or systemic questions. I describe this procedure in more detail in chapter 9.

References

Carpenter, H. (2006), Reconceptualizing communication competence: high performing coordinated communication competence: a three-dimensional view. PhD dissertation, Fielding Graduate University, Santa Barbara, CA.

Clottes, J. (2001), Chauvet cave: France's magical ice age art, *National Geographic*. Retrieved from http://www.nationalgeographic.com/ngm/data/2001/08/01/html/ft_20010801.6.html on September 7, 2006.

Cowan, C. and Todorovic, N. (2006), Spiral dynamics gateway. Retrieved from http://www.spiraldynamics.com/ on September 7, 2006.

Debold, E. (2002), Epistemology, fourth order consciousness, and the subject–object relationship or . . . how the self evolves with Robert Kegan. *What is Enlightenment Magazine*, 22. Retrieved from http://www.wie.org/j22/kegan.asp?pf=1 on November 6, 2005.

Equal Rights Amendment (2006), Retrieved from http://www.equalrightsamendment.org/ on September 7, 2006.

Fort, D. and Skinner-Jones, A. (1993), *The Great Divide*. A film by DNA Productions, Santa Fe, NM.

Geertz, C. (1975), On the nature of anthropological understanding, *American Scientist*, 63: 43–57.

Gergen, K. J. (1991), *The Saturated Self: Dilemmas of Identity in Contemporary Life*, New York: Basic Books.

Heise, D. R. (1970), The semantic differential and attitude research. In G. F. Summers (ed.), *Attitude Measurement*, Chicago: Rand McNally, pp. 235–53.

Hobbes, T. (1651), *Leviathan*. Retrieved from http://oregonstate.edu/instruct/phl302/texts/hobbes/leviathan-contents.html on March 9, 2006.

Kegan, R. (1994), *In Over Our Heads: The Mental Demands of Modern Life*, Cambridge, MA: Harvard University Press.

McNamee, S. and Gergen, K. J. (1999), *Relational Responsibility: Resources for Sustainable Dialogue*, Thousand Oaks, CA: Sage.

Mezirow, J. (1991), *Transformative Dimensions of Adult Learning*, San Francisco: Jossey-Bass.

Moxey, K. (1999), The history of art after the death of the "death of the subject," *Invisible Culture: An Electronic Journal for Visual Studies*. Retrieved from http://www.rochester.edu/in_visible_culture/issue1/moxey/moxey.html on November 6, 2005.

Pearce, W. B. and Littlejohn, S. W. (1997), *Moral Conflict: When Social Worlds Collide*, Thousand Oaks, CA: Sage.

Pearce, W. B., Littlejohn, S. W., and Alexander, A. (1987), The New Christian Right and the humanist response: reciprocated diatribe, *Communication Quarterly*, 35: 171–92.

Seel, R. (2005), Story and conversation in organizations: a survey. Retrieved from http://www.new-paradigm.co.uk/story_&_conversation.htm on January 5, 2006.

Sociology graduate students, University of Colorado (n.d.), The emergence of the schools of symbolic interactionism. Retrieved from http://socsci.colorado.edu/SOC/SI/si-schools.htm on September 7, 2006.

Vygotsky, L. S. (1978), *Mind in Society*, Cambridge, MA: Harvard University Press.

Chapter 8

Relationships and Relational Minds

Preview

Relationships and relational minds emerge from the dynamic dance of coordinated actions and managed meanings. This chapter describes both the way we make relationships in communication and, once made, the way these relationships shape our patterns of communication. In this spiraling, reflexive process, relational minds emerge.

Some minds are more sophisticated than others. While I'm tentative about naming these various levels or stages of development, I'm more definite about some of the characteristics of preferred forms of relational minds.

The chapter demonstrates the use of three of CMM's concepts: the hierarchy model, strange loops, and the LUUUUTT model.

The Difference between Being Related and Being in Relationship

Each of us is born into patterns of pre-existing relationships that we did not choose and that will shape our lives in important ways. We are, through no virtue or fault of our own, brothers and sisters, sons and daughters, and distant cousins. We often punctuate the stories of our lives by the relationships we form, stress, break, and redefine. We enter into temporary alliances on the playground as children, contractual relationships in marriage and business, and sworn relationships in professions such as the military and police and in activities such as courtrooms and financial representation.

As I'm using the term in this chapter, relationships include all sorts of things that are usually treated separately. I certainly mean to include friendships, marriages, and aunts and uncles, but I also mean larger, less personal relationships such as corporations, cities, religions, and tennis clubs.

To the extent that it is possible to separate episodes, selves, and relationships, the quality of our lives is most directly a function of our relationships. Consider the experience of two men. Knowing that he was about to die of cancer, Raymond Carver (2000) wrote a short poem titled simply "Last Fragment." In it, he asked the question that many people have asked: did you get what you wanted from life? His answer is jarringly different than what I expected as I continued reading the poem. "I did!" he said, going on to say that he had come to love himself and to feel himself loved. If you know his personal history, you'll know that he knew well the lack of love, and thus was positioned to appreciate it when he found it (Liukkonen n.d.). The other example is the famous line in Jean-Paul Sartre's (1989) play *No Exit*. One of his characters delivers the angry, bitter judgment that: "Hell is other people." While these comments may seem to contradict each other, what they have in common is the strong affirmation that the quality of our relationships is directly related to the quality of our lives.

Let me bring in a third voice. Paul Tsongas, the junior Senator from Massachusetts, was diagnosed as having cancer. Shortly afterward, he resigned from the Senate. I watched the televised news conference in which he announced and explained his decision. Quoting from a letter received from a friend, he said, "No man ever said on his deathbed, 'I wish I had spent more time in the office.'"

How can we make the kind of relationships that enable us to say, at the end, that we got what we wanted from life? How can we make relationships that support the evolution of higher forms of consciousness and better forms of communication?

Relationships and Minds as Objects in Our Social Worlds

Like selves, relationships emerge in patterns of social interaction. Unlike selves, they are not tied to a specific biological being, enabled and constrained by that being's capabilities. Again like selves, relationships have emergent characteristics that possess powers not held by any of the components parts. With a tip of the hat to Gregory Bateson (1979), call this emergent unity "mind." Unlike selves, minds do not have consciousness, but like selves, they are (more or less) self-regulating, coherent entities that perceive, process information, and act.

This is a very unusual concept of relationship, so let's build to it in three steps. The first is to distinguish "things that are related" from "things that are a part of a relationship." The point I'm making was expressed indirectly by poet Billy Collins (2005: 3–4), who asked whether the salt and pepper shakers standing side by side for many years have become friends.

In one sense, everything is related. Salt and pepper shakers stand in a certain relationship to each other and are perceived as separate parts, both necessary, of a set. At this same level, all of us share subatomic particles that move freely among us and we are all caught up in a web of physical forces. But the serious answer to Collins's deliberately naïve question underscores the more complex relationships among humans.

Our genes connect us. In the largest sense, we all share the same genetic inheritance: so we see and hear in the same bandwidth; we are capable of similar emotional and cognitive experiences; we all can enjoy a sunset or a glass of cold water on a hot day. We all have mothers and fathers; we all need to eat, sleep, and laugh. Opinions differ about how far to extend this list, but this is enough to make the point.

Language connects us. All human beings are enmeshed in language, and language is consequential. There is a special affinity between human beings and language. If you raise a child and a puppy in a home, the child will learn to speak whatever language the adults in that home use, but the puppy won't. It is impossible to prevent a human infant from learning, not only a few words or phrases, but the complex grammar and syntax of any human language to which it is exposed. And language is not a neutral instrument. The vocabularies of all languages reflect the experiences and perceptions of their users; their grammars embody cosmologies. Learning to use a language is a process of being shaped into a complex mold until we are "fit" for interaction with other users of that language – and simultaneously disabled from the same quality of interaction with users of other languages. As Bakhtin (Morson and Emerson 1990) points out, meaning runs through language; most of us will never use a word that hasn't already been used by thousands of other people who did not mean what we mean by it. While we can twist and tweak the common language to serve our individual purposes, we don't own it.

Being joint-tenants of a finite planet also connects us. After discovering that the world is bigger than we had thought,[1] we are coming to realize that it is smaller than we ever imagined.[2] Given the communication and transportation technologies now available, everything that happens anywhere is relevant to all of us everywhere, and the sheer number of us, coupled with our capacity for breaking and making things, has shifted our relationship to the planet. We still cower at the might of natural forces. I wrote this in the calendar year in which a tsunami caused unprecedented destruction in the nations bordering the Indian Ocean, an earthquake caused great damage in Pakistan, and Hurricane Katrina destroyed the city of New Orleans, among many more "ordinary" demonstrations that human society is fragile, living on the outside of an unstable, spinning, gas-covered ball. However, we have also become one of the forces able to level mountains, divert rivers, and change fertile fields into sterile deserts, and vice versa. Among other things, we are physical bodies that occupy shared space. Those natural resources you consume are now no longer available to me; and the sludge that I might pour into my part of the river affects your drinking water. We are related.

But are we in relationships? If so, it is because we have made those relationships. Unlike salt and pepper shakers, we might name our relationship as friends or strangers. (The action of naming them, perhaps even more than the names given, separates "a relationship" from "being related.") We might develop our relationship so that our actions flow together smoothly, or collide violently. The stuff of human relationships is expressed in another part of Billy Collins's (2005: 3–4) poem in which he addresses "You, the Reader":

> I wonder how you are going to feel
> When you find out
> that I wrote this instead of you.

Jointly enacting episodes seems to be a necessary but not sufficient condition of developing a relationship. From an individual's perspective, we start taking the others into account; patterning our behavior around theirs; naming the relationship; doing things for or because of the relationship; etc. From an observer's perspective, the relationship develops a mind of its own. The relationship itself acts in ways that uses those in it for its purposes, shapes the selves of those in it, and monitors and maintains itself.

I was working in Bogotá, Colombia, with a group of civic leaders. They suggested that we apply some CMM concepts to a recent event in which a government minister was found guilty of using his position to enhance his own personal fortunes. Two things brought this to the attention of my Colombian colleagues: (1) they knew this person and knew him to be an idealistic, responsible person and could not imagine how he had become corrupted; and (2) this person was just the latest in a long line of people in this position who had been indicted and convicted of the same crime.

As we discussed it, we realized that we were the prisoners of a story about individualism. We were forcing these events through a conceptual funnel that treated individuals as moral actors and institutions as neutral spaces in which the dramas of individuals played out. But, we wondered, how often do we need to observe good men go bad when put into this position before we begin to change our stories and describe the mind of the organization itself as corrupt and corrupting?

Using Bateson's (1979) notion of the extra-somatic (literally, outside-the-body) social mind, we began looking at the patterns that connected various aspects of the organization in which these men found themselves. We began looking at this particular governmental office as a whirlpool or tornado of logical force, pulling the people appointed to it in the direction of committing these crimes, and seeing the persons appointed as having to resist this pressure with the strength of their character. Framed in this way, the struggle seemed unbalanced: a deeply textured organization, intricately interwoven with all of the other branches of government, and that pre-existed the appointment of the new minister on one side, and the strength of the personality of the newly appointed minister on the other.

We began playing with metaphors that would describe the mind of the pattern of relationships into which good men and women were appointed as minister. One compelling metaphor portrayed the organizational mind as a factory for producing felons. Another engaging metaphor was that the mind of the governmental organization is greedy, and uses the individuals in it as tools to accumulate what it wants.

This discussion made Bateson's (1979) notion of mind very vivid and showed some practical implications of paying attention to "the pattern which connects" one thing to another. It started me on the path to seeing this class of objects in our social world as not just "being related" but as "being in relationships," and the patterns in those relationships as comprising relational minds.

Using this insight, my colleagues in Bogotá and I started thinking about how we could make better social worlds. We decided that trying to find a still more honest person to put in the position of this government ministry or exhorting the next person appointed to try harder to resist the pressures toward illegal activities was not likely to be effective. Rather, the most constructive act would be to change the relational mind of this office, making it less greedy and impelling officials toward honesty rather than toward illegal activities. As an exercise in this workshop, we spent some time imagining what might be a critical moment and how we might act into it wisely.

Colombia did rewrite its constitution a few years later, in 1991.[3] This process might have been such a critical moment. I have absolutely no evidence that any of the participants in our exercise in disciplined imagination were involved in the revision, but at least some parts of the new constitution look like it took a more systemic perspective than the one it replaced.

Relationships as Contexts for the Way We Communicate

Once made, relationships govern and guide the way we communicate. Among other things, they function as contexts into which and out of which we act.

As I was writing this sentence, a 125-pound wolf came into my study and repeatedly flipped my arm away from the keyboard with his muzzle. He then stared at me and growled. If I didn't know the context for this event, I'd be confused and a bit alarmed. But I am in a relationship with this wolf. I named him (Yukon), I feed him, play with him, and take him for walks. I think he's named me, too; while I can't spell that name, I can recognize it when he growls it. I'm not sure exactly how to name our relationship, but it has developed a mind of its own and has changed both of us.

We found Yukon in the custody of the Society for the Prevention of Cruelty to Animals when he was about six weeks old. They told us only that he was a stray and probably a wolf; we believe that they were going to destroy him. When we insisted that we would take him home, the officers told us many scary things about attempting to domesticate a wolf and, as standard procedure, required us to fill out "adoption papers" that prescribed the responsibilities that we were accepting when entering this relationship.

At first, we were in relation to each other but didn't have a relationship. Yukon was genuinely oblivious to our intentions and desires about his behavior. It wasn't that he was rebellious; he simply didn't care about us. But wolves are inherently predisposed to be members of a pack and we

Relationship: cross-species friendship

Flipping arm with muzzle; $\longrightarrow$ request for episode: go to park
certain kind of growl

Figure 8.1   Relationship as a context for interpreting speech acts

deliberately acted in ways that invited him to join our family as his pack. He responded to the invitation and, as wolves will do, made a bid to be the leader of the pack, which we had to thwart. Over time, we've developed a strong relationship. In ways that go beyond my ability to articulate, we are sensitive to each other's moods and needs, and all of us have been changed by being a part of this relationship.

This relationship is a context for managing the meaning of specific acts. You should find the diagram in figure 8.1 familiar. We have a frequent episode of "going to the park together." His behavior in flipping my arm and growling is intended to have the implicative force to change the episode from one in which I'm working at my desk and he sleeping at my feet to one in which I'm walking and he's running, sniffing, and attending to other canine duties. This behavior is unique to our relationship. I'm not the only one in our family who takes him to the park, but I'm the only one that he treats this way. In this particular instance, I've treated it as an invitation that I've refused, choosing to stay at my desk and write these lines. Disappointed, he is now lying at my feet, sighing deeply and making me clearly aware of how disgusted he is with me.

In more complicated situations, what we do in any given moment is not only a part of conversational triplets (bounded by what others did and will do in response) but is doubly contextualized by both the "episode" of which it is a part and the "relationship" in which it occurs. Even more interesting, we can manage our meanings by exploring whether the episode is the context for the relationship or vice versa.

A scene from the movie *Good Will Hunting* illustrates a pattern in which "friendship" is the context for "episode," as shown in figure 8.2.[4] While

Relationship: friends

Episode: one of your friends is in a fight

Speech acts: join the fight

Figure 8.2   Relationship as the context for an episode in *Good Will Hunting*

Episode: one of your friends is in a fight

Relationship: friends

Speech acts: ???

Figure 8.3   Episode as the context for relationship in an alternative version of *Good Will Hunting*

watching a neighborhood softball game, Will saw a man who used to bully him when they were children and told his friends about this part of his history. While driving away from the game, Will saw the man again, and told the driver (Chuckie) to pull over, a clear signal to the others that he was going to fight. One of Will's friends, Morgan, protested on very practical grounds: "Ah, Will . . . we just seen the guy 15 minutes ago at the ballgame. If we was gunna' fight him we shoulda' fight him then, but we got snacks, now." Chuckie enforced the relational rules, in this case that the whole group support Will if he gets involved in a fight: "Let me tell you somethin'. If you're not out there in two fuckin' seconds, when I'm done with them, you're next." All four men jumped out of the car and assaulted the former bully.

The situation depicted might have gone differently if the relational mind had a different configuration; for example, if the episode was the higher level of context, as shown in figure 8.3. In this case, Chuckie, Morgan, and Billy might have hesitated or chosen not to join in the unprovoked street fight. In fact, we might imagine Chuckie or Morgan physically restraining Will or reminding him about the negative consequences of street fighting, particularly for someone already known to the police as a brawler.

Identifying whether the story of the episode is the context for the relationship, or vice versa, helps in understanding what is going on in specific situations. But the hierarchy model also helps to understand changes over time. For example, consider the development of a romantic relationship. Let me diagram it in figure 8.4 and then give a verbal description. When two people begin dating, it's likely that the episode (what happens on the date) is the context for their relationship. If the date goes well, they may think that this is a good person with whom to form a relationship; if it does not, they may break off the relationship and date other people. After a series of dates that go well, something happens, depicted by the arrows in figure 8.4. Now the relationship is the higher context. If they have another date that goes badly, they might shrug it off, thinking that this is just one unfortunate episode in a cluster of highly prized and desired episodes. The relationship continues, surviving the bad date in a way that it would not if "episode" were the higher context.

The arrows in figure 8.4 indicate "implicative force," the effect of an action or combination of actions on the contexts in which they occurred. Not shown in the figure is a further possible change in the relationship. If there are a sufficient number of unwanted episodes, or if the unwanted episodes are sufficiently disastrous, they may exert sufficient implicative force to change the pattern of contextualization yet again. Episode or self might become the highest context and the relationship might terminate.

Used this way, the hierarchy model can show both the configuration of relational minds and their changes over time. But relational minds are not necessarily or even usually logically consistent or well ordered. CMM's notion of "loops" was developed to explain certain patterns of disorder.

People often oscillate between contradictory behaviors. For example, a teenaged boy might show patterns in which he acts very normally and others in which he displays an inability to comprehend things around him. If we were not using CMM or a similar conceptual lens, we might ask the question, "What's the matter with him?" and be puzzled by the oscillating pattern. But from a CMM perspective, we would at least entertain the hypothesis that his symptoms are being co-created, and ask what about what he is doing *together with* the others with whom he is in relationships. It's possible that the behaviors we are observing are the function of the relational mind, not something "wrong" with one person in this complex set of relationships.

John Burnham (W. B. Pearce 2002) described how he and his team used this idea in understanding what was going with a fourteen-year-old boy diagnosed with Asperger syndrome, a mild form of autism (Kirby n.d.). They were not certain of the diagnosis and, in fact, were not certain that

Figure 8.4   Changes in contextualization in the development of a romantic relationship

making a "diagnosis" was in the boy's best interest. They noted that the boy sometimes seemed better and sometimes worse. They also noted that the boy's father's behavior oscillated in a manner similar to that of his son. At times, the father accepted the therapeutic team's diagnosis and acted toward his son as if he were "sick." At other times, he rejected the diagnosis and expected his son to act normally.

The idea that father and son were coordinating to make episodes that neither of them wanted or perceived as a whole gave the therapeutic team an important clue. In my terms, they began to think that the relational mind had a curiously twisted structure that was thwarting the attempts made by both father and son to act in a mutually productive way. They described the state of this relational mind in terms of what CMM calls a "strange loop," as shown in figure 8.5.

In a strange loop, mutually exclusive meanings exist at each of two or more levels of contextualization of actions. For example, at the level of the diagnosis, the son may be said to either have or not have Asperger syndrome. For a strange loop to form, people in these relationships must affirm both diagnoses at different times, and in response to other parts of the loop. In addition, there is an oscillating pattern of mutually exclusive behavior: sometimes the son's symptoms of Asperger syndrome increase and at others they diminish. Finally, each side of the oscillating behavior has sufficient implicative force to shift to the "other" set of meanings (as indicated by the diagonal arrows).

In this specific case, the team developed the hypothesis that the son's symptoms decreased when his father was more caring and patient. When the son's behavior improved, the father became convinced that he was

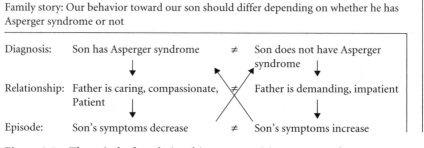

Organizational culture: Diagnosis is important

Family story: Our behavior toward our son should differ depending on whether he has Asperger syndrome or not

Diagnosis: Son has Asperger syndrome   ≠   Son does not have Asperger syndrome

Relationship: Father is caring, compassionate, Patient   ≠   Father is demanding, impatient

Episode: Son's symptoms decrease   ≠   Son's symptoms increase

Figure 8.5   The mind of a relationship as comprising a strange loop

"normal" and became more demanding and impatient of the remaining symptoms. The father's changed behavior had sufficient implicative force to cause the son's symptoms to increase, leading his father to change his mind and conclude that his son in fact did have Asperger syndrome and became more caring and patient . . . and so it goes.

The strange loop in the mind of this relationship, like others we've studied, is robust. Efforts that either father or son might make to change the pattern that connects them are likely to be redefined as just unusual ways to continue it, and if either father or son were to leave the relationship, the mind would seek to recruit someone else to fill the missing role.

The team also noted that this strange loop is held in place, in part, by their own organizational/professional culture that values making diagnoses. (In the model, this is the highest level of context, the story that is the context for the whole strange loop.) This belief is institutionalized beyond the clinic in the process by which therapists are certified as qualified to make diagnoses, the interconnections with other arms of government prepared to act in certain ways on the basis of these diagnoses, and the father and son themselves who have been disciplined to respect the authority of therapists and to frame issues like these within a "medical model" of illness and treatment.

Using Kegan's (Debold 2002) terms, the members of this team were "self-authoring." That is, they were able to ask, "What is our role in making/sustaining this strange loop?" That question helped them discern a critical moment. They decided not to make a diagnosis; for principled reasons, they refused to declare whether the boy either had or did not have Asperger syndrome. Instead, they framed both father and son as doing as well as they could in a relationship that was strangely looped, and acknowledged their own (the team's) part in co-constructing this episode. Among other things, this collapsed the strange loop and called attention to the contingency between the father's mode of parenting and the son's symptoms. The team's hope was that awareness of this contingency would reveal critical moments in the family relationship into which father and son could act wisely.

Because they recognized their own role in creating the strange loop, the therapeutic team began to question their own organizational culture, particularly their practice of diagnosing patients in an individualist manner. This discussion became a critical moment in their treatment of other clients.

Making Relationships in Communication

Some relationships have highly articulated stories: think of the contract drawn up to specify every possible contingency in the relationship between business partners, employers and employees, or insurance providers and people insured. As an independent consultant, I recently received an RFP ("request for proposal") from a local government in which the description of the project filled about a half page; the description of the relationship into which they were prepared to enter filled twelve pages of small print written in language that only a lawyer could love. Every possible contingency was imagined, with stipulated penalties for nonperformance; required assurances of liability insurance; prior agreement to use arbitration to handle conflicts; etc. I chose not to submit a proposal even though the work itself was interesting; I simply didn't want to enter such a restricted relationship.

In the past decade or so, it has become common to understand organizations by looking at the narratives that structure the relationships in them. This research has found an important difference between what Barbara Czarniawska (2004: 40) calls "work stories" and "organizational stories." "Work stories" are unfinished, unpolished, told in bits and pieces; they assume a lot of tacit knowledge, and are often interrupted and redirected by the storytelling efforts of others in the organization. On the other hand, "organizational stories" are told from beginning to end with well-developed plots and with elements of aesthetic and political/commercial value.

I think this is a useful distinction. First, to the extent that it is better described by its "work stories" than by its "organizational story," this indicates that a relationship or organization is messy, and includes many different voices. Second, the distinction focuses attention to the work done within a group to move to a more consensual story. In a formal sense, this might be an organizational Strategic Initiative to develop a "mission statement." In other contexts, it might be a less formal and perhaps more spirited competition among various persons to persuade others to accept (or otherwise manage to impose) their "working story" as the "organizational story."

Making a similar distinction, we might say there will always be a tension between what we might call "stories lived" (the episodes we enact in coordination with each other) and the "stories told" (the narratives that we use to make meaning of the lives we lead, including the episodes in which we participate). From the CMM perspective, we assume that all of us are trying simultaneously:

- To act in such a way that we call into being those episodes that we want or need and to preclude the enactment of those episodes that we hate or fear;
- To tell ourselves stories that:
  - Are coherent with each other; and,
  - Are consistent enough with the episodes in which we live to make them comprehensible.

Among other things, this way of thinking suggests that the tension between the stories we live and the stories we tell is one of the powerful drivers fueling the development of our relationships. This tension can be represented as shown in figure 8.6. If the gap between our stories lived and stories told gets too great, we'll need to do something, either by re-authoring our stories or by changing our actions.

The tension between stories lived and told is also affected by the manner of our storytelling, as shown in figure 8.7. There are many ways of telling the stories in which we make meaning of our lives, and each carries with it some consequences. For example, we might tell stories in a manner that treats the plots that we have developed as if they are accurate descriptions of an unchanging reality. If we do, and if, to the contrary, reality is largely fluid and half paradoxical, then there will be frequent and probably

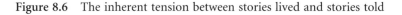

Figure 8.6   The inherent tension between stories lived and stories told

Figure 8.7   Storytelling as a mediator of the tension between stories lived and stories told

disquieting senses of discrepancy between our stories lived and stories told. Another manner of storytelling disconnects our ideals or beliefs from our daily experience. If this is the manner of our storytelling, we can be faithful to our beliefs no matter how much those beliefs are contradicted by our experiences.

The LUUUUTT model shown in figure 8.8 is a heuristic for exploring the complex dance among stories, patterns of coordinated actions, and ways of storytelling. While parts of the model formalize what many systemic practitioners do, a distinctive feature is the extent to which it calls attention to storytelling. LUUUUTT is an acronym for (1) stories *Lived*, (2) *Unknown* stories, (3) *Untold* Stories, (4) *Unheard* stories, (5) *Untellable* stories, (6) stories *Told*, and (7) story *Telling*.[5]

Storytelling is a rich and complex art, and many books could be profitably devoted to it. Here are just two examples that indicate the richness of this topic: the rhetoric of being a victim and the discourse of appreciation.

Some stories are told in a discourse of victimization (Burke 1969; Lucaites and Lewis 1998; Kell and Camp 1999). Regardless of what others do, these storytellers manage to portray themselves as the victims of other people's cruelty or of complex conspiracies. While this seems counterproductive, victims have a privileged position of not having to accept responsibility for what is happening (it's someone else's fault) and being granted a pre-emptive exoneration for evil things that they do (it was a pardonable response to the other person's outrageous behavior).

The organizational development process called appreciative inquiry (AI) is grounded in the claim that good things are achieved when a special form of storytelling is used (Cooperrider and Whitney 1999). It uses specific forms of questions and meeting design to change "the arduous task of intervention" into "imagination and innovation." When this works, "instead of negation, criticism, and spiraling diagnosis, there is discovery, dream, and design."

Figure 8.8   The LUUUUTT model

Sometimes stories or storytelling give rise to relationships; at other times coordinated action precedes the stories that make it coherent. In some relationships, it isn't clear how the relationship should be named or what story should be told about it. People begin acting together and only later – if at all – name the relationship or enhance its story. The relationship between Tevye and Golde in the play *Fiddler on the Roof* is an example. While it was clear that they were husband and wife, the story of their emotional relationship was untold. After talking with his love-struck daughter (Hodel), Tevye noted that "It's a new world" and asked his wife Golde if she loved him. She treated the question as if it was strange: "Do I love you? With our daughters getting married and this trouble in the town? You're upset, you're worn out. Go inside, go lie down! Maybe it's indigestion." Tevye persists, and Golde describes their life together: "Do I love you? For twenty-five years I've washed your clothes, cooked your meals, cleaned your house, given you children, milked the cow. After twenty-five years, why talk about love right now?" Finally, Tevye reminds her of their wedding day; it was an arranged marriage and they had not previously met. They both remembered how nervous they were, and Tevye asks if she's grown to love him. "I suppose I do," she replied, and they sang in unison, "It doesn't change a thing but even so, after twenty-five years, it's nice to know" (*Fiddler on the Roof* n.d.).

The pedantic professor in me would quibble with Tevye and Golde's comment (in the duet) that telling a previously untold story about their relationship doesn't change a thing. Once developed (and whether named or not), the stories in relationships powerfully affect the episodes that occur.

The Evolution of Relational Minds

I believe that relational minds evolve in much the same way as patterns of communication (described in chapter 6) and forms of consciousness (described in chapter 7). We're hindered in describing these evolutions by the lack of a good vocabulary describing the process and naming various moments in it, and, our underdeveloped ability to describe these evolutions hinders our efforts to foster the emergence of more sophisticated relationships.

Even though it does very well what it does, most of the scholarly work on relationships that I know serves us poorly if our purpose is to create better social worlds. Reflecting what Elspeth MacAdam (personal conversation) once called our cultural "acquired fascination with deficit discourse," most of it is focused on relationships that are mad, bad, or sick, and might help us get from bad to good, but not from good to great. Much of that research treats relationships as a variable, something that one can have more or less of, or enter farther into or extricate oneself from. Approaches exploring the dialectics of relationships (Baxter and Montgomery 1996) or deliberately constructing a vocabulary for naming levels in the evolution of relationships seem more useful.

Spiral Dynamics is an interesting attempt to construct a model of the evolution of what they call Value Systems and I call mind. They have developed a spiral model with eight color-coded patterns, each of which represents a "meme" or "world view, a valuing system, a level of psychological existence, a belief structure, an organizing principle, a way of thinking, or a mode of adjustment" (Lessem 2006: 4). The first tier of the system includes six memes:

- *Beige* requires subsistence needs to be met in order to remain alive.
- *Purple* is nurtured through observing rituals, finding reassurance, and by expressing a sense of enchantment in life's mystery.
- *Red* is excited by stories of company heroes, by celebrating feats of conquest, and by evidence of respect.
- *Blue* is reinforced through appeals to traditions, fair treatment for all, and by honoring length of service and loyalty.
- *Orange* is exercised by displaying symbols of success, individuals being recognized for their achievements, and challenges for improvement.
- *Green* is enhanced by stressing the importance of the people, responsiveness to feelings, and a caring socially responsible community.

(Lessem 2006: 11)

Yellow and *Turquoise* comprise the second tier, in which "competence and functionality and qualities of being, not having or even doing, within the context of flexible and open systems" is possible (Lessem 2006: 11).

The developers of Spiral Dynamics want to be understood as describing, not evaluating, these levels. They insist that each is a response to a set of lived conditions and does not reflect intelligence, or character, or temperament. Because our lived experience changes, the level at which we function can be expected to ebb and flow.

I appreciate Spiral Dynamics as a way of creating a vocabulary in which we can make some of the distinctions that will serve us well as we set ourselves to stimulate the "upward" development of society. At the same time, I think that this is an unfinished process, and certainly would not want to treat this model or the attendant vocabulary literally. Specifically, the "communication perspective" focuses attention on the patterns of communication in which we move through cultural evolution, rather than on naming the various stages through which we are moving.

My energies are taken by the task of creating patterns of communication that enable and demand higher levels of consciousness and relational minds. I find myself using "cosmopolitan communication" and "dialogue" interchangeably to describe the form of communication that I think best accomplishes this challenging purpose.

I'm using a technical sense of "dialogue" here. I do not mean just talk. Rather, I'm referring to a particular quality of communication in which a relationship is formed in which each participant remains in the tension between standing your ground and being profoundly open to the others (Pearce and Pearce 2004).

In dialogic communication, it makes sense to say, "We disagree? Wonderful! How did you come to hold your position?" Dialogic conversations enlarge perspectives rather than constrict them; enable us to discover more about our own positions than we had originally known; permit us to address the "gray areas" as well as the things about which we are certain; and, paradoxically, in the absence of the attempt to persuade, we often come to agree with each other.

But that's not the way we usually treat disagreements in our personal or professional lives. Twenty-five years ago, I realized how much I tried to avoid disagreements. After attending the annual conference of the International Communication Association, I went to a conference where Gianfranco Cecchin, Carl Tomm, Vern Cronen, and I were leading a workshop. As we met, Gianfranco asked where I had been. When I told him, he asked if it had been a good conference and I replied "Yes." "Oh?" he said, "what did you learn?"

The question stunned me. The criteria by which I was accustomed to evaluate academic conventions depended on the extent to which I was able to move my own agenda forward. I would have felt comfortable with questions such as "Did your presentation go well?" and "Did you get to meet Professor X?" Learning from – not just about – other people and their work was not what I expected to do. Dialogue is a way of being in relation to the other that makes "What did you learn?" an obvious question; avoiding disagreements shuts us off from the positive effects that dialogue can have on our evolution as selves and in relationships.

My own professional discipline was formed in patterns of communication that had little to do with dialogue, and we've paid a high price for it. For fifty years – from 1911 to the early 1960s – my discipline organized itself into competing and confrontational schools of thought referred to as the Cornell School of Rhetoric and the Midwestern School of Speech. As it turned out, it did not matter which of these schools was right. While the careers of particular individuals waxed and waned based on their abilities to attack or defend the opposing positions, the discipline found itself in a pattern of communication that many practitioners call DAD, or Decide–Advocate–Defend. Highly intelligent, articulate men and women decided which school was right, advocated it, and defended it against the attacks by the other. Among other things, this pattern of communication impeded progress in our thinking about communication, reduced our contributions to society, and made us vulnerable to the series of hostile takeovers by ideas and individuals from outside our discipline that started in the 1960s (Pearce 1985).

Taking the communication perspective, I believe that *the pattern of communication in which we handle our differences, more than the positions we take on the issues or who wins the arguments, will shape the evolution of our social worlds.* I believe that this holds true for the evolution of relational minds in marriages and organizations and for the evolution of consciousness in selves.

Dialogic communication is the most radical alternative to the DAD model. In dialogue, individuals are called to listen, inquire, understand, explain, and find ways of moving forward together. Disagreements and differences are seen as sites for mutual learning, not intellectual pugilism. The art of posing questions is valued at least as highly as that of expressing one's own opinions. The narrative forms of self-disclosure and inquiry are more highly prized than that of advocacy. Had my discipline used this form of communication, it would have developed more quickly and more robustly and would have made a much greater contribution to the world.

Making Better Social Worlds

I want to link two ideas here: Kegan's claim that the most sophisticated level of consciousness, like the least sophisticated level, includes a powerful

affirmation of oneness, and my suggestion that the "stuff" of relationships is an emergent mind that, like consciousness, evolves. With these
two ideas on the table, I want to ask how we would coordinate and make
meanings if we were to find ourselves, even if only momentarily, in the
best of all possible social worlds.

It's a good question, and any answer I can think of seems inadequate.
I'm tempted to invite you to live with the question rather than rush to premature answers, or to make some claim that clearly and deliberately
mocks itself, like this:

(1) *Student:*   Master, what is the nature of enlightenment?
(2) *Teacher:*   A bowl full of snow.
(3) *(Pause)*
(4) *Student:*   Ah! *(And goes away, enlightened.)*

But my intellectual roots lie in pragmatism as well as mysticism and I can't
be satisfied with this, so let me end this discussion of relationships by
responding to the question (not "answering" it) by telling a story (what
else did you expect?).

In June 1972, people all over the world were shocked when their
newspapers carried a photo of five children running toward the camera,
screaming. Nine-year-old Kim Phuc – naked, burned, and terrified – was
in the center of the photo. She was running from her village in Vietnam,
on which napalm bombs had been dropped. Clearly visible in the photo
behind the children strode three soldiers, carrying weapons.

Like all things, whether mundane, tragic or sublime, this image was
grabbed by minds and fit into stories. Some "familiar" story-forms would
cast Kim Phuc in the role of victim and tell a story of trauma. If this story
were lived out, she might have been a life-long user of psychiatric services.
Another familiar story-form would cast the teller in the role of hero-avenger,
setting him- or herself to punish the guilty and prevent a recurrence of the
outrageous barbarisms. Hollywood filmmakers have lived well for years off
the proceeds of such stories. Yet another familiar story is the morality-tale,
in which the teller takes the role of sagacious observer and comments –
whether wryly, sadly, or angrily – about politics, human nature, or the
tactics of guerrilla warfare. Other stories, some less familiar, can certainly
be developed, and this is a fateful process. Both the story told and the
manner of its telling are parts of the creation of the social worlds in
which we all live.

But one aspect of storytelling is that it is never "finished." What some call "narrative unity" is always challenged by subsequent events. This story is no exception.

In 1996, 24 years after she was bombed and burned by napalm, Kim Phuc participated in a Veteran's Day ceremony at the Vietnam Veterans' Memorial in Washington, DC. She said, in halting English, that if she ever met the pilot who bombed her village, she would urge him to join her in working for world peace. A member of the audience, former Army Captain John Plummer, now a Methodist minister, wrote on a scrap of paper "I am that man." The note was passed to her and moments later they publicly embraced. "I'm sorry," he said, crying; "I forgive you," she replied.

This was a wonderful event, but life goes on and, as I said before, storytelling is never finished.

A cynical reporter named Bowman investigated Plummer's service record and found that he was not and could not have been the pilot that bombed Kim's village. While Plummer was a pilot stationed in Vietnam on the day of the bombing (June 12, 1972), he flew helicopters, not the type of fixed-wing aircraft that bombed Kim Phuc's village. In fact, on that day, he had a staff assignment and did not fly at all. Further investigation reveals that he did not order the strike on Kim Phuc's village, nor was he authorized to do so. As it turned out, the pilot of the plane that bombed the village was Vietnamese, not American (Bowman 1997).

I know nothing about these people except from the public record, so my interpretations are inferences based on very little information. That said, it's clear that Bowman and Plummer were working at different levels of consciousness in their understanding of relational minds. For Bowman, Plummer, and Kim Phuc were related but not in relationship. He was interested in whether they were standing side by side on a particular day – like the salt and pepper shakers in Billy Collins's poem.

On the other hand, Plummer's statement "I am that man" can be understood as an affirmation that there is a relational mind that connects them even if they were not physically at the same place on that fateful day. In this interpretation, Plummer's statement is the kind of speech act *about* something that makes it true *by* saying so.[6] I think he was speaking literally when he said "I'm sorry," but in a far more profound way when he said "I am that man," and that Bowman's tin ear could not discern the differences between the two. Plummer identified himself with the war of which he was a part, although he was not involved in this specific event. In an interview with the literal-minded reporter who accused him of perpetrating a hoax, Plummer said, "Every time I saw that picture, I said, 'I did that. I'm responsible.'" Asked why he wrote "I am that man" on the note to Kim Phuc, Plummer said, "I felt tremendous remorse that a little girl was hurt in something I was involved in, remote as it may be . . . I still feel the connection to what happened there – because I was involved in the process" (Bowman 1997).

Plummer was speaking in what Joseph Campbell (1959) called a mythic voice, and this is serious business indeed, because

> mythology is no toy for children. Nor is it a matter of archaic, merely schol-arly concern, of no moment to modern men of actions. For its symbols (whether in the tangible form of images or in the abstract form of ideas) touch and release the deepest centers of motivation, moving literate and illit-erate alike, moving mobs, moving civilizations. . . . For surely it is folly to preach to children who will be riding rockets to the moon a morality and cosmology based on concepts of the Good Society and of man's place in nature that were coined before the harnessing of the horse! And the world is now far too small, and men's stake in sanity too great, for any more of those old games of Chosen Folk (whether of Jehovah, Allah, Wotan, Manu, or the Devil) by which tribesmen were sustained against their enemies in the days when the serpent could still talk. (1959: 12)

Plummer was speaking in a voice of a highly evolved consciousness about a sophisticated relational mind in which each of us should love our neighbor as we love ourselves. Using the language of Spiral Dynamics, his was a "green" rather than "blue" value system; one of noncontingent compassion for others rather than a social exchange of this for that. He was capable of joining Raymond Carver in answering the question "did you get what you want out of life?" with an emphatic "yes," not because he had amassed the most toys but because his ability to "want" had evolved beyond physical toys or literal meanings.

Although everyone I know would want to surround this statement with important qualifiers, we now have convincing evidence that certain kinds of stories and certain patterns of coordination make better rela-tionships than others. Better stories move "from blame and labeling to positive connotation and contextualization and from linearity to cir-cularity (Seligman 1997); they are future-oriented, dreaming, imagining, and appreciative (Lang and McAdam 1997); they don't get bogged down in "problem-solving," rather they work with "the positive presumption – that organizations, as centers of human relatedness, are "alive" with infinite constructive capacity (Cooperrider and Whitney 1999); and they usually feature directional shifts in time, space, causality, interactions, values, and telling (Sluzki 1992). Better patterns of coordination are inclusive, respectful, and dialogic (K. A. Pearce 2002).

The evolution of better social worlds involves a reciprocal pattern, in which participation in better relationships and engagement with more highly evolved consciousness enables us to perceive critical moments in our meaning-making and in our coordination. And good choices in these critical moments stimulate the further evolution of our relationships and selves.

I believe that Kegan has something importantly right when he said that the first and last stages in the evolution of consciousness are, in a particular way, alike: neither sees hard and fast separations between self and the rest of the universe. In much the same way, I believe that when minds, consciousness, and patterns of communication evolve into higher forms, they become less differentiated from each other. As they emerge, they converge. And at last, they are one.

From a less developed perspective (like that of journalist Bowman?), this state of affairs looks like the problem of relativity. Nothing is fixed! There is no one truth or one right way! The center does not hold! What shall we do? From a more developed perspective (military pilot turned minister Plummer?), the same state of affairs is perceived as the affirmation of the richness of polysemy. Nothing is what it seems; there are deeper significances beyond the mere facts. Our own perspective precipitates the potentiality of the universe into a particular social world; and so do the perspectives of all of the other people with whom we share our social worlds.

As a social theory, CMM intends to foster the evolution of better worlds by providing tools and concepts that analyze (that is, cut into parts; display the pieces of) the process of communication. Its purpose is to help us understand and act intelligently into the social world, thus making it better. All the concepts and models mentioned in this book are intended to be used as scaffolds enabling us to identify those things holding back our evolution and to function as if we were more highly evolved than we are. With delight, I note the irony that if these tools do their work well, they become less important. When the gates of enlightenment are opened, one throws away the now-unnecessary brick that one used to knock on it. Until I reach enlightenment, however, I find these concepts and tools very useful and invite you to use them as well.

Notes

1   There have been many moments when an existing human population discovered that the earth continued beyond the boundaries of what they knew.
I'm thinking of whatever African ancestors of us all who ventured into what
is now Europe and Asia and then through the South Pacific and perhaps to
South America (see Jacobs 2000).

2   I'm thinking of the view of the earth from space that enabled many of us,
for the first time, to comprehend the world as a limited, spherical whole
rather than an infinitely extended horizontal expanse. Some astronauts have
described their deep spiritual experiences, and others have popularized the notion
of "spaceship earth." See Firth and Smith (2002).

3   A copy of the constitution, and its amendments since ratification, can be found
online at http://pdba.georgetown.edu/Constitutions/Colombia/col91.html.
Retrieved on August 22, 2006.

4   I'm drawing from the transcript of the movie rather than from the published
script. See http://www.un-official.com/GWH/GoodWillT.html (retrieved on
November 1, 2005).

5   Kim Pearce and I first developed this model while working with a particular
client; we needed a CMM tool that we didn't have, one that focused on
storytelling and its relationship to untold stories. The image of the musical
instrument bards used to accompany themselves with as they told their
stories appealed to us, so we worked to develop the acronym LUTE. As we've
continued to use the model in our work, it has continued to grow. We
published the model as LUUUTT with three Us (Pearce and Pearce 1998). Based
on their work with CMM in corporate contexts, Beth Fisher-Yoshida and Ilene
Wasserman have made convincing demonstrations of the usefulness of
"untellable stories" as a fourth "U" and I'm pleased to include it here. In 2003,
a participant in one of my seminars in Aarhus named Vibeke (I cannot remember or find her last name) developed what she called "A Narrative Model
of Storytelling" that included five "Us." Two of the additions were "Unlived
stories" (dead stories) and "Undynamic stories" (those that have little life or suck
the life out of those who enact them). These are very interesting suggestions.

6   Technically, a perlocutionary act. This concept is commonly used among
those studying speech acts.

References

Bateson, G. (1979), *Mind and Nature: A Necessary Unity*, New York: E. P. Dutton.
Baxter, L. A. and Montgomery, B. M. (1996), *Relating: Dialogues and Dialectics*,
New York: Guilford Press.

Bowman, T. (1997), Vietnam vet's tale called a hoax, *San Francisco Chronicle* (December 18): A3.

Burke, K. (1969), *The Rhetoric of Motives*, Berkeley: University of California Press.

Campbell, J. (1959), *The Masks of God: Primitive Mythology*. New York: Viking.

Carver, R. (2000), Last fragment. In *All of Us: The Collected Poems*, New York: Vintage.

Collins, B. (2005), You, Reader. In *The Trouble with Poetry, and Other Poems*, New York: Random House.

Cooperrider, D. L. and Whitney, D. (1999), *Appreciative Inquiry: Collaborating for Change*, San Francisco: Berrett-Koehler Communications.

Czarniawska, B. (2004), *Narratives in Social Science Research*, London: Sage.

Debold, E. (2002), Epistemology, fourth order consciousness, and the subject–object relationship or . . . how the self evolves with Robert Kegan. *What is Enlightenment Magazine*, 22. Retrieved from http://www.wie.org/j22/kegan.asp?pf=1 on November 6, 2005.

Fiddler on the Roof Soundtrack Lyrics (n.d.), Do you love me? Retrieved from http://www.lyricsondemand.com/soundtracks/f/fiddlerontherooflyrics/doyoulovemelyrics.html on November 2, 2005.

Firth, P. and Smith, B. (2002), Spaceship Earth. Retrieved from http://www.sciencenetlinks.com/lessons.cfm?DocID=295 on September 7, 2006.

Jacobs, J. Q. (2000), The "replacement" or "out of Africa 2" hypothesis: the recent African genesis of humans. *Paleoanthropology in the 1990s: Essays by James Q. Jacobs*. Retrieved from http://www.jqjacobs.net/anthro/paleo/genome.html on September 7, 2006.

Kell, C. and Camp, R. (1999), *In the Name of the Father: The Rhetoric of the New Southern Baptist Convention*, Carbondale: Southern Illinois University Press.

Kirby, B. L. (n.d.), What is Asperger Syndrome? O.A.S.I.S.: Online Asperger Syndrome Information and Support. Retrieved from http://www.udel.edu/bkirby/asperger/aswhatisit.html on September 7, 2006.

Lang, P. and McAdam, E. (1997), Narrative-ating: future dreams in present living jottings on an honouring theme, *Human Systems*, 8: 3–12.

Lessem, R. (2006), Introduction. In D. E. Beck and C. C. Cowan, *Spiral Dynamics: Mastering Values, Leadership, and Change*, Malden, MA: Blackwell Publishing, pp. 1–13.

Lucaites, J. and Lewis, W. (1998), Race trials: the rhetoric of victimage in the racial consciousness of 1930s America. In J. F. Klumpp (ed.), *Proceedings of the Tenth SCA/AFA Conference on Argumentation*, Washington, DC: Speech Communication Association, pp. 269–74.

Liukkonen, P. (n.d.), Raymond Carver – in full, Raymond Clevie Carver. Retrieved from http://www.kirjasto.sci.fi/rcarver.htm on November 1, 2005.

Morson, G. S. and Emerson, C. (1990), *Mikhail Bakhtin: Creation of a Prosaics*, Palo Alto, CA: Stanford University Press.

Pearce, K. A. (2002), *Making Better Social Worlds: Engaging in and Facilitating Dialogic Communication*, Redwood City, CA: Pearce Associates.

Pearce, W. B. (1985), Scientific research methods in communication studies and their implications for theory and knowledge. In T. Benson (ed.), *Speech Communication in the Twentieth Century*, Carbondale: Southern Illinois University Press, pp. 255–81.

Pearce, W. B. (2002), CMM: reports from users. Paper presented at the Western States Communication Association convention. Available online at: http://www.pearceassociates.com/essays/reports_from_users.pdf.

Pearce, W. B. and Pearce, K. A. (1998), Transcendent storytelling: abilities for systemic practitioners and their clients, *Human Systems*, 9: 167–85.

Pearce, W. B. and Pearce, K. A. (2004), Taking a communication perspective on dialogue. In R. Anderson, L. A. Baxter, and K. N. Cissna (eds.), *Dialogue: Theorizing Difference in Communication Studies*, Thousand Oaks, CA: Sage, pp. 39–56.

Sartre, J.-P. (1989), *No Exit and Three Other Plays*, New York: Vintage International.

Seligman, P. (1997), Sprouts, jigsaws and acorns, *Human Systems*, 8: 14–16.

Sluzki, C. (1992), Transformations: a blueprint for narrative changes in therapy, *Family Process*, 31: 217–30.

Chapter 9

Afterword: Something of a Guide for Using CMM

Warning!

One purpose for writing this book is to make it easier to use CMM. In the Preface, I used a metaphor from manufacturing: I wanted to reduce the "first unit cost" of putting CMM in practice – that is, how much you have to invest before using it for the first time.

In 2005, I was teaching a two-day course for consultants. At the end of the first day, one of the participants said that he needed some specific advice for how to deal with a situation in his company. "Fine," I told him. "We'll have an opportunity for coached practice tomorrow. Let's use this situation then." "No, you don't understand," he replied. "I'm leaving here for a meeting at my office and have to deal with this situation tonight. I want to use what I'm learning here, but I'm not sure just how." I responded by saying, "When you don't know what else to do, start with the time-line and use the serpentine model . . ."

Please understand what I've written in this Afterword in that spirit. Perhaps the title should be "What to do when you don't know what to do."

If you read this book with an eye for them, there are many examples of how CMM can be used. Frankly, I'm more comfortable with a flurry of examples than a wallet-sized card with a numbered list of steps to take in any given situation. I firmly believe that the world is polysemic and in a state of continual creation, and that we are storytellers, and tellers of many interrelated stories simultaneously. With such entities in such a world, any "one size fits all" description of how to use CMM inevitably distorts and disarms the user. But I also know that we need a different kind of support when we are learning to use a tool than when we have mastered it, and when we are in a challenging situation than when we are in our comfort zone. So . . .

Reluctantly, with the need to caution you, and with a good bit of nervousness, I've decided to offer the following description of how to use CMM. If you learn these steps well and practice them, you'll grow increasingly dissatisfied with them as your own competence grows.

Ways of "Using" CMM

When I think of using CMM, I think of two purposes and three contexts.

One purpose is presented in chapter 1 of this book: discerning critical moments and choosing wisely how to act into them. The other purpose is highlighted in chapters 6, 7, and 8: providing a scaffolding that supports the evolution of better patterns of communication, more sophisticated forms of consciousness, and higher states of mind.

These purposes can be realized in three contexts, usefully marked by the person-position (first, second, or third) that you take in them. In a first-person position, you might use CMM to examine your own role in particular situations, understanding them so as to choose wisely what to do and/or to stimulate the evolution of patterns of communication, forms of consciousness, and relational minds. In a second-person position, you might act as a friend or consultant to someone else, helping them to achieve these same purposes. In the third-person position, you might act as a researcher, describing, critiquing, and suggesting effective action in ways that join conversations that achieve these purposes.

Of course, the specific things you do will vary in terms of which purpose is the more important at the moment and which person-position you take. However, I think that there are strong family resemblances among what you might do in all of these. These family resemblances constitute the CMM tradition of practice, enabling us to recognize each other when we are using CMM rather than some other approach, or to coach each other in how to use these methods better.

In what follows, for the purposes of this guide, I'm going to focus on a second-person consulting relationship as a way of helping the client choose wisely what to do in a specific situation.

How Do You Know if You've Used CMM Well?

I hope that you will not only read this Afterword, but will put it into practice. If you do, then I can answer the question posed in the heading of this section. You've used CMM well when the person you are consulting knows how to go on and is better equipped to choose wisely how to act into a situation. You've used CMM well when you've supported the continuing evolution of preferred patterns of communication, more sophisticated forms of consciousness, and more highly developed relational minds. That is, the evaluation of how well you have done comes from its effects.

Philosophically, this is a restatement of Pragmatism. The test of CMM lies not in the truthfulness of its claims but in how useful it is in helping us understand the social worlds we live in, identify critical moments, and act wisely in them. That is, CMM's "truth" is not so much a matter of how well it *represents* the social world (and, if our social worlds are as many, fluid, and polysemic as CMM describes them, how could they be represented?) as how well it *guides action* into the world.

This emphasis on the effects of what we do seems scandalous to many people. It seems (repeat: seems, from their perspective) to disregard virtues such as honesty, accuracy, and integrity, and to dismiss our ability to know the world in which we live. As I've talked about this approach with many of these scandalized people, I've found that they are usually thinking of a one-time assessment of the effects of an action, while I'm thinking of a continuing process of action and reflection. The continuing process of acting, observing the consequences of our actions, and learning from them, I believe, is the site in which honesty, accuracy, and integrity are formed, and in which the ability to know a changing, polysemic world can be developed.

I'm not interested in arguing the philosophical legitimacy of Pragmatism. I'd rather point to its implications for what you and I do in specific situations. To take one example, when I'm training people to facilitate dialogic communication, we use the technique of coached practice in which they work with others who are playing roles – usually as the most difficult people the facilitators-in-training will ever meet. Typically, the facilitator will ask "Did I do that correctly?" and, in the role of coach, I will reply, "I don't know. Let's ask the others." Turning to the group: "In the role you were playing, when [the facilitator] said . . . , what response did that elicit from you?"

Note the paradigm shift in this pragmatic response. Instead of comparing the performance of the facilitator-in-training against an ideal of what a facilitator should be or do, or against a list of how to ask questions or make comments, this approach assumes that there may be any number of "right" ways of facilitating, and that the determination of what is "right" comes from the response it elicits.

Intellectually, I hope that you'll see that "using CMM" isn't a matter of fitting yourself into a predetermined profile, but of joining in the unfinished, unfolding, interactive, and polysemic patterns of communication with other people. All the concepts in this book – speech acts, episodes, the tension between stories lived and told, the untold and unheard stories in a situation, etc. – are designed to help you sense and name these patterns.

As a person putting these ideas into practice, I hope that this reminder will free you from the trap of trying to fit an abstract description or do it "by the numbers." It is much more important that you be responsive to the other people in the situation than try to make the situation fit a textbook description.

A Typical Four-phase Sequence in Using CMM

You are tired of hearing this, but here it comes again: this four-phase sequence is an idealized abstraction for the purposes of giving you something to do in those situations where you don't know what to do. In reality, using CMM is a spiraling, reflexive process responsive to the specific opportunities and demands of the situation. Now, with that said, again . . .

Description

The first phase of any CMM work is to describe what is going on. This affirms that CMM is about specific situations, not situations (or people, problems, institutions, etc.) in general. However, the extent of the descriptive phase may differ. In some cases, you'll only want the minimal amount of information in order to engage with the client; in others, you'll want a lot more. (For example, if you are taking a third-person perspective as a researcher, you'll spend far more time in this phase than you might if you are working as a consultant.)

In this phase, CMM practitioners usually seek multiple descriptions, taking each as partial and unfinished. This expresses the idea that social worlds are polysemic, and that every saying and doing is multiply interpreted (not only by different people, but by each person), and that every saying and doing is always open to reinterpretation. As a result, CMM practitioners treat the answer to the question "What did you mean by that?" as an expression of what the person NOW, in the present, thinks that she or he meant, not necessarily what they meant at the time. Meaning, like everything else in our social worlds, moves on.

Particularly when the CMM practitioner is in the first- and second-person positions, "description" is always "re-description." That is, remembering and reflection, particularly as guided by systemic questioning or CMM models, is a re-construction of the experience and often is a sufficient intervention to enable a client to know how to move forward.

I'll come back to this phase below, and suggest three starting points. Let me end now by saying that this phase isn't "over" when it is over; rather, you might keep cycling back to add to or revise the description as you continue.

Interpretation

Social worlds are meaningful, and humans are storytellers. And the kinds of situations in which clients seek consultation are usually those in which the stories are not working; they are somehow blocked, unable to move forward. Articulating the meanings that clients have for the situation, the jumble of other stories, and the other conversations in which they participate is part of the "descriptive" phase of CMM practice. However, clients seldom if ever tell all of the story, and never all of the stories, that relate to the situation for which they seek help. So, the next phase of CMM practice is to help the client tell their story more fully, better aligned with the story they are living, and/or with a different grammar that enables them to move forward.

Three major strategies may be used in this phase.

First, using the serpentine model as the primary analytic tool, the consultant and client may construct a time-line of the sequence of events leading up to the decision the client needs to make and begin adding in the various stories (in their appropriate hierarchical relationship) that each event expresses and re-constructs. My experience is that clients always leave out significant events in their first description of the time-line, and that, when we start working through the interpretation of those events, they "remember" the missing events. So we go back to the descriptive phase, insert the remembered events, and continue with the interpretation. The effect of this process is to de-emplot or re-punctuate (using the concepts introduced in chapter 6) their stories, freeing them to re-author their stories in a more effective manner.

Second, using the LUUUUTT model as the primary analytic tool, the consultant and client may focus on the manner of storytelling, the tension between the story told and story lived, and/or the various "Us" (untold, unheard, untellable, unknown stories) in the situation. In my experience, when clients and consultants work through the LUUUUTT model, the client always ends up with a richer understanding of the situation than she or he had before, and is better positioned to act wisely into the situation.

Third, using the daisy model as the primary analytic tool, the consultant may use systemic questioning to invite the client into a different and more sophisticated epistemology such as described in chapters 7 and 8. This epistemology involves seeing the whole system, not just a part of it, and invites the client to look at it from various perspectives. In the process, systemic questioning de-centers the description of the situation from the client's perspective, helping the client to discover that other people have stories different from his or hers, that these stories include information not available from the client's perspective, and that the client's interpretations of specific events or objects in the social world are only some of many possible ones (Cronen and Pearce 1985; Pearce 1995).

Systemic questioning is my term for a process developed by four brilliant practitioners collectively known as the "Milan School" of systemic family therapy (Cecchin 1987). They called the process "circular questioning," and it has developed over the years (Tomm 1985, 1987a, 1987b, 1988). Since I've given more examples of the use of the serpentine and LUUUUTT models in previous chapters, I'll focus on systemic questioning in this chapter. Of course, in any instance of real practice, you would probably use all three approaches to various extents.

Critique

It is more accurate to say that CMM has a critical edge rather than that it is a critical theory. The key difference is that CMM performs immanent critiques (based on factors inside the process itself) while the more well-known "critical theory" performs external critique (based on the a priori assumption that power is the basic structure of social relationships and that the relevant question is who is oppressed by whom). CMM's critical edge comes from the thick description of what is being made and how it is being made.

The paradigmatic questions for CMM are "What are we making?" "How are we making it?" and "How can we make better social worlds?" CMM's unusual, technical vocabulary is intended to help answer those questions. For example, the question "What are we making?" can be answered in the vocabulary of speech acts, episodes, selves, relationships, forms of communication, forms of consciousness, and minds. The question "How are we making it?" can be answered with the use of the serpentine, daisy, hierarchy, and LUUUUTT models and the concept of logical force. The question "How can we make better social worlds?" uses all of these, along with the notion of critical moments.

The critical edge in CMM practice comes from connecting the dots. For example, the description and interpretation of specific events might well disclose a contradiction between espoused values or purposes and the outcomes (what is being made). By bringing this contradiction into discourse with the client, CMM performs a critical function. To change the example, use of the LUUUUTT model might bring the tension between stories lived and stories told into discourse, and in so doing perform a critical function.

The process of communication (coordinating actions and making/ managing meaning) is so complicated that I have never done an analysis of a specific situation without (1) losing my ability to have easy critical answers (of the nature, "it's entirely his fault!"), and (2) finding openings for re-authoring and for intervention through wise actions. So, I'm not concerned about whether CMM practice will have a critical edge. In fact, my concern is that the practitioner (and the client) postpone the fateful moment of thinking that they are ready to make a judgment until they have a sufficiently rich understanding of the situation. I firmly believe that a sufficiently rich description of the situation is a critique powerful enough to enable us to move on toward better social worlds.

Putting it into practice

Whatever is done in this phase of the process needs to be soundly grounded in a thick description of the situation itself. It is hard to say anything "in general" except to remember, when choosing what to do, to remain consistent with the epistemology that was developed in the descriptive, interpretive, and critical phases of the process.

In consulting, it is often enough to help the client move through description, interpretation, and critique. The client is the "expert" and will decide what to do next. However, consistent with the communication perspective, CMM practitioners may be seen as architects or facilitators of specific forms of communication. In designing specific meetings or long-range communication processes, CMM practitioners create the scaffolding that enables clients and others to participate in patterns of communication more sophisticated than they could have constructed for themselves, and in doing so, to evolve as persons and in relationships.

Entry Points for CMM Practice

The first question, of course, is how to begin. The answer, of course, depends on how the client approaches you and what are the specific aspects of the situation. But in general, there are three entry points.

In chapter 4, you learned that CMM conceptualizes communication as having two faces, inseparable but different: coordinating actions and making/managing meaning. As shown in table 9.1, these sort out some of the things you might listen for or observe in the first few minutes of a consultation, and some of the questions that these might raise for you. For example, if you notice that there are robust patterns of coordinated action in the client's life or organization, your curiosity might be directed to the forces that keep this pattern together despite all those things that might cause it to fall apart. How are new participants "recruited" into the pattern? How are "deviations" dealt with? Who is doing what episode-work? You might decide to start with a sequential description of the pattern, using the serpentine model.

Or, you might notice that a particular story is being told all through the organization. In various forms, you hear it from those with the highest paygrades as well as those with the lowest. What processes of ante-narrative (described in chapter 6) did the organization go through in order to select this as its work-story? What other candidate narratives didn't make it? Which of these remain as untold, unheard, or untellable stories? Where does this story fit in the hierarchy of other stories? Is it the story that contextualizes many of the others, or is it at a fairly low level of contextualization? You might start with the LUUUUTT and hierarchy models, perhaps teaching

Table 9.1   Entry points for CMM practitioners

Coordinating action	*Making/managing meanings*
Robust patterns – how sustained?	Stories – what? Which? How told? In what contexts? When? To whom?
Unusual/fragile/beautiful/valuable patterns – how achieved?	
Powerful moves/skillful play – what – why so powerful?	Relationships among stories – hierarchy? Nested? Loops?
People/institutions with affinities for particular patterns – how? What? Why?	With what logical forces?

these concepts and models to your client and then doing the analysis collaboratively.

Table 9.1 identifies the two faces of the communication process, but there is a third element: the relationship between the two faces. Perhaps what strikes you first is the gap between the stories lived (coordinated actions) and the stories told (making/managing meanings). Using the LUUUUTT model, perhaps in connection with the serpentine, you might describe and interpret the situation, bringing this gap into discourse. However, the gap might be more than just a single situation, and you might want to explore the grammar of the client's social world. ("Grammar" is a term that CMM took from Ludwig Wittgenstein. In this sense, it means the configuration of stories and actions linked together by logical force.) To explore the grammar, you might use systemic questioning.

An Example of Consulting Using Systemic Questioning

Let's assume that I am asked to consult with a company that has a number of branch offices, one located in Phoenix, Arizona. The following is a totally fictional account, designed to illustrate the use of systemic questioning by a consultant. In what follows, I'll put my questions in italics to separate them from my comments about what I'm doing. If this example works for you, your perception of the densely textured social world of this office will begin to take shape as you imagine the answers given to my questions.

Just who hired me for this job, and what commission I'm given makes a lot of difference. In this case, I'm hired by a vice-president who told me that her assignment is to improve the overall productivity of the branch offices. When she received this assignment, she noted that there was a surprisingly large difference between productivity at the highest- and lowest-achieving branch offices, and she thinks that she can get the biggest bang for the buck (her metaphor) by raising the performance of the lowest-achieving offices rather than trying to increase the productivity of the highest-achieving offices even more.

The office in Phoenix has had the lowest productivity of any of the branch offices during the past five years. *I asked her what story she has about the Phoenix office.* I did not ask "why" the office has such low productivity or what the "problem" is. My question is more open-ended, as well as planting the seed of the idea that this is "her story," not what is "really" the case. She told me about the productivity levels and added, "They have had poor leadership. It's not that any of their managers have been bad, just that the turnover has been so great that they haven't been able to whip the office into shape." *I asked, "What story do you have about the turnover?"* "I'm not sure. Most of them said that they liked the office, but that they found other positions more attractive." *"From your perspective, what would 'whipping the office into shape' look like?"* As she responded, I followed up with questions focusing on what she saw and heard and paid little attention to her generalizations about the office itself. My interest lay in the interaction between her and the branch office.

When I arrived in Phoenix, I treated the vice-president's story about "managerial turnover" as "the presenting problem," not the "truth" about what is going on. This is a way of reminding myself not to accept her description uncritically. I've almost always found that the supervisor's story of what is going on is not very useful, except to know it as part of the richer description of the situation. If the supervisor's story was "right," then the organization would probably not need a consultant.

I meet with all the employees in the Phoenix office in an off-site meeting room, hoping that this will serve as "neutral turf" and help them think outside the usual channels. My first step is to get a general description of the system that I have in view. I use the term system-in-view as a way of reminding myself that the people in front of me do not necessarily comprise the whole system. Drawing the boundaries of the system is an interpretive act. I start by asking about their stories and about who is involved in them.

Other than the people in this room, who were the first people who noticed that something was going on in the Phoenix office?

I'm doing several things in this question. I'm testing the boundaries of the system by asking about people not present who are connected by means of "noticing what's going on." I'm also deflecting attention away from the people in the room. I assume that each person has his or her own story and I'm not interested in giving them yet another opportunity to express it. Instead, I want them to tell their story in an unusual, more systemic manner, and will ask questions that invite them to do so. In addition, I'm resisting the temptation to assume that either the clients or I know "what" is going on. I'll be interested to see how much description they give me of "what" is happening even though I just asked "who noticed."

How did they name what was going on?

One aspect of systemic questioning involves using the words from the client's answer in the following question. So, if this was a real intervention rather than an example, I'd replace the pronoun "they" with the names of the people given me in the previous question.

How did ____ name what's going on?
How did ____ name what's going on? Etc.

These questions invite the group to begin exploring various interpretations of "what" is going on. It includes the embedded suggestion that whatever "it" is, it is named differently by different people. Notice that I am continuing to deflect away from their own stories; I asked them to describe how other people "story" the situation.

One of the defining characteristics of systemic questioning is the exploration of differences, such as more or less, before and after, and from here and from there. I begin to explore these differences by asking members of the group to compare the way other members name what is going on.

Did ____ and ____ know that they were naming it differently?

I'm still deflecting them from telling their own stories while inviting them to think, probably more specifically than they have before this interview, about the configuration of similarities and differences across the system. Now I introduce the "difference" of before and after.

> *When did they first notice that they viewed what was going on from different perspectives?*

I'm taking advantage of the power of questions. I could have asked about their "disagreement" or their "differences of opinion" but I chose to embed the suggestion that each of the people in the office has a "perspective" that makes the office and the relationships in it look differently.

> *What conversations have they had about their different perspectives on what is going on?*
> *What learnings have come from these conversations?*

I'm putting an appreciative spin on these conversations, which might well have been pretty ugly, by asking for positive outcomes.

Thus far, I'm just getting a description of the situation, but you can clearly see that the four phases of the process are not neatly separated. I'm also embedding suggestions, getting interpretations, and generally inviting the group to re-author their story while telling it to me.

The next series of questions continues to elicit descriptions of the situation, but also brings in potential critical perspectives based on what is getting made by the actions that various people took.

> *When ___ (fill in from answers above) noticed the low morale here in the Phoenix office, how did he/she show his/her concern?*

This question includes two embedded suggestions (or invitations to a different epistemology). First, it suggests that "notice" equals "concern" – I'll monitor carefully to see if this suggestion (or any of the other, similar ones) gets picked up. Second, it introduces the idea that the present situation, whatever it is, is already the result of what people have said and done, and invites the client to see this as a continuing process, not a static "state" about which nothing can be done. In addition, it invites the clients to use the term "shows" rather than "feels" or "thinks" or any other intrapsychic term. This focuses attention on what people actually say and do, and leads to the follow-up questions that link actions to perceptions of difference.

To whom did he show this concern first?
To whom did he show this concern most frequently?
To whom did he show this concern least?
Were there any people from whom he deliberately tried to hide his concern?
Who might have or should have noticed what was going on in the Phoenix office, but did not?

I'm initiating a set of questions about the "dark side" of the system; to see if there are some stories about ways in which the system is not functioning well. This is dangerous; it can elicit the typical rhetorics of blame and victimage. To avoid this, I ask first for event-by-event sequences, moving only later to abstract, summarizing stories.

What did they say or do that showed that they did not know what was going on?
Who responded to that?
What did they do?
What happened next?
Does everyone here agree that this was the sequence of events?
What's your story about what's going on?

Notice how vague my questions are. In the actual interview, I would use indefinite pronouns when I want to avoid premature naming of persons or events, but as soon as the persons being interviewed supplied the vocabulary, I would work hard to use their terms in the stems of my questions.

By now, I've invited the client group to a different epistemology in which to think about what is going on in their office, and I've developed a pretty good picture of what is going on. Only now am I ready to invite the members of the group to tell the stories from their own perspective (I still don't want to get their rehearsed story that they brought with them). And I'm going to continue to block this by starting this part of the interview with the lowest-ranking person present.

Who is the newest member of this team?
How do the people in this office name what is going on?

Do you agree with that way of naming it? Or do you have a different story about what is going on?

I'm starting with the person least authorized to be the team storyteller. If my purpose is to co-construct a new story that will enable the team to move forward together, then I want to avoid giving them an opportunity to tell, one more time, the "old" story. By starting with the person who "first" noticed or the team leader, I run the risk of initiating a well-rehearsed "telling." To avoid that, I might start with the person who "last" noticed, or the newest member of the team, or the lowest-ranking member of the team. In what follows, let's assume that this person says that the group describes what is going on as "low morale" and that he agrees with that label.

When did you first notice the low morale?
What was going on at the time?
What called your attention to this aspect of what was going on?
When you noticed that something was going on, did you at first call it "low morale" or did you call it something else?
When did you change from calling it ___ to low morale?
To whom did you show your concern?

When I think the time is right (a judgment call!), I'll turn to the next person.

Who is the next newest member of this team?
Is your relationship to "low morale" different than ___'s?

I'm beginning to set up an "exteriorization" of the problem, treating it as an event or object in the social world that is "made." Among other things, this reduces its power. We make it; we don't "have" it or it "have" us.

Who is the third newest member?
How about your relationship to "low morale"?

Etc. to include all members of the team . . . As I go, I'll be sensitive to differences among the various people. I'll note these differences or contradictions, and ask them what story they have about those differences. By asking "what story you have . . . ," I'm inviting them to author a story. If I were to ask "why do you differ?" this is less likely to result in answers that empower the client to move forward.

I'd probably take a break now. I might let the team spend a bit of time alone to let some of this new information enter into their discourse. Then, if I was working with a partner – and this is my preferred way of working – we might invite the team to listen while we engage in a reflective conversation about what we've learned and develop some hypotheses. Let's assume that one of the hypotheses I've developed is that "low morale" has had a positive effect on the team because they don't feel that they have been working well together – everybody is working individually on their own projects – so having "low morale" is a way of building team unity because it unites them. My partner and I might develop three or four other hypotheses, none of which we really believe but all of which suggest new ways of connecting the dots, specifically ways that give a positive connotation to the system by describing how "the problem" was made as a constructive resource to deal with a challenge. We've worked hard to describe the system as an extrasomatic (this is Bateson's term; it means "outside the body") mind, not something about individual's beliefs, attitudes, or values.

After my partner and I reflect with the team listening, I ask if anyone has anything to say. After listening without comment to whatever they say, I would pick one of the members on the basis of my feeling at the moment – perhaps this is a decision-maker, the most respected observer, the youngest/most junior member of the group, or the oldest/most senior member of the group. Let's assume that the comments made by members of the office following our reflections picked up this silly hypothesis about "low morale" being a useful member of the team. I've already "exteriorized" the problem and offered an embedded suggestion that this problem is serving some positive functions. Now I'm going to offer the suggestion – through my questions – that it is time for this member to leave the team.

> If "low morale" were to go away, who among you would be the most disturbed by its absence?
> To whom would you show how much you miss "low morale"?
> How would you show that you miss it?
> Who would be most happy if low morale were to go away?
> To whom would you show your happiness?
> What would you do differently?
> So, looking at the things that low morale is doing for you, how much longer should you keep it?

In all of these questions, I'm focusing on what people can actually say and do, and not allowing "morale" to be some intrapsychic state about which nothing can be done. I'm also inviting the clients to see themselves as "agents" who can decide what to do about this problematic team member rather than be the victims of it. My follow-up questions will have to do with how they will know when it is time for "low morale" to go. Before this time, who should do what or do things differently to keep "low morale" alive and well? Who should say when it is time for "low morale" to go? Should they have a "farewell party" for low morale? Etc., etc. I'll carry this visualization just to the point of absurdity.

Now, in this scenario, my commission derived from the vice-president, and I'll have to report back to her. One of the things I like about working with CMM is that I don't have to hide anything from my clients. In this particular case, I might tell them that I need to report back to the vice-president (they already knew that) and invite them to help me construct a story about what is going on in the Phoenix office. That story might be a drawing, a short story, a formal report, or a filled-out CMM model – anything that would allow them to express their re-authoring of their story.

I will be mindful of how this report changes the interaction between the Phoenix office and the vice-president, and give some attention to the pattern of communication between them.

This is a Test . . .

. . . and it counts 100 percent of your grade. True or false: there is only one way of working with CMM. If you answered "true," turn back to page 1 of this book and start over. We'll wait until you're gone.

OK, now we've got that taken care of. Working with CMM is an opportunity for artistry, not for conformity. In this book, you've seen short examples of how to work with CMM from a number of perspectives and in a wide variety of contexts, from interpersonal relationships to events that shape the entire world. I urge you to try these ideas out. Reflect on what they enable you to do. Revisit the material in this book – I'll bet that you get something out of it the second time that you did not the first.

Be adventurous. Push the limits. When I learned to ski, I was embarrassed because I fell so often. A patient instructor gave me good advice. The goal is not to stay standing; it is to learn how to ski. You do this, he said, by skiing on the edge of falling, and when you go over the edge, you get up and try again. It's good advice for skiing – and for using CMM in your practice.

References

Cecchin, G. (1987), Hypothesizing, circularity, and neutrality revisited: an invitation to curiosity, *Family Process*, 26: 405–13.

Cronen, V. E. and Pearce, W. B. (1985), Toward an explanation of how the Milan Method works: an invitation to a systemic epistemology and the evolution of family systems. In D. Campbell and R. Draper (eds.), *Applications of Systemic Family Therapy: The Milan Approach*, London: Grune and Stratton, pp. 69–86.

Pearce, W. B. (1995), Bringing news of difference: participation in systemic social constructionist communication. In L. Frey (ed.), *Innovations in Group Facilitation: Application in Natural Settings*, Cresskill, NJ: Hampton Press, pp. 94–115.

Tomm, K. (1985), Circular interviewing: a multifaceted clinical tool. In D. Campbell and R. Draper (eds.), *Applications of Systemic Family Therapy: The Milan Approach*, London: Grune and Stratton, pp. 33–45.

Tomm, K. (1987a), Interventive interviewing: Part I. Strategizing as a fourth guideline for the therapist, *Family Process*, 26: 3–13.

Tomm, K. (1987b), Interventive interviewing: Part II. Reflexive questioning as a means to enable self-healing, *Family Process*, 26: 167–83.

Tomm, K. (1988), Interventive interviewing: Part III. Intending to ask lineal, circular, strategic or reflexive questions, *Family Process*, 27: 1–15.

Index

Page numbers for notes and figures are in italics.